AF594313

草間彌生 Art Book

Hi, Konnichiwa

Yayoi Kusama

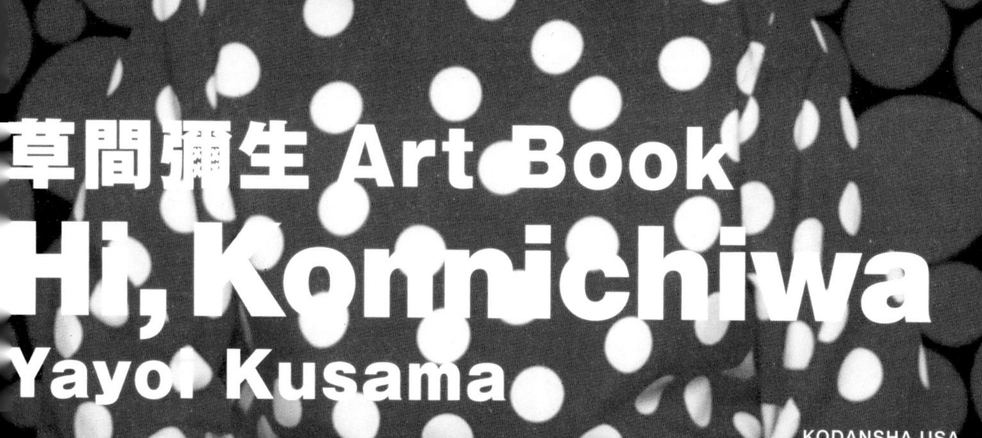

KODANSHA USA

ハーイ、コンニチワ！

あなたたちに青春がやって来るということ
そんなに大それたことを知っているの？
青春は死と生を共にたずさえて
あなたの背後から音もなくしのび寄ってくる
私は暗かった前世をふり捨てて、再生し、
いま運命から与えられた時のしじまに
心から生の賛美を歌いあげたい。

私の手の中が一杯になったほど
芸術のはしくれたちが
ハーイ、コンニチワと私にそっとささやいてくれる。
人の世の入口で、青春のかげりをちらつかせて
私に大きな宿題をこの人生にもちこんできたとき、
未知への怖れや不安でくめどつきない生と死の斗い
そして私の果てしない夢を今夜こそ見いだしたい。

草間彌生

Hi,Hello!

Do you know that outrageous news
that youth is coming to you all?
Youth, carrying with it both death and life,
creeps up on you soundlessly from behind.
I forsake my previous, dark life, regenerate
and in the time of stillness granted me by my destiny,
I want to sing in praise of life from the bottom of my heart.

Fragments of art fill my hands,
gently whispering, 'Hi, Hello.'
At the entrance to the world of mankind,
when they show me the shadow of youth
and bring an important assignment into my life,
amidst the fear and anxiety of the unknown
that causes the never-ending struggle between life and death,
I wish to discover my boundless dream tonight.

Yayoi Kusama

未来への心の位置を高めたい。

そのため、私は芸術をそれへの手段として選んだ。

これは一生をかけての仕事である。

I want to lift my heart toward the future.
I have chosen art as the means of accomplishing this.
It is a task that will last a whole lifetime.

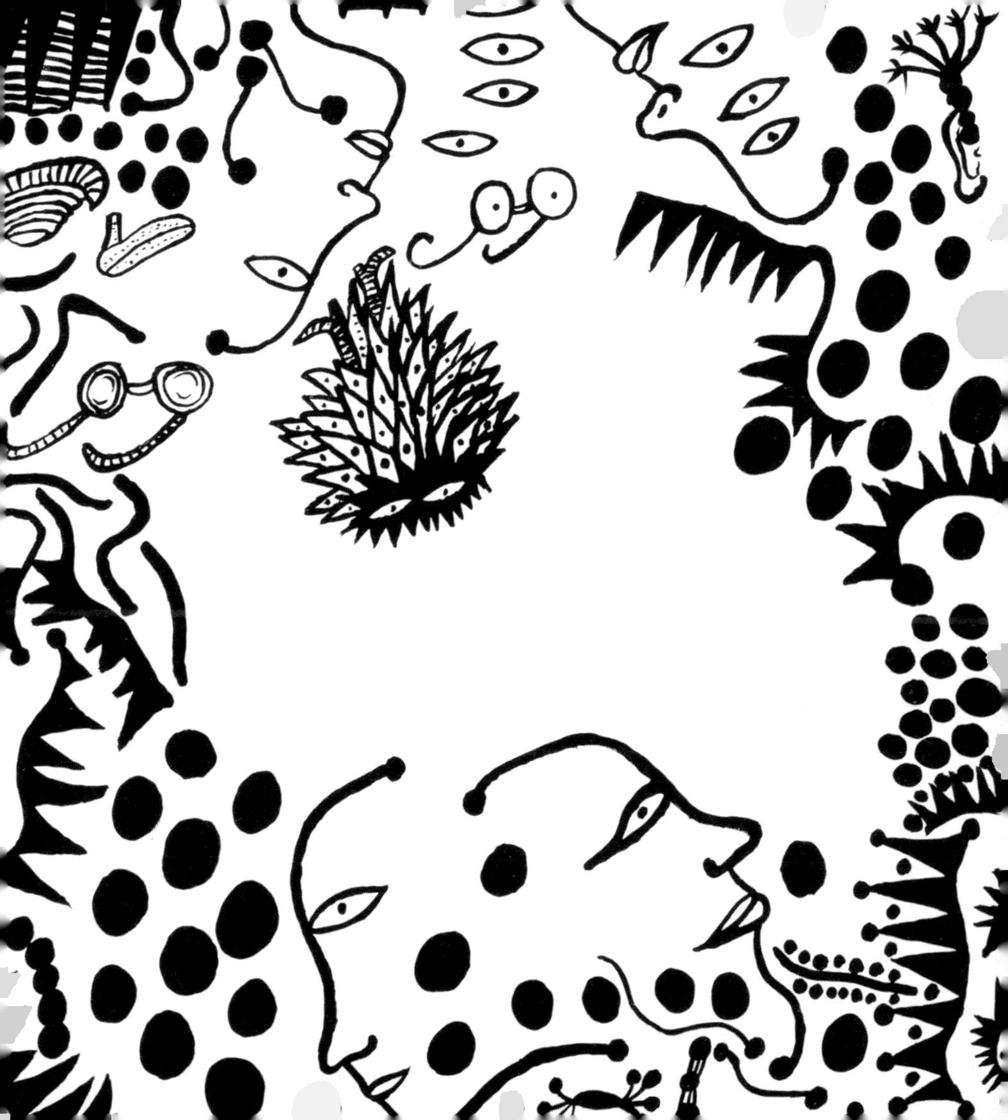

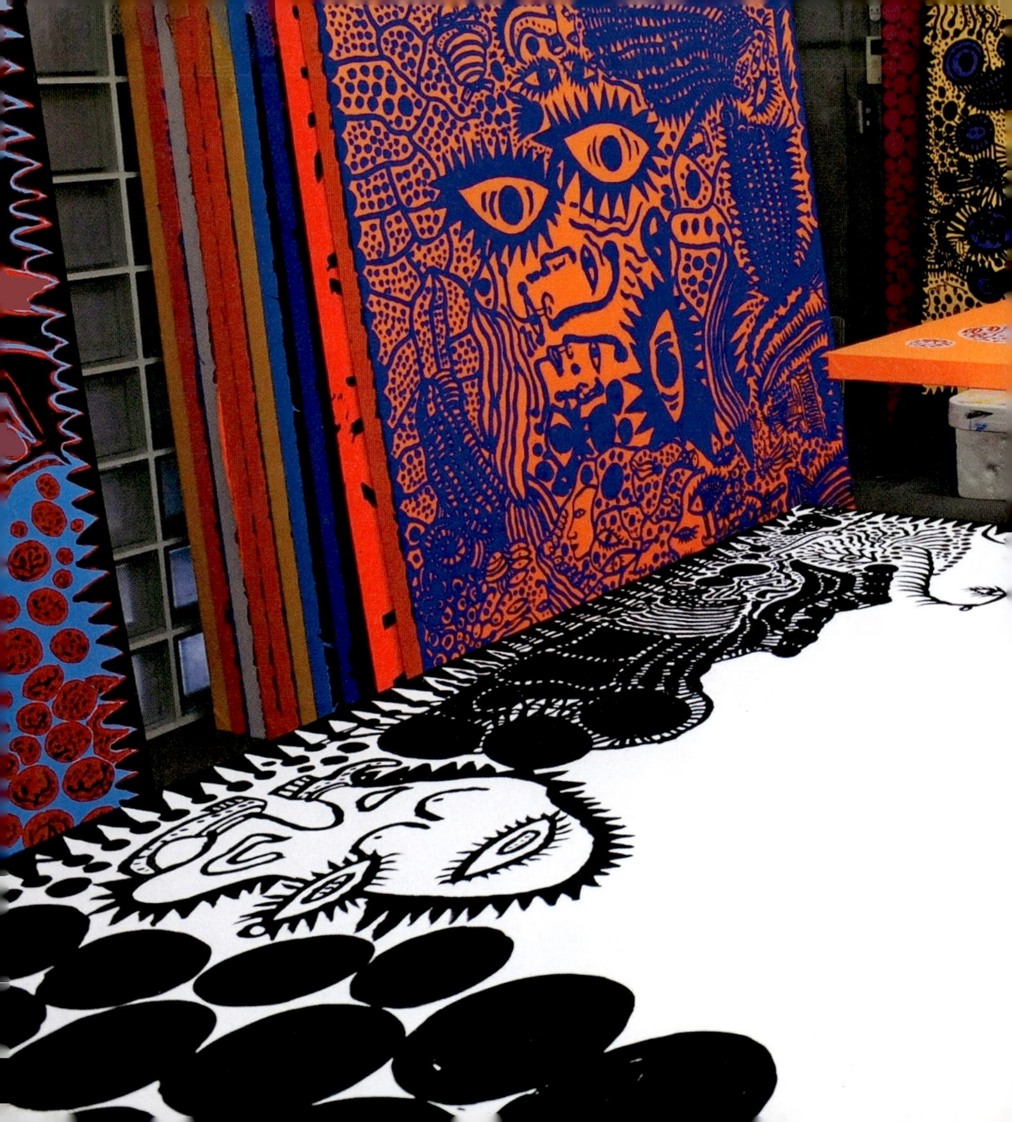

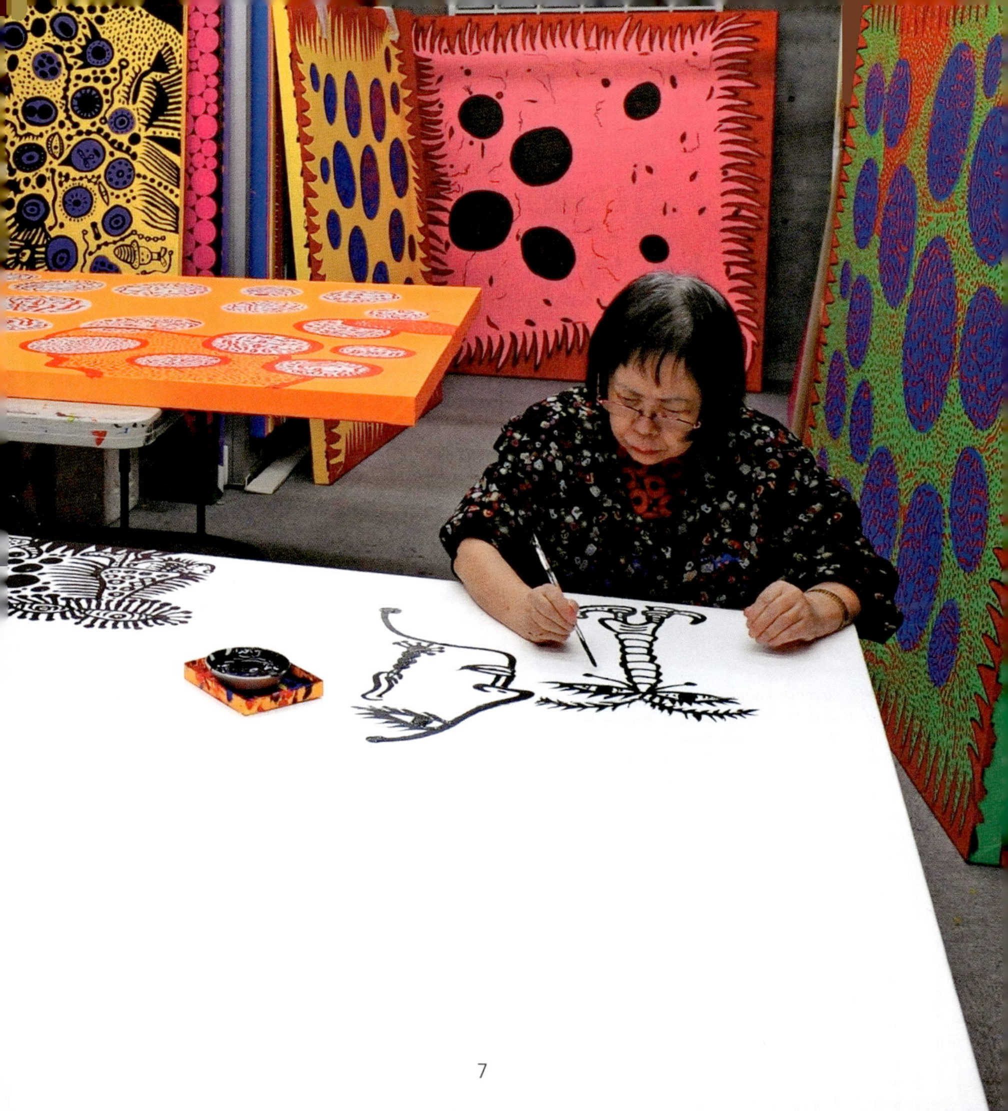

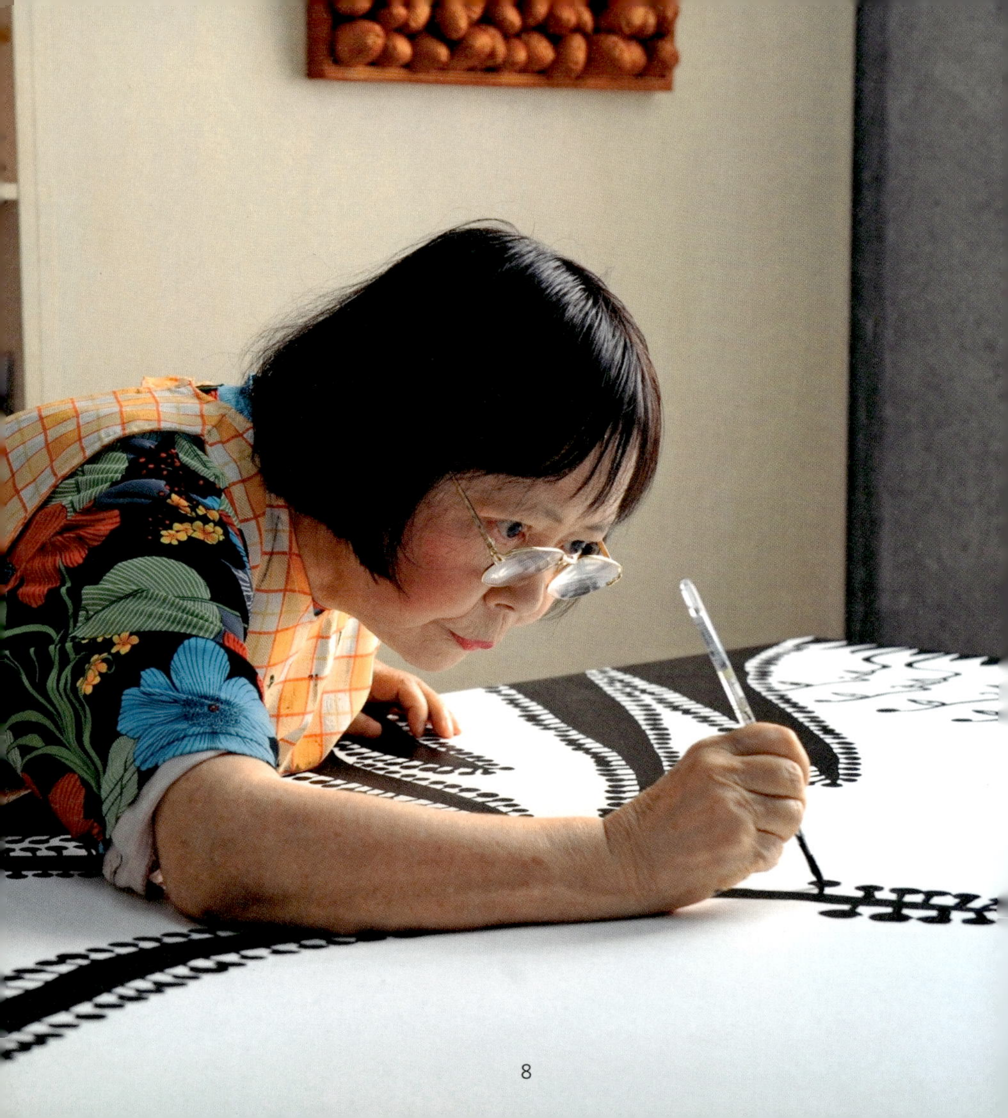

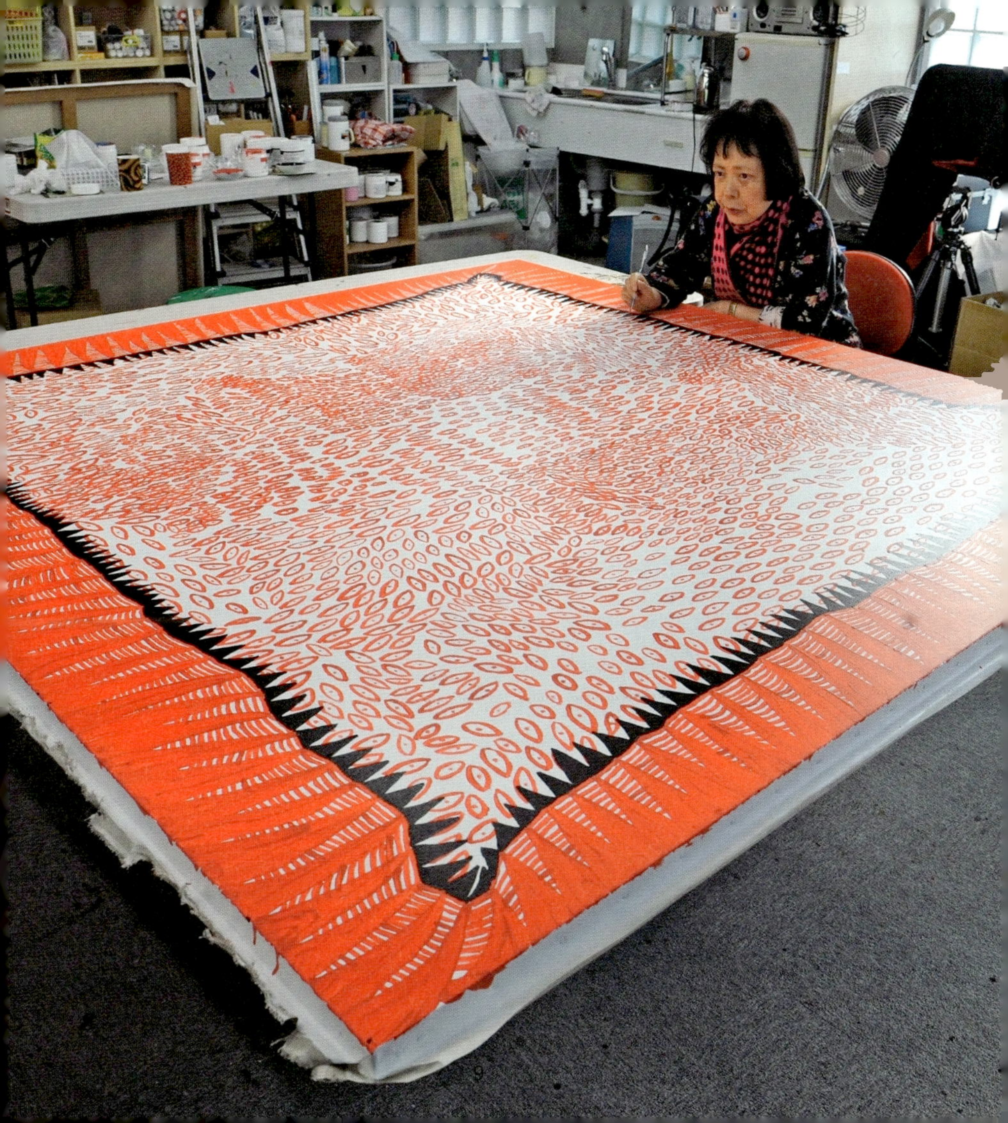

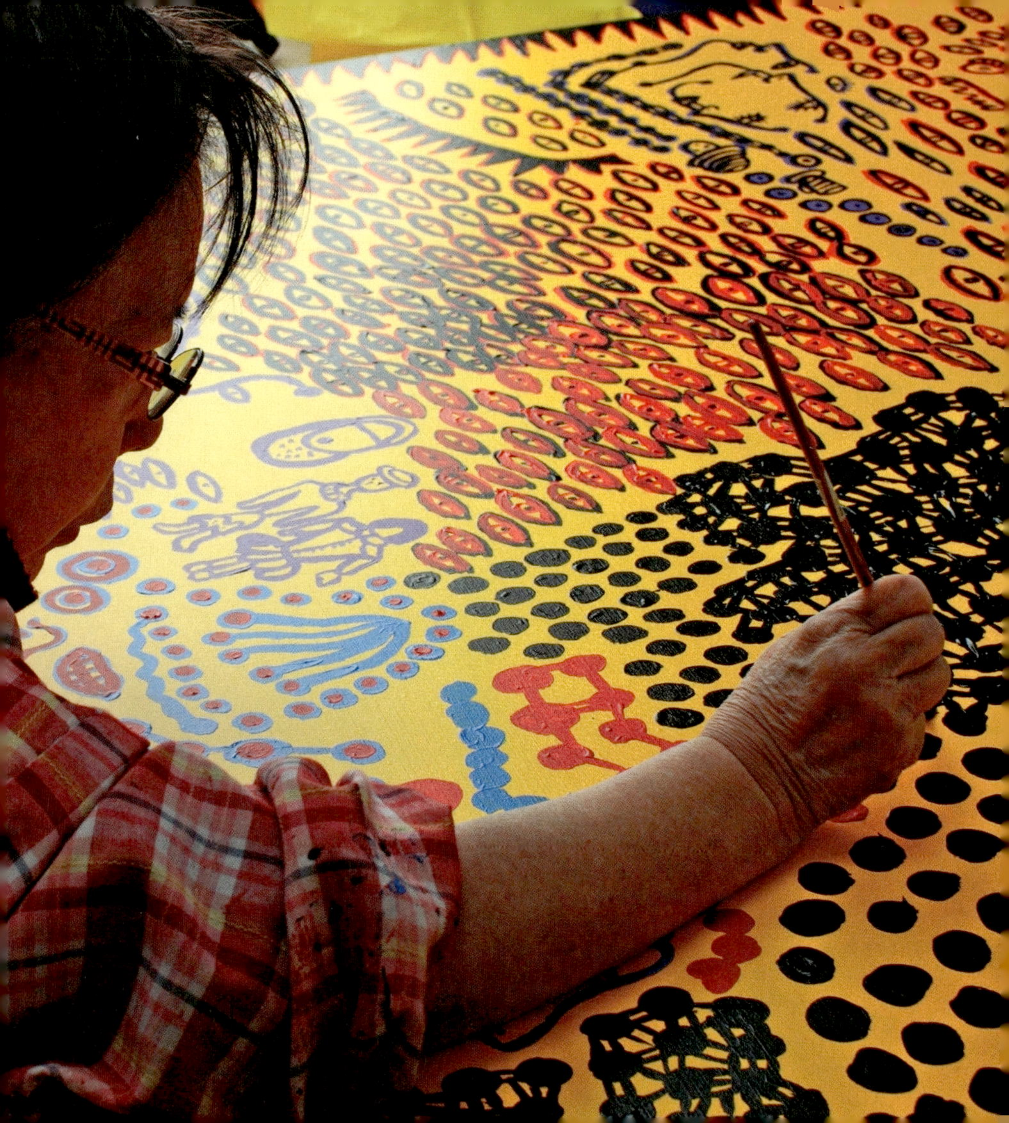

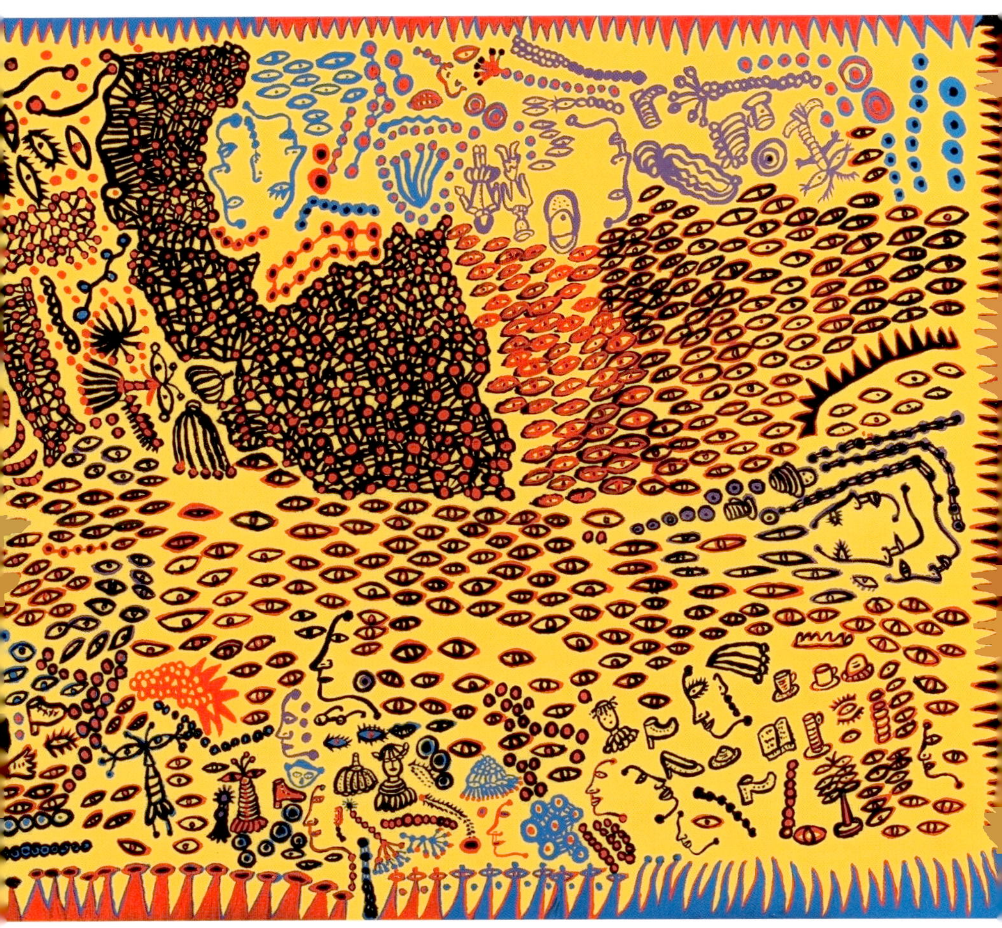

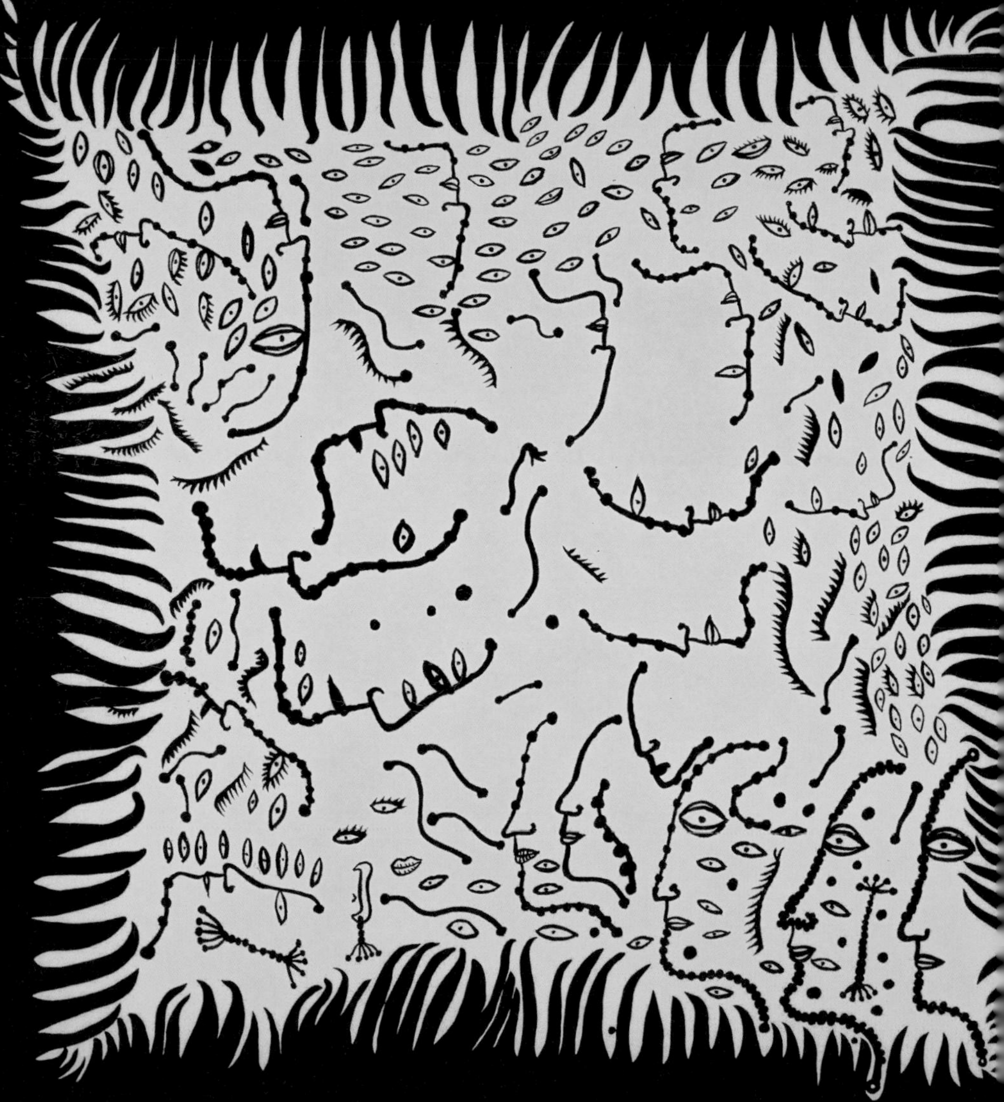

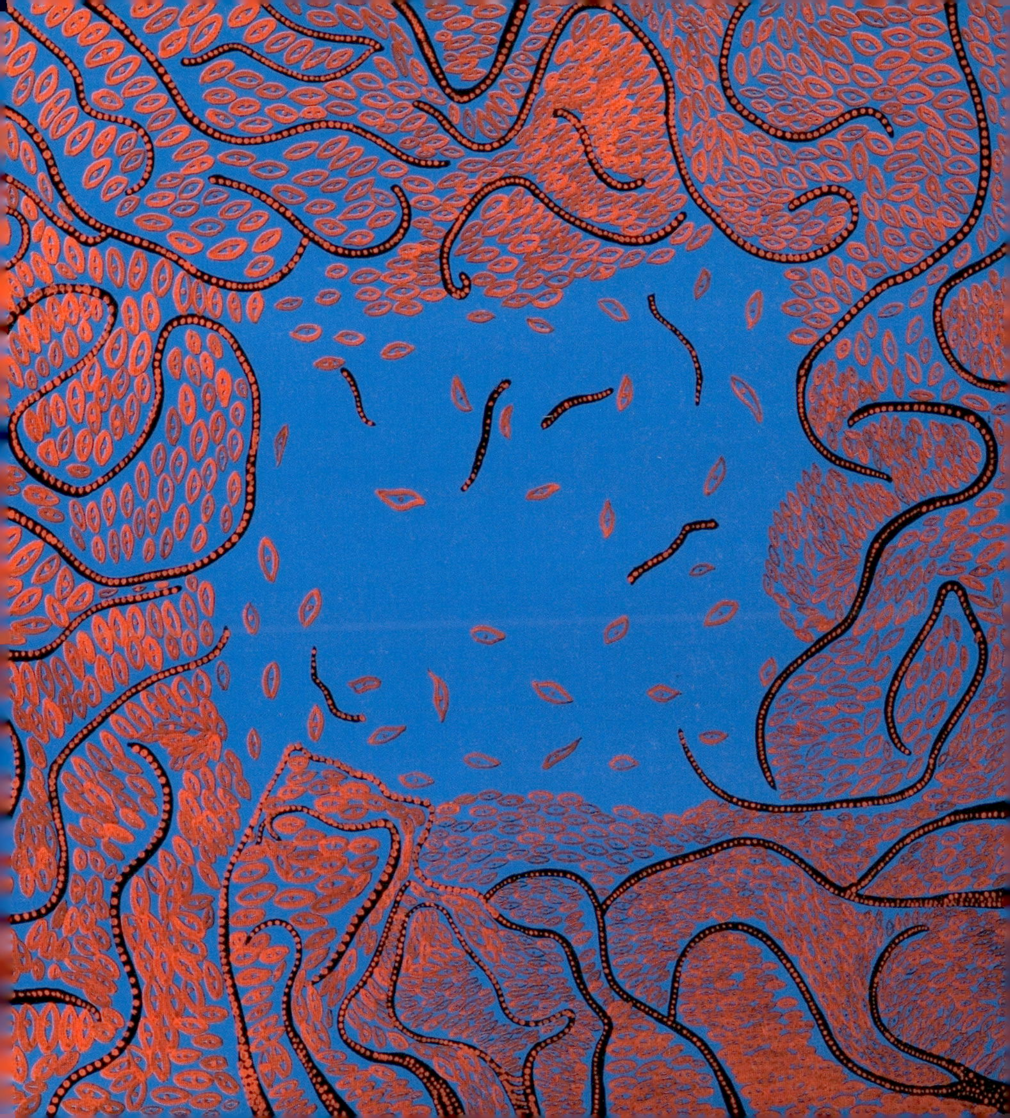

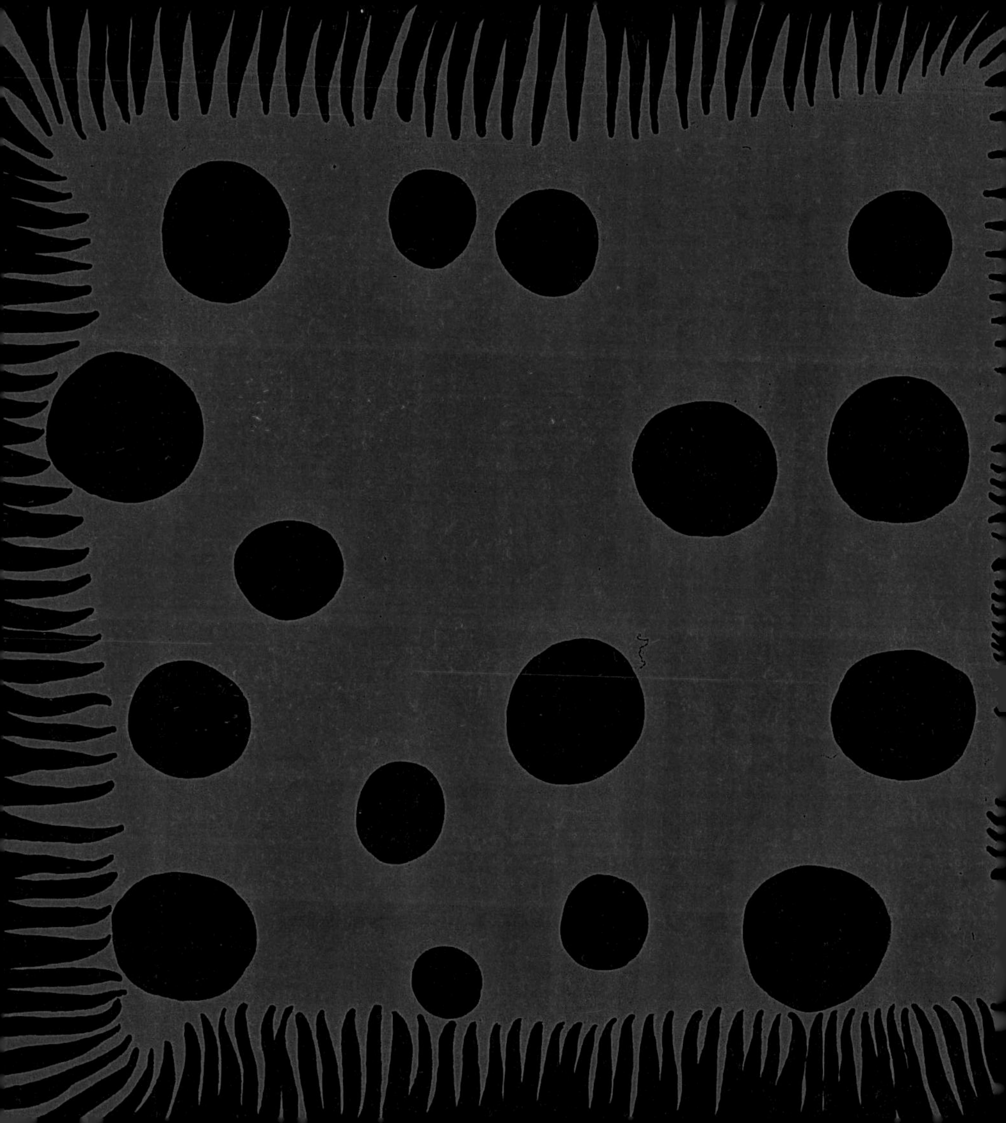

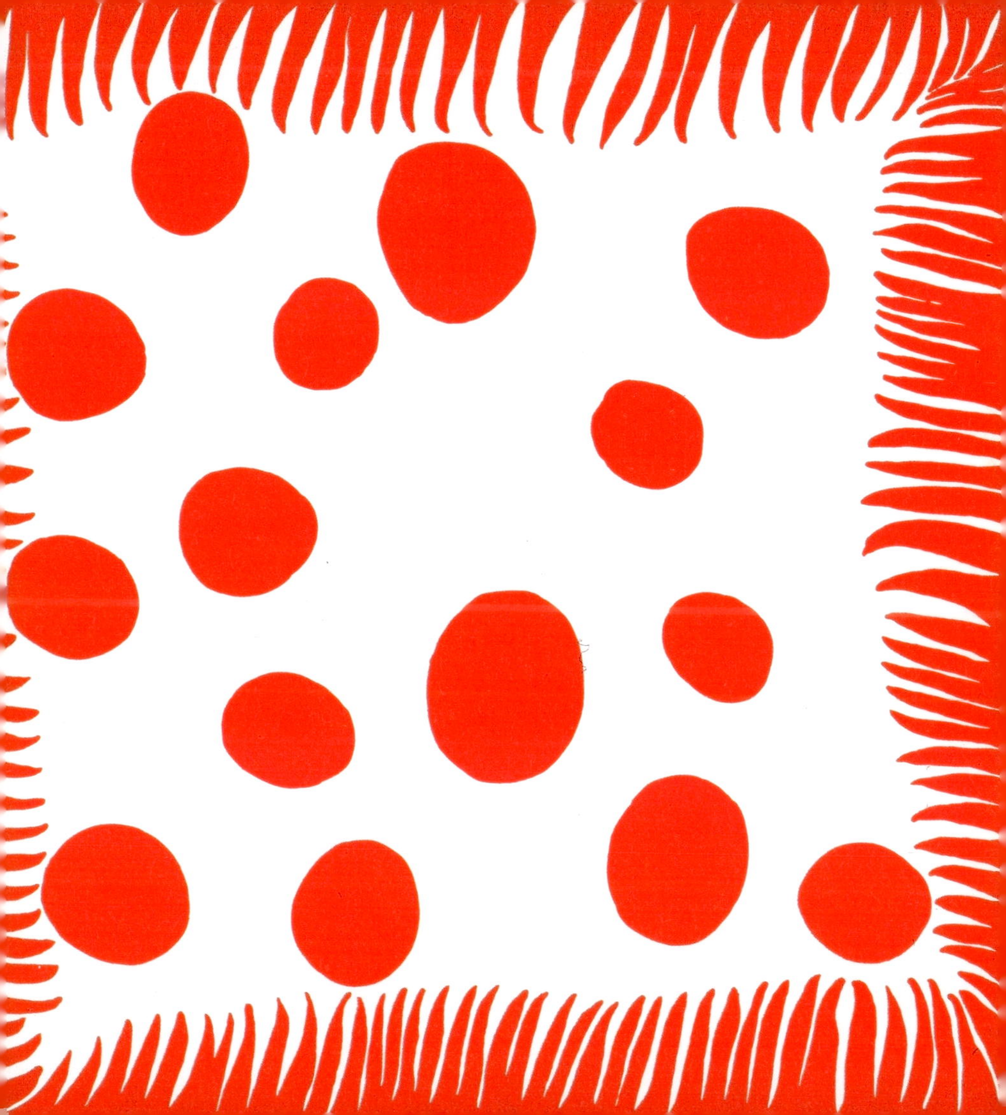

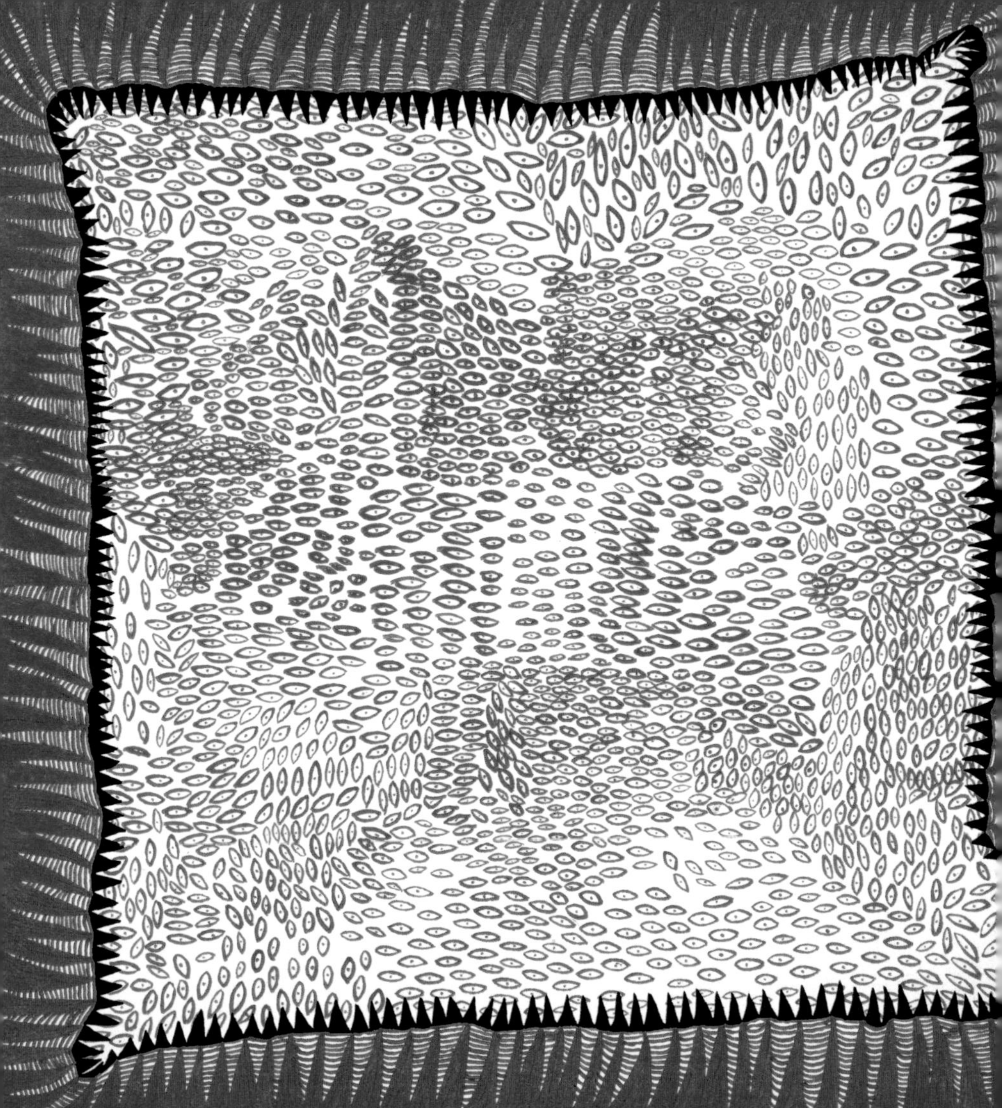

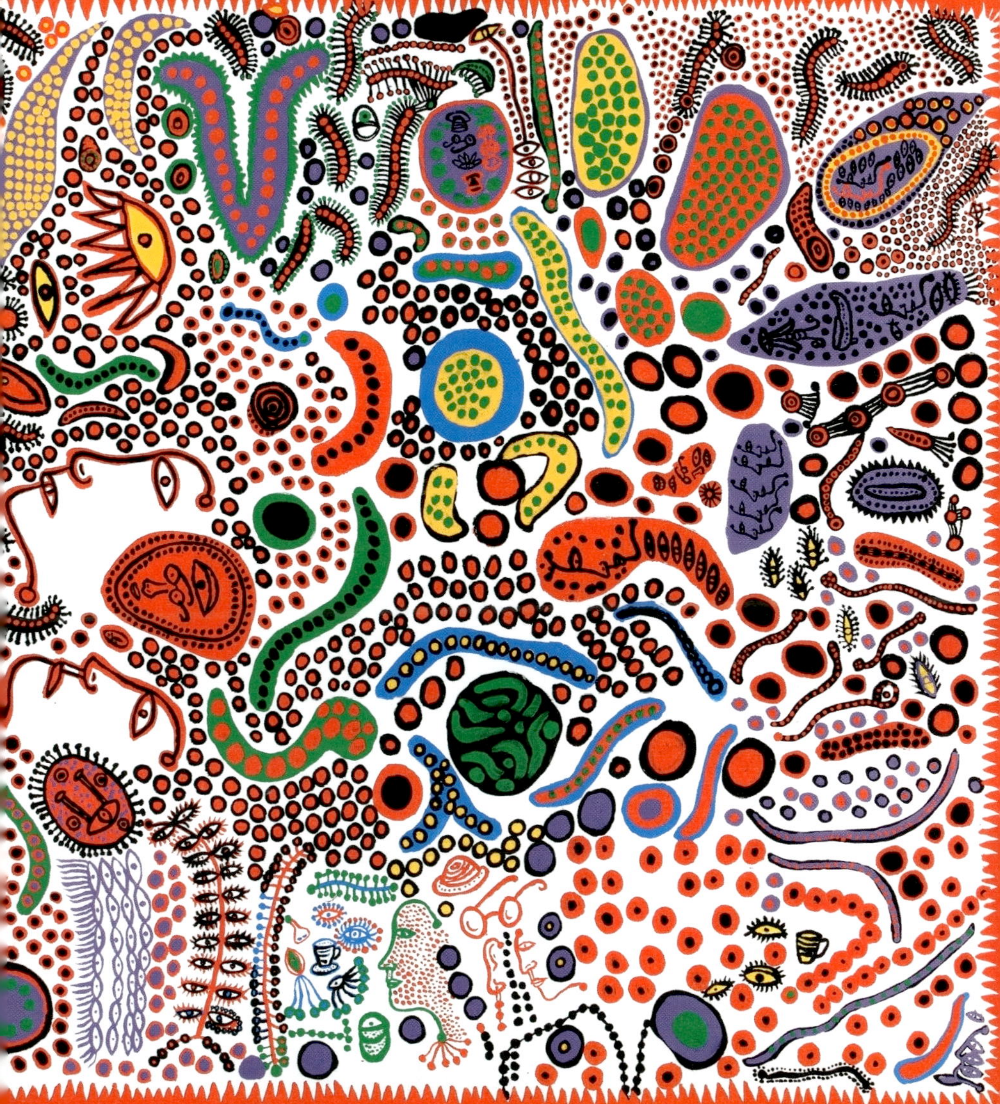

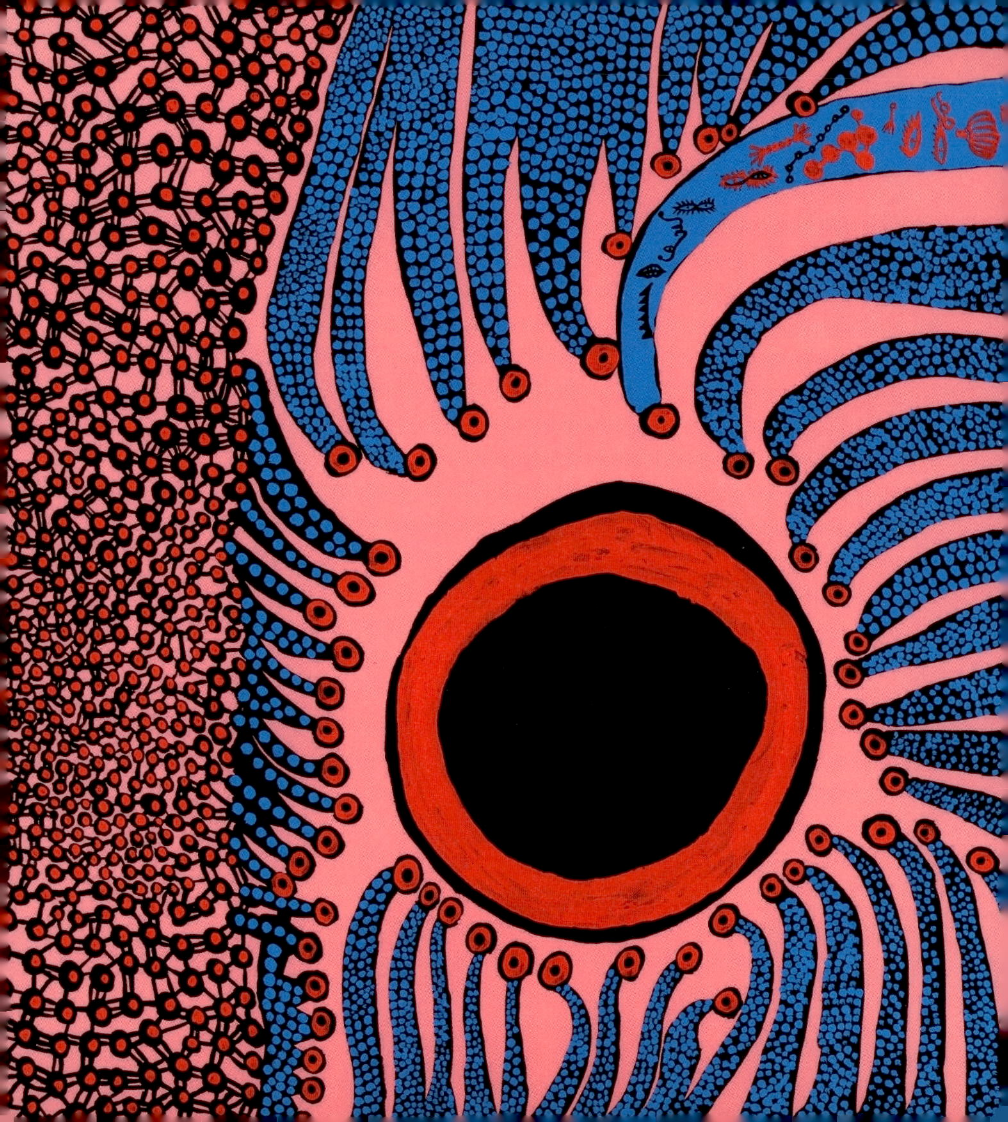

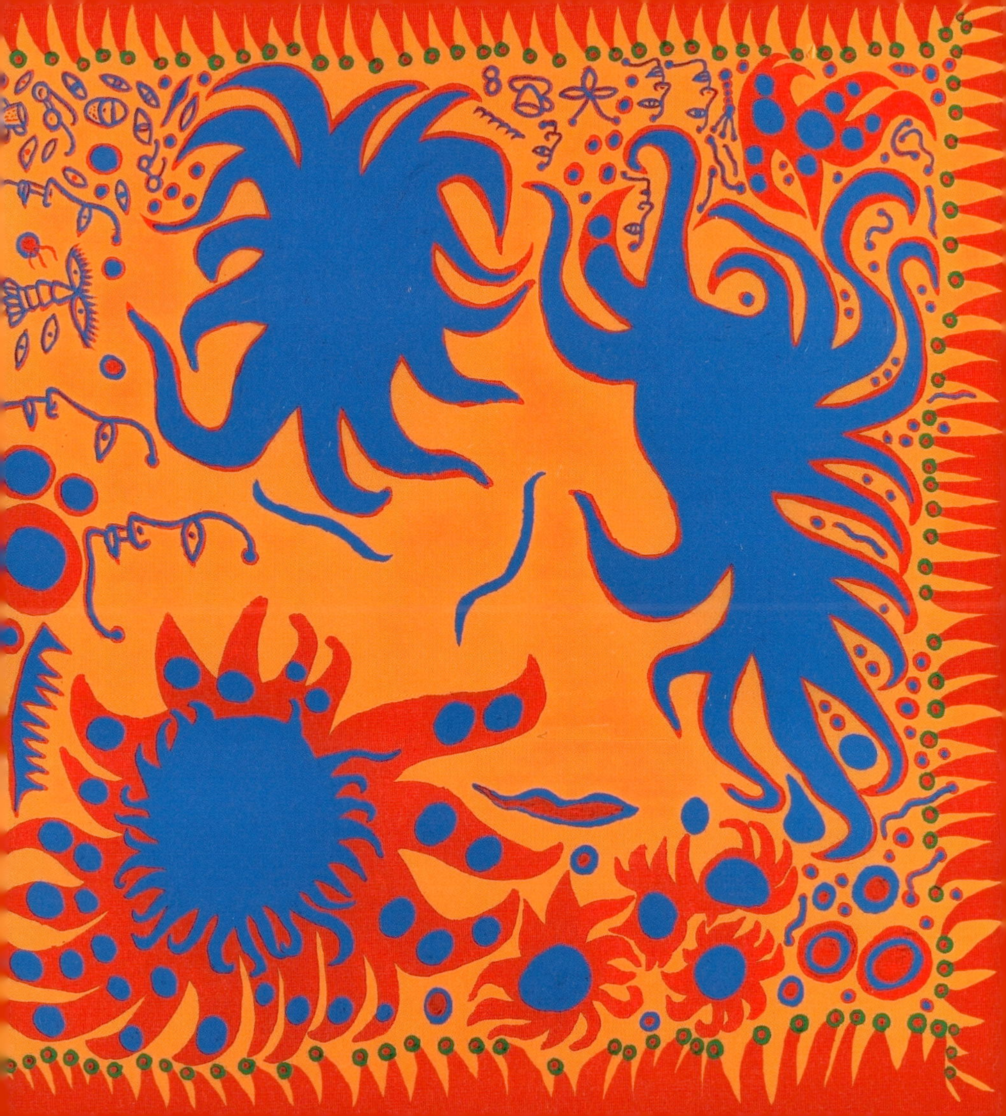

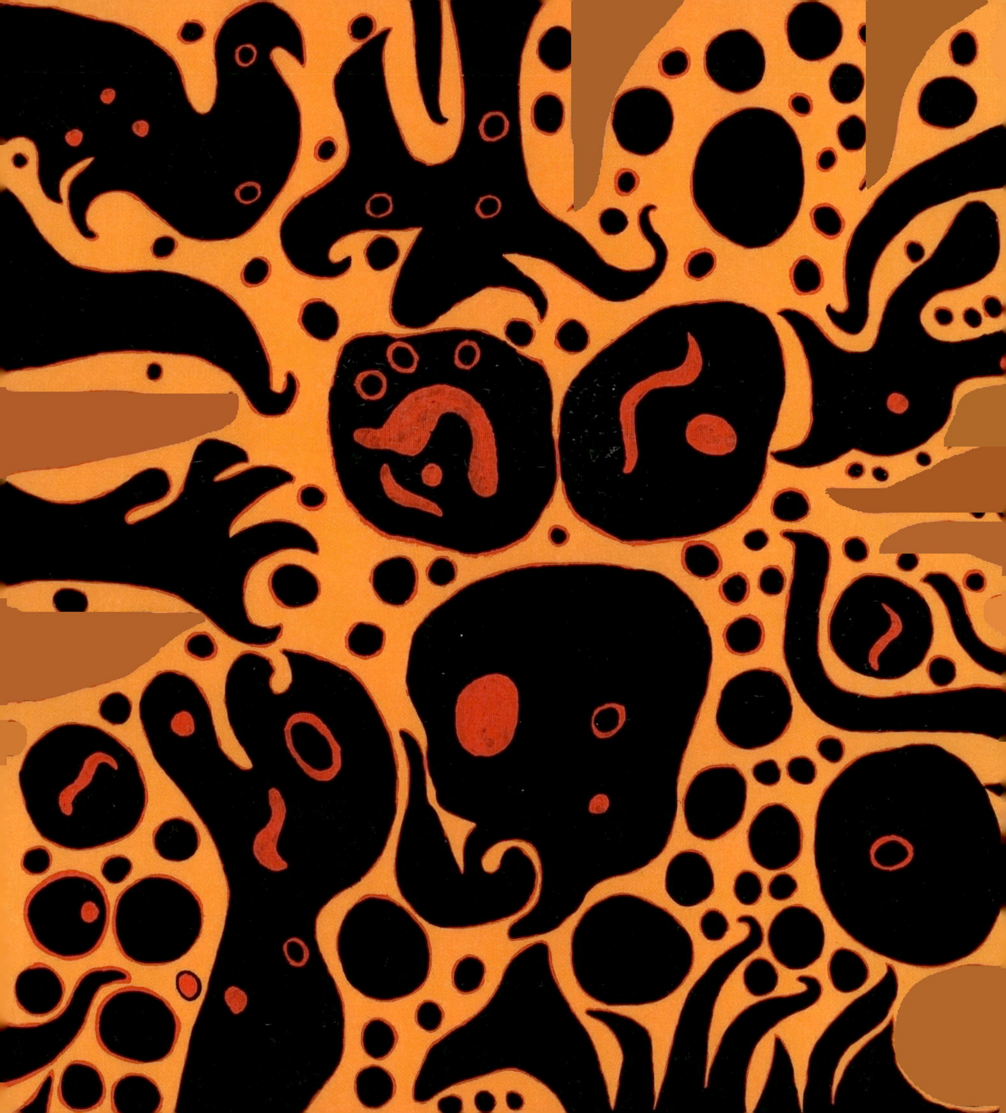

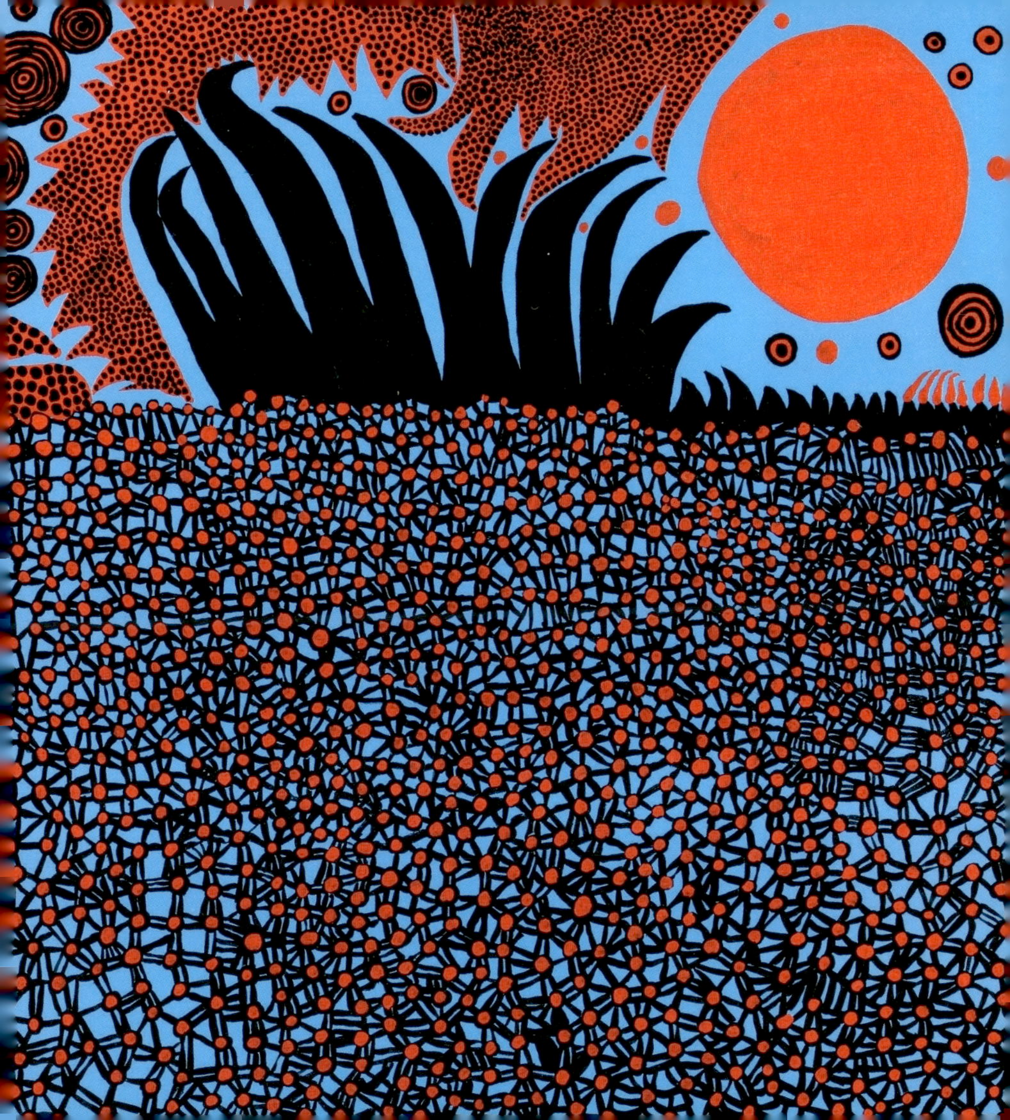

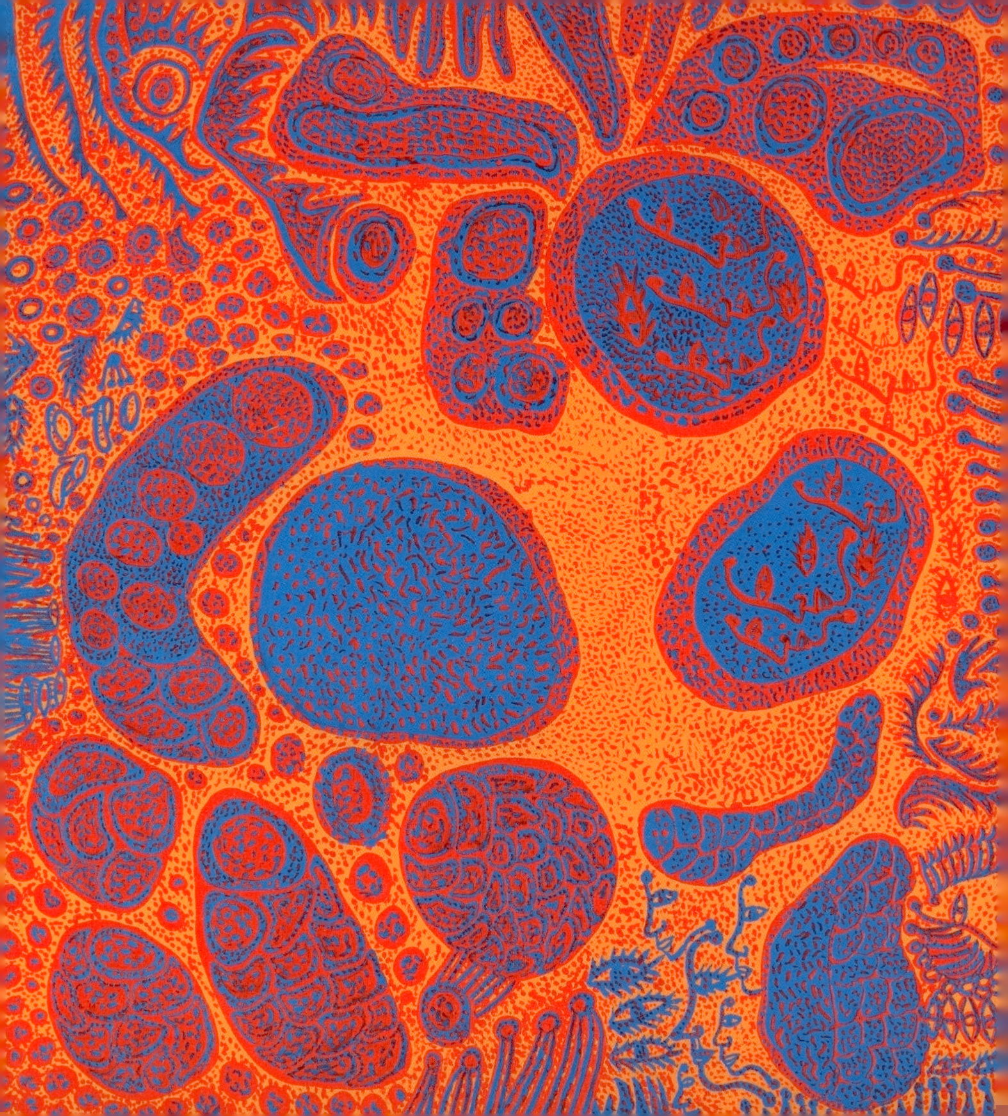

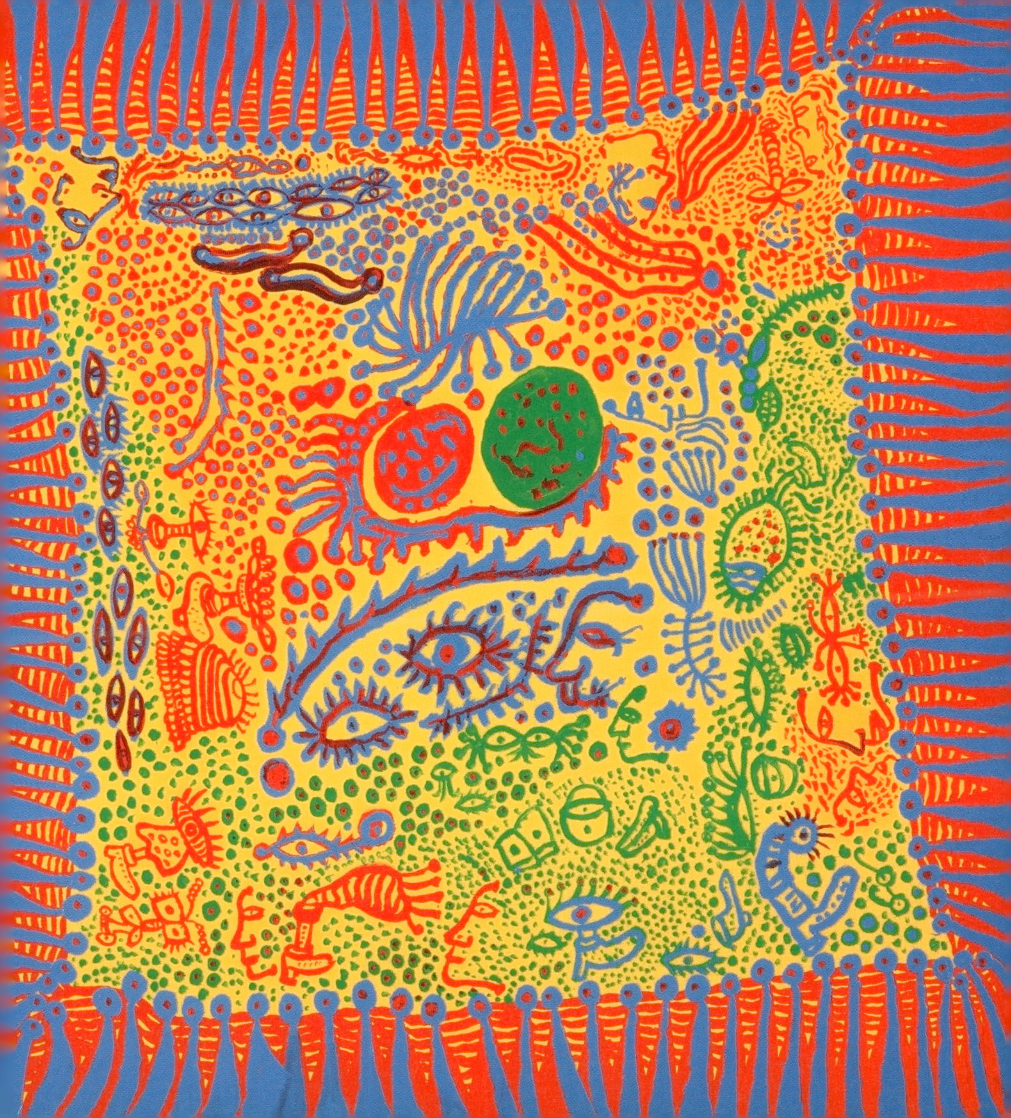

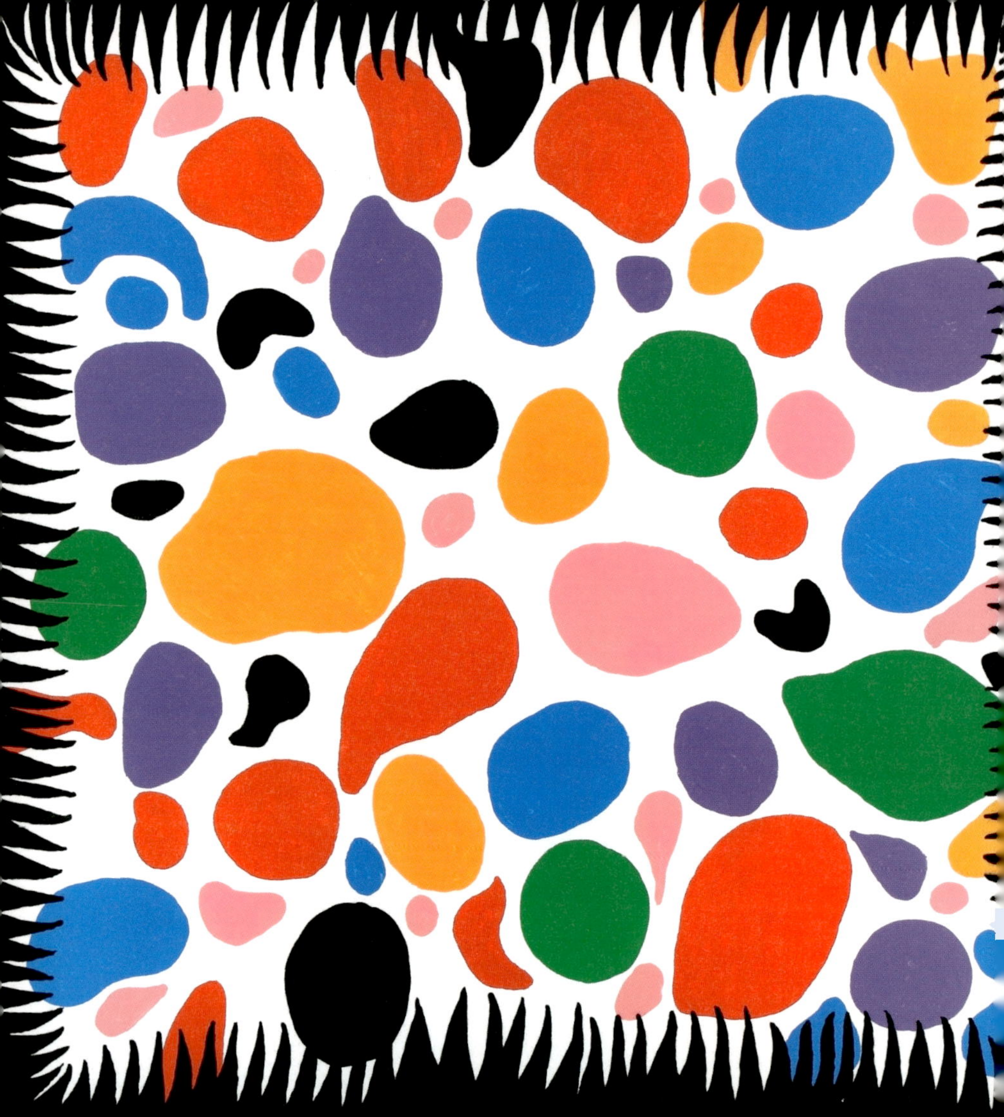

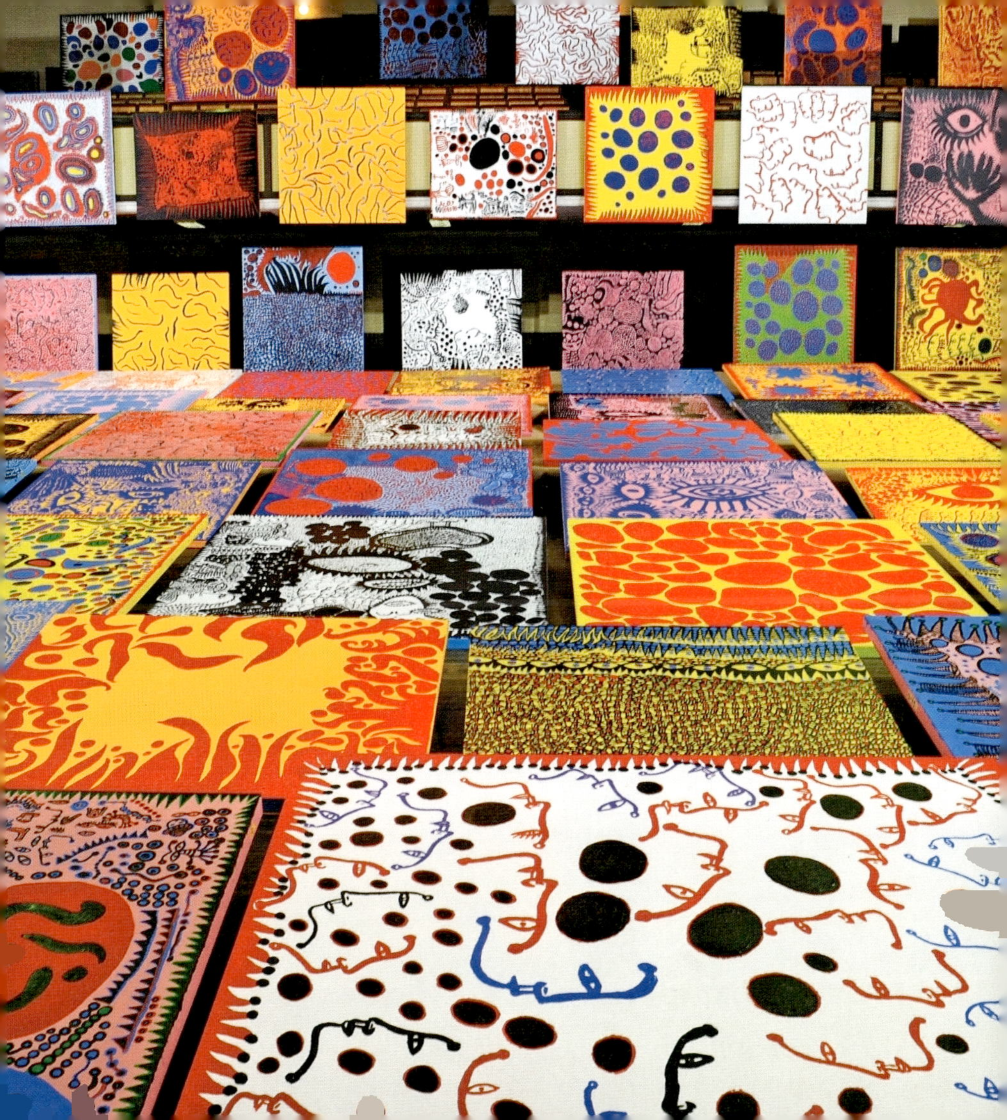

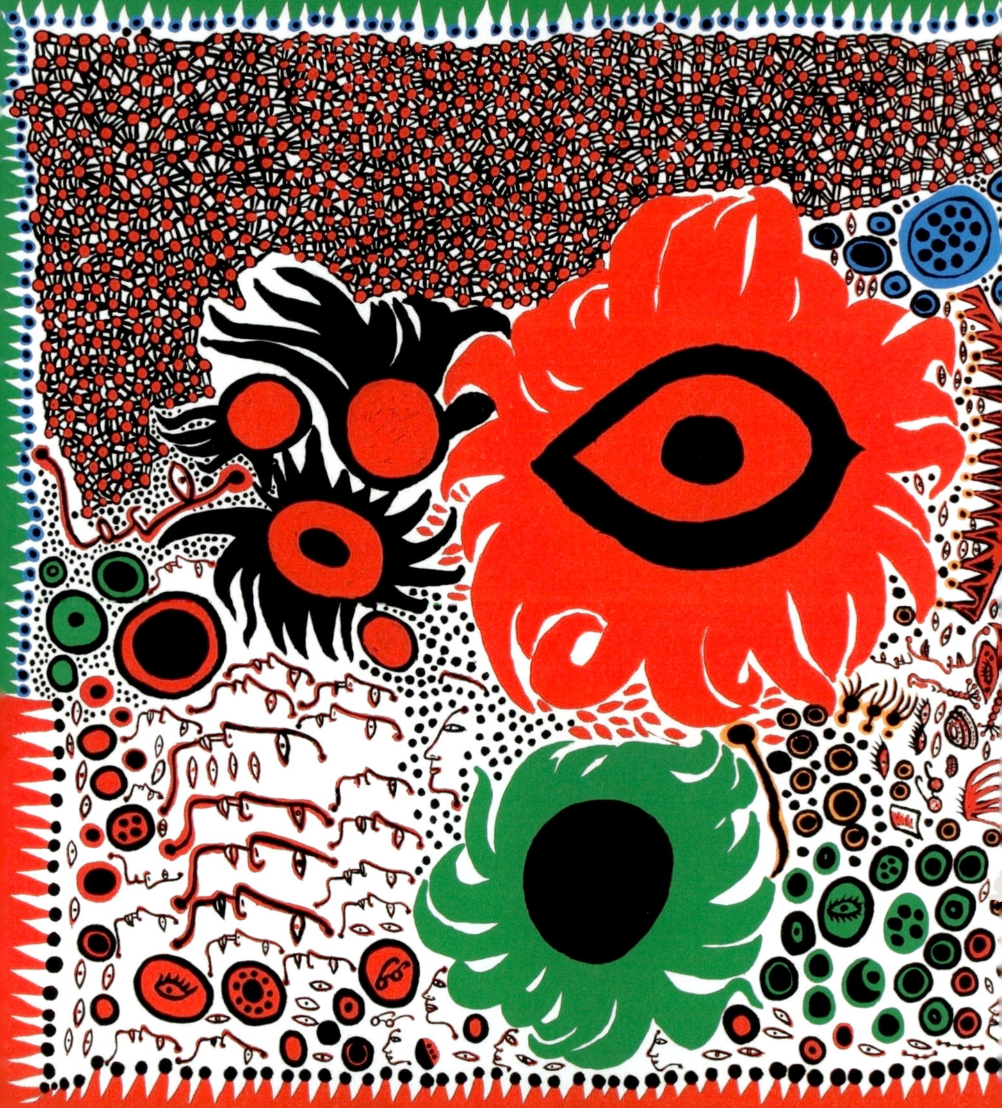

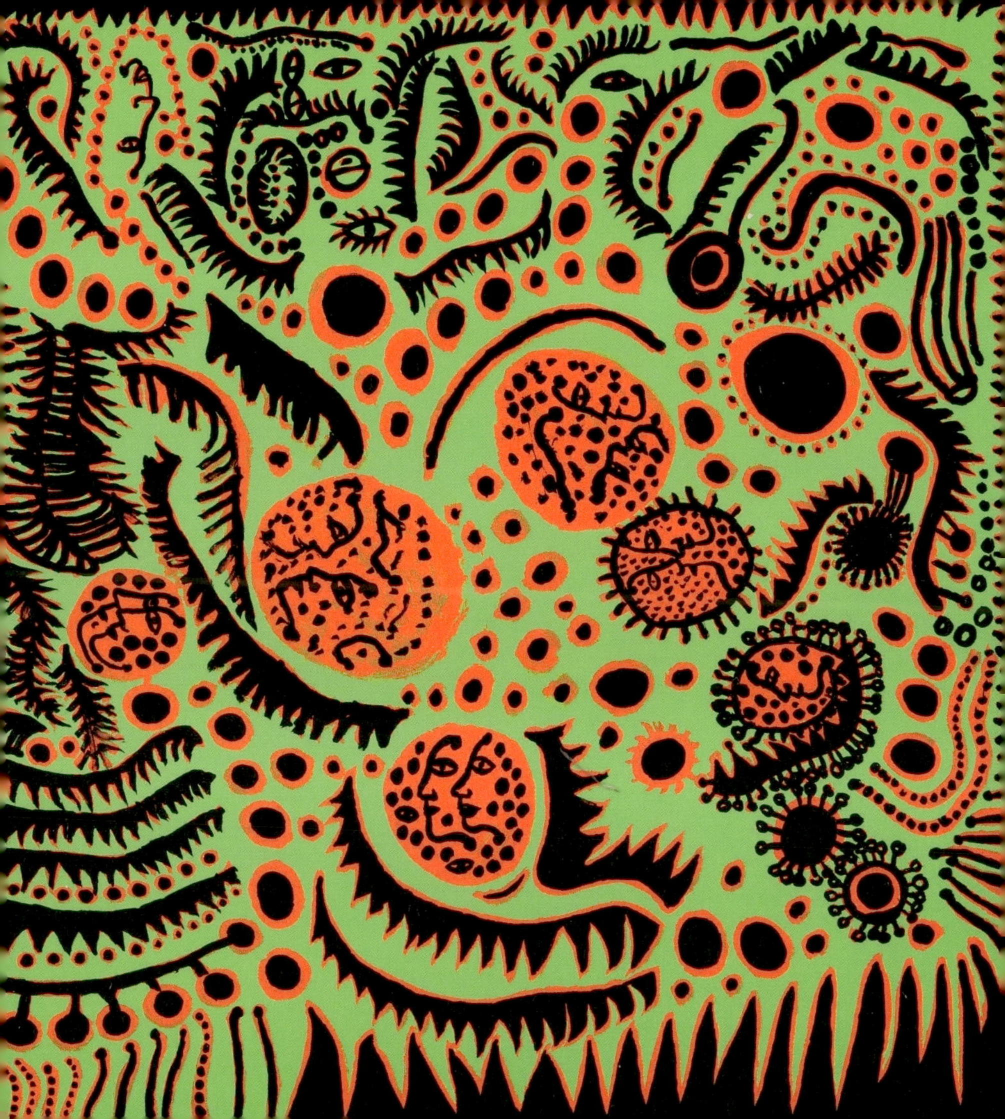

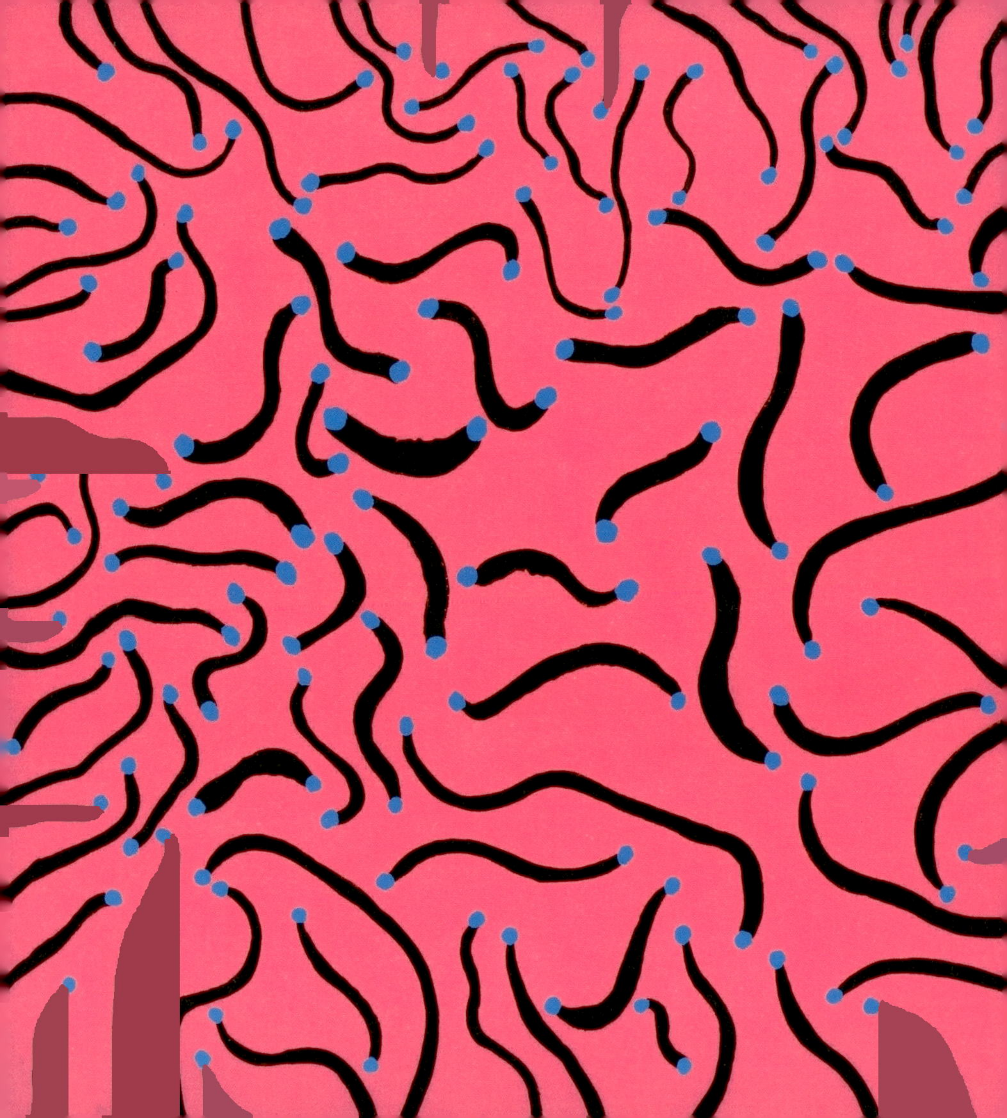

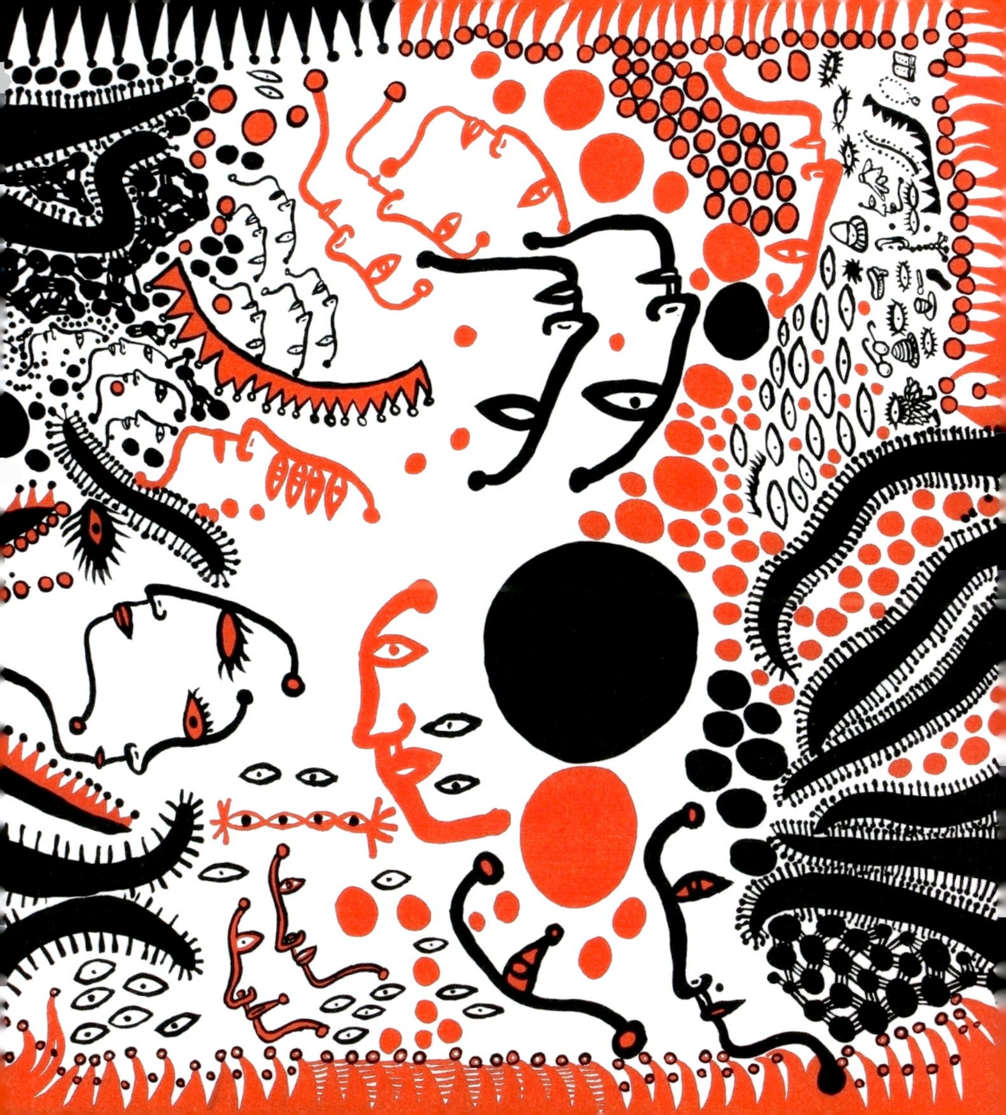

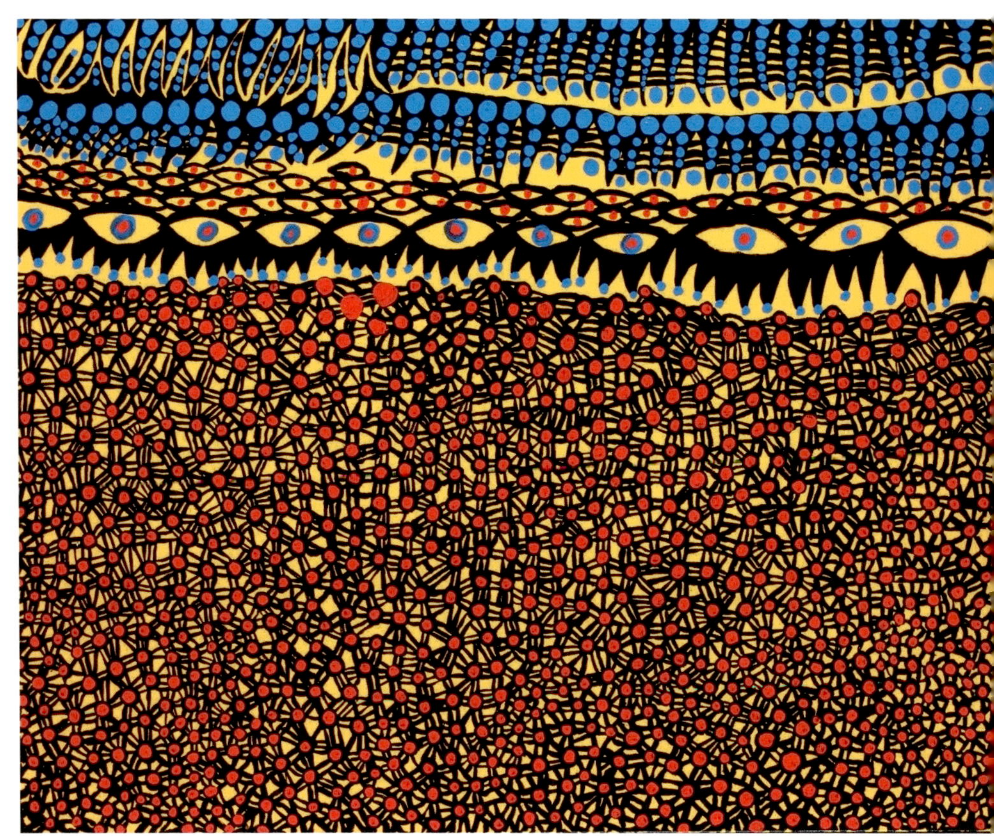

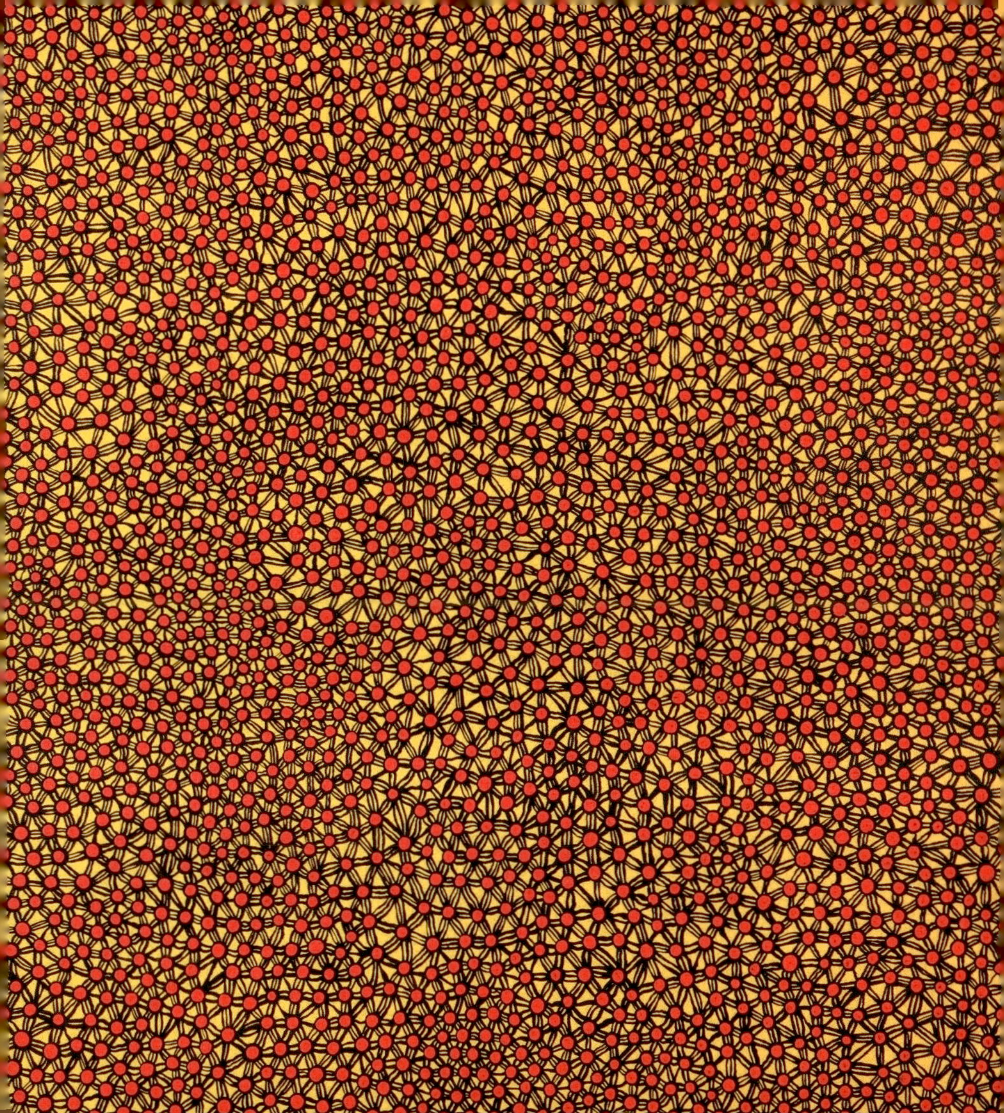

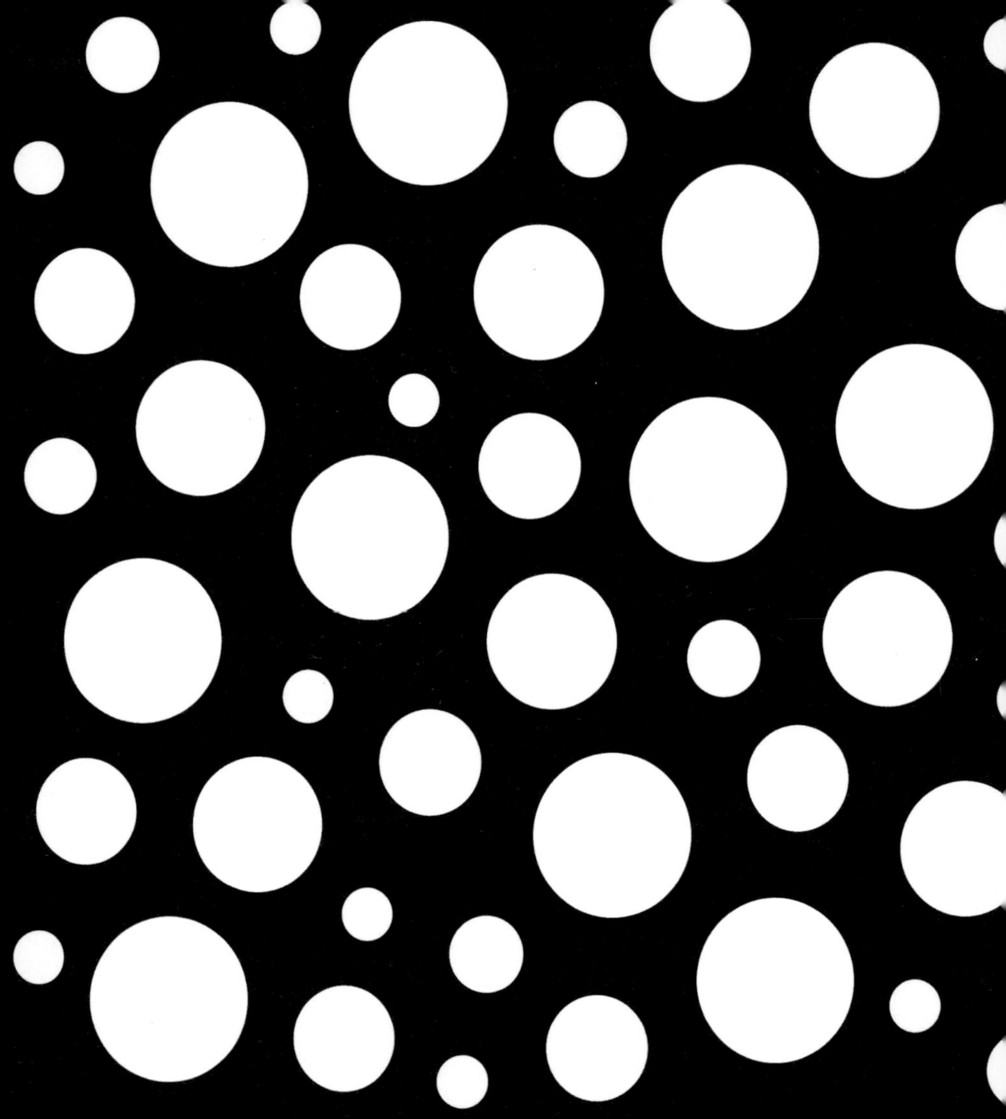

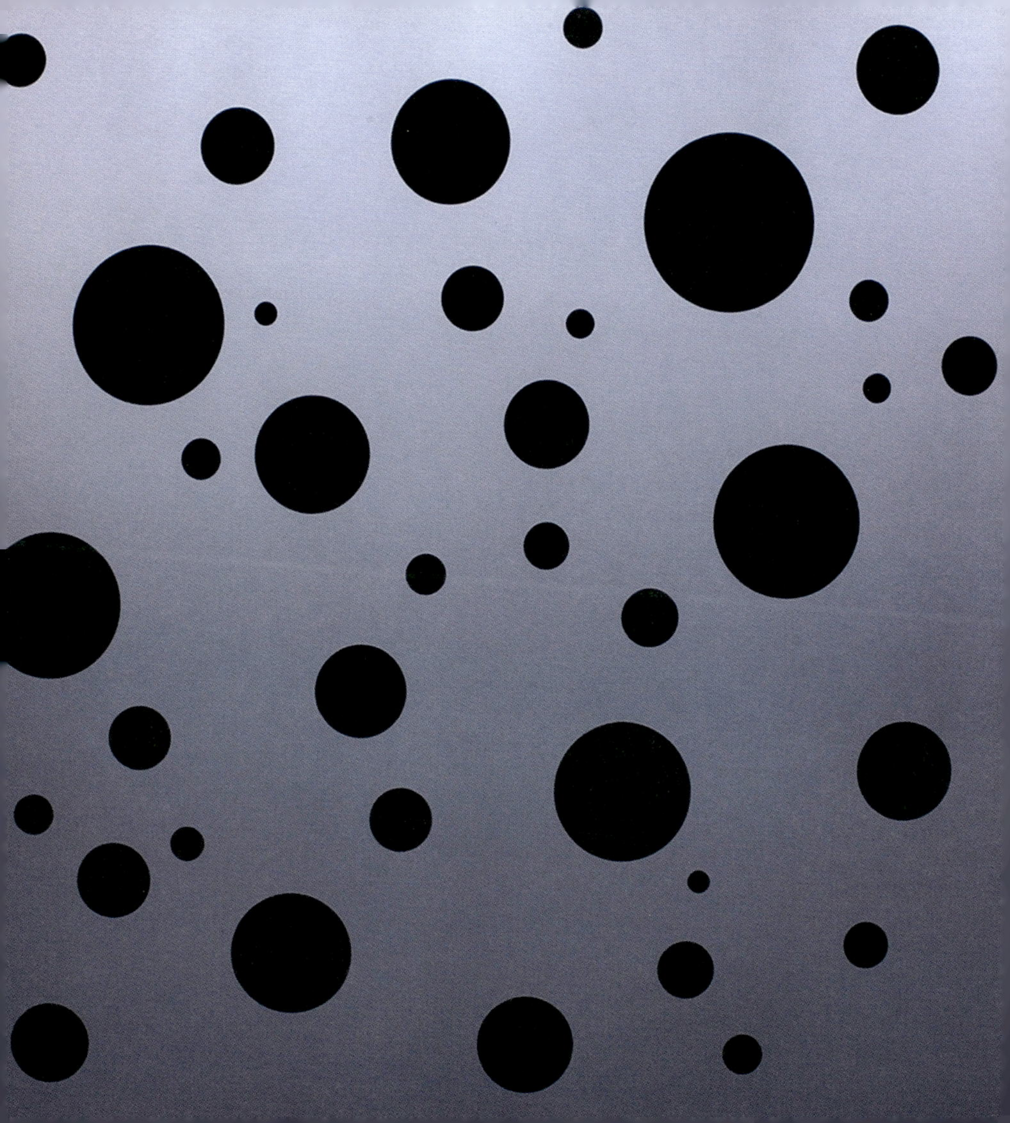

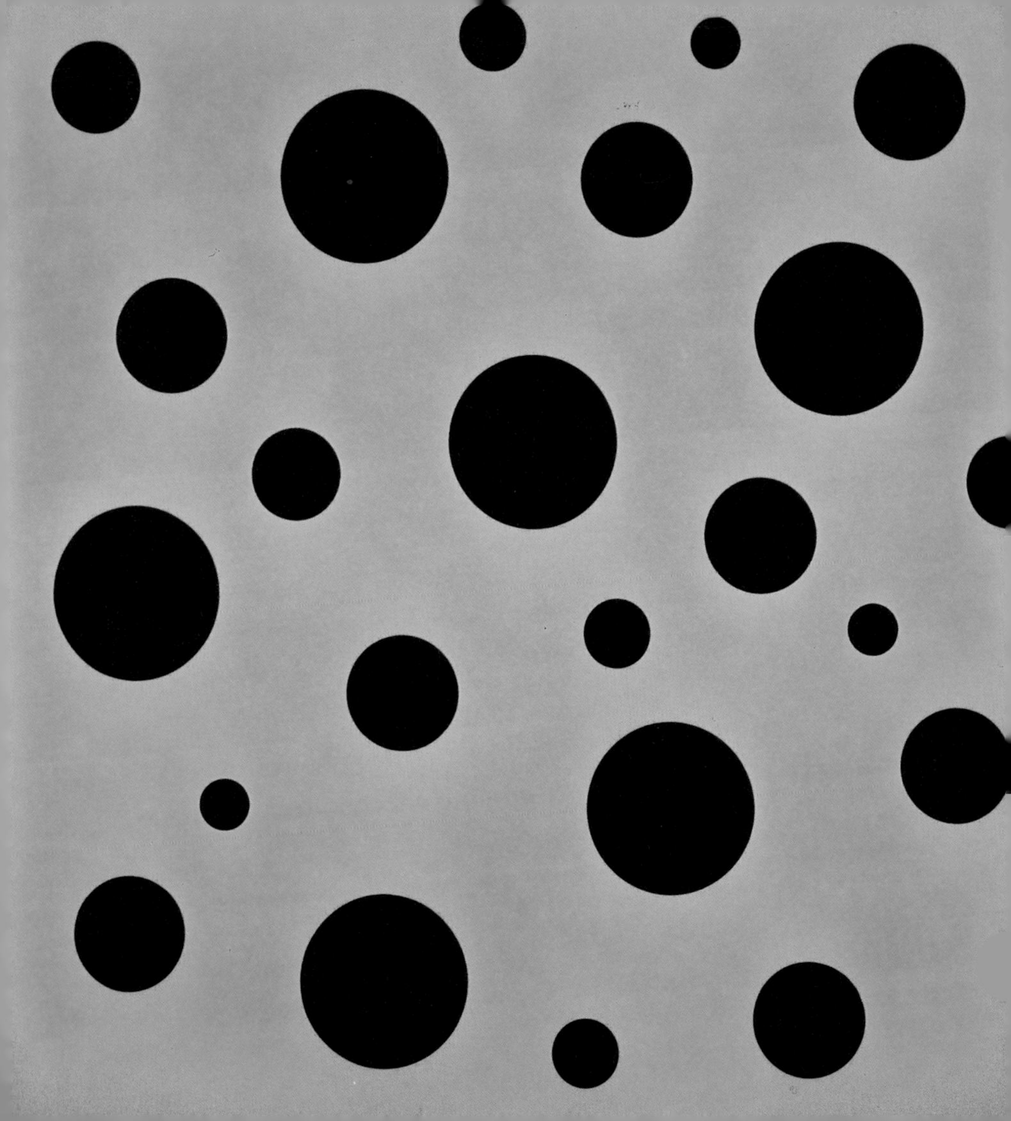

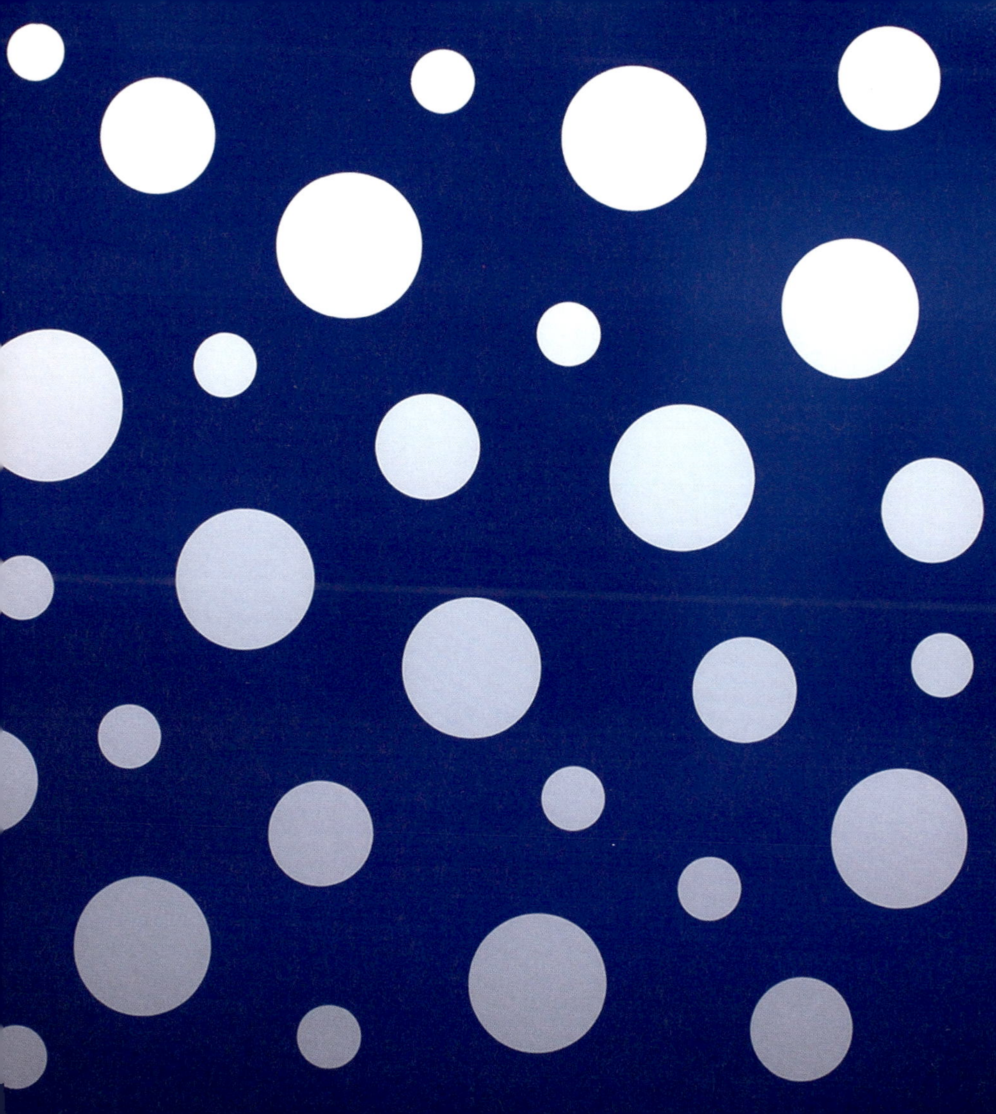

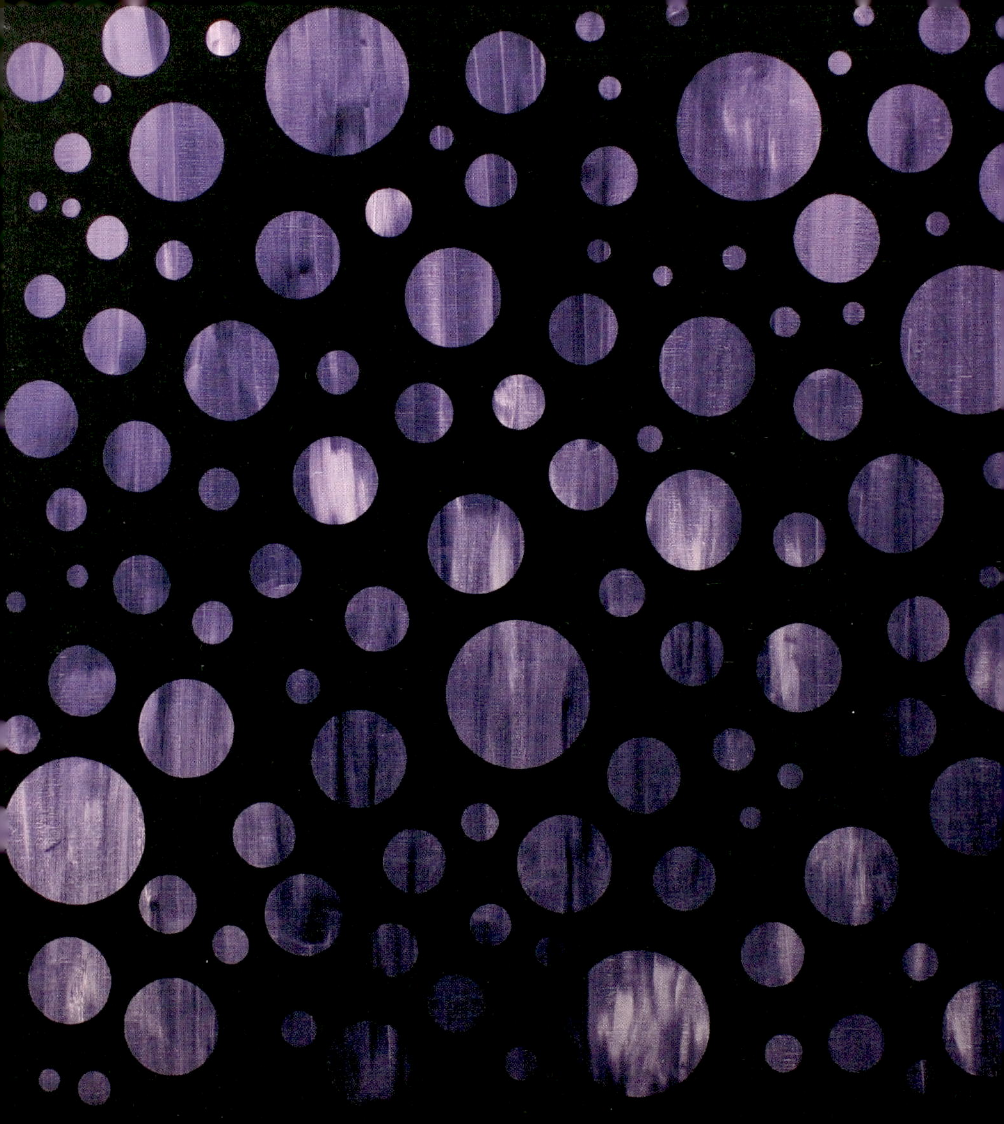

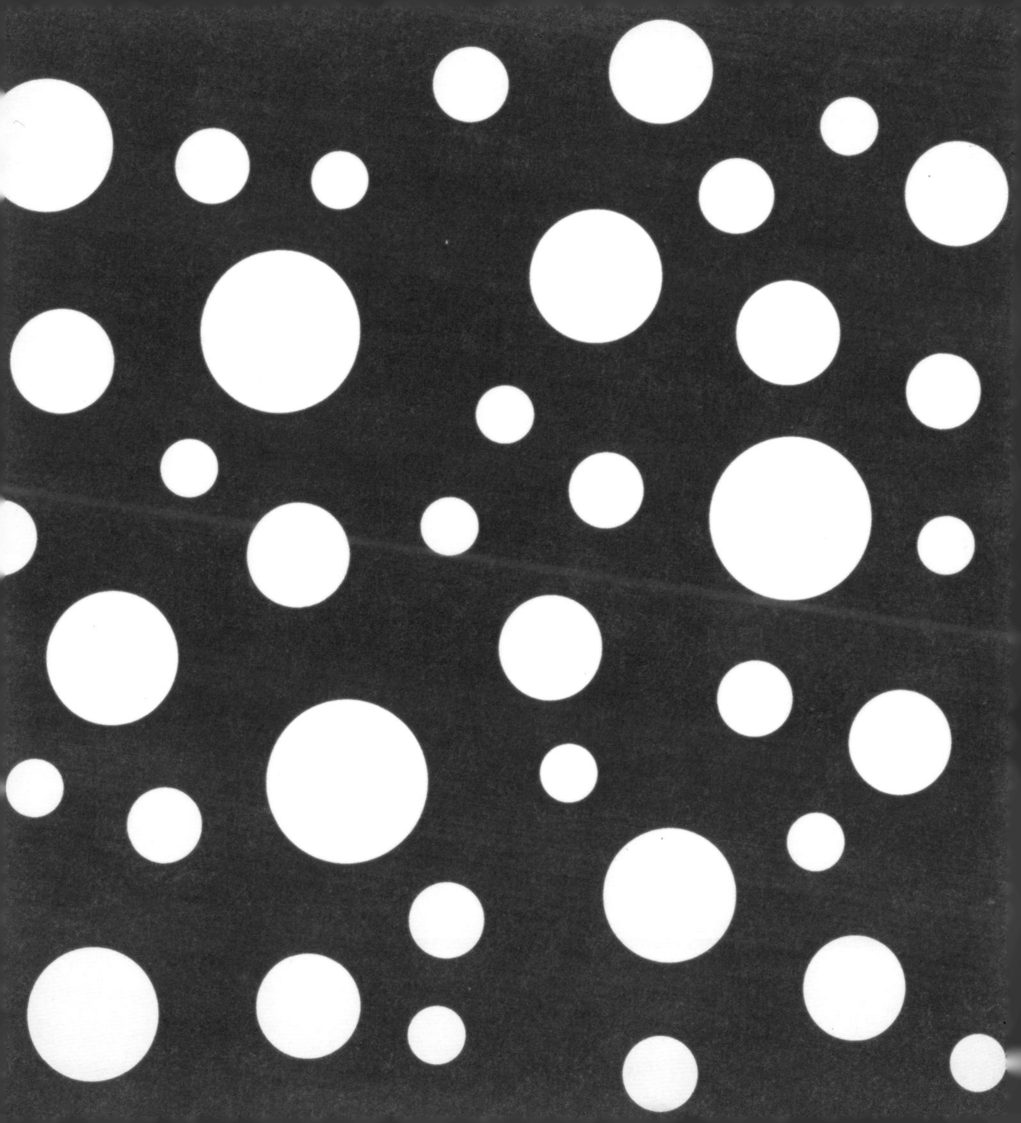

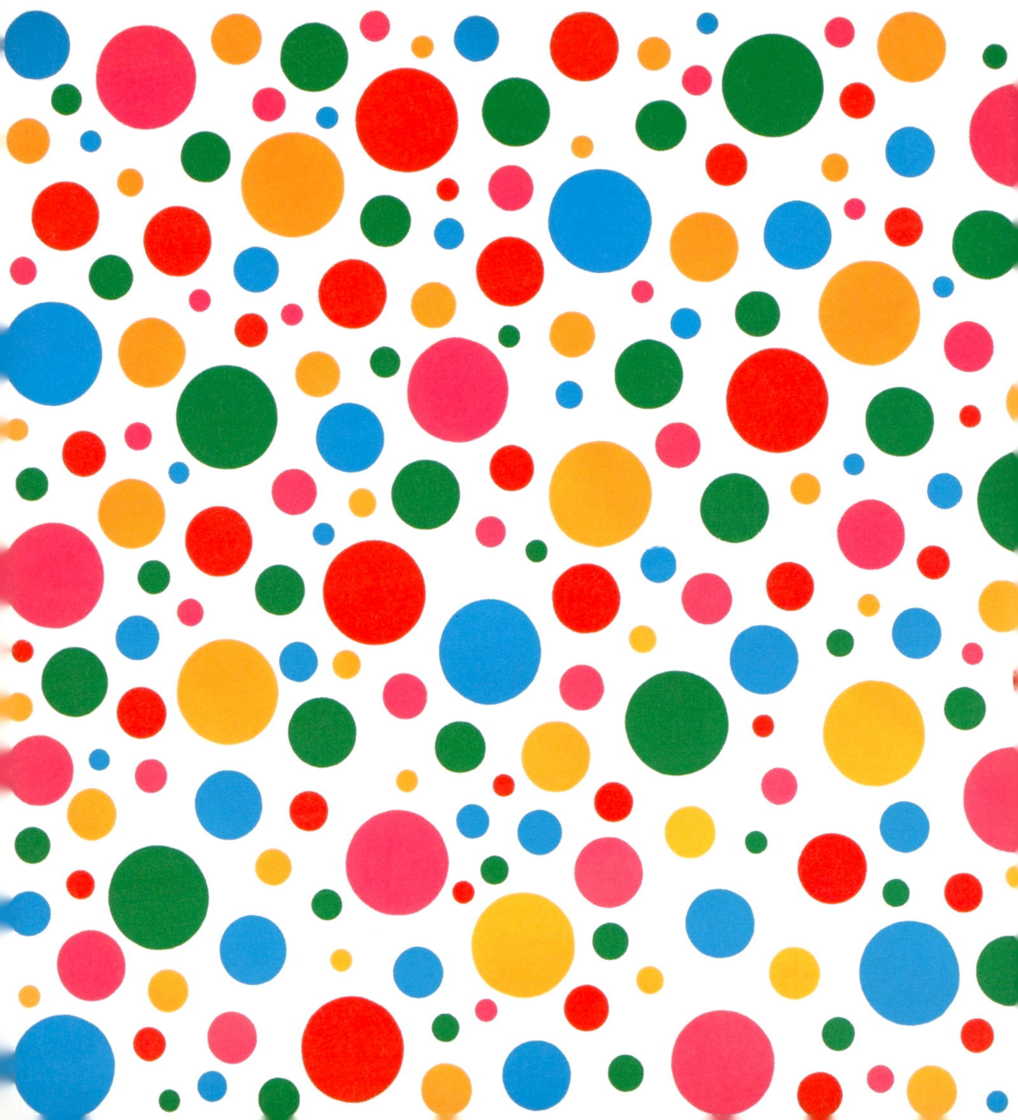

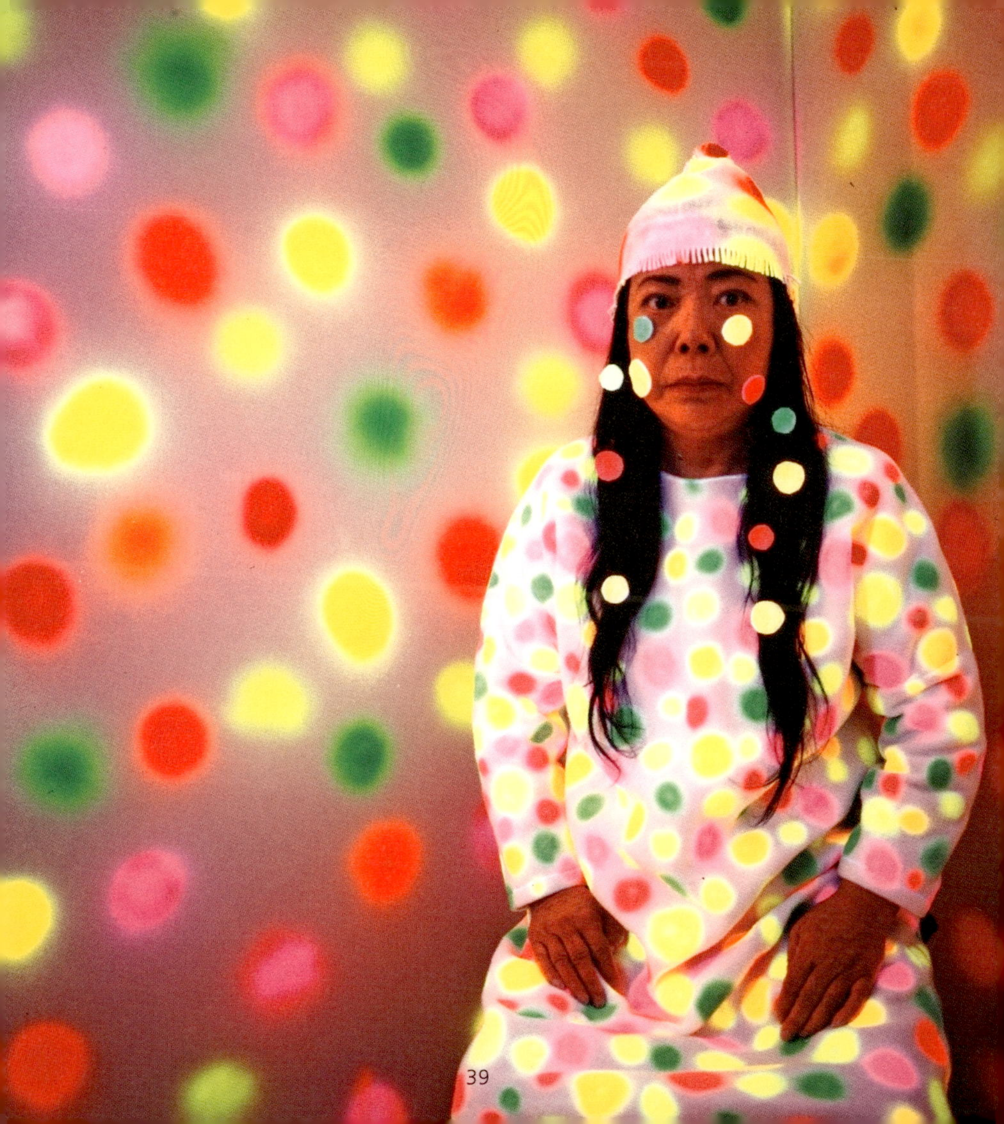

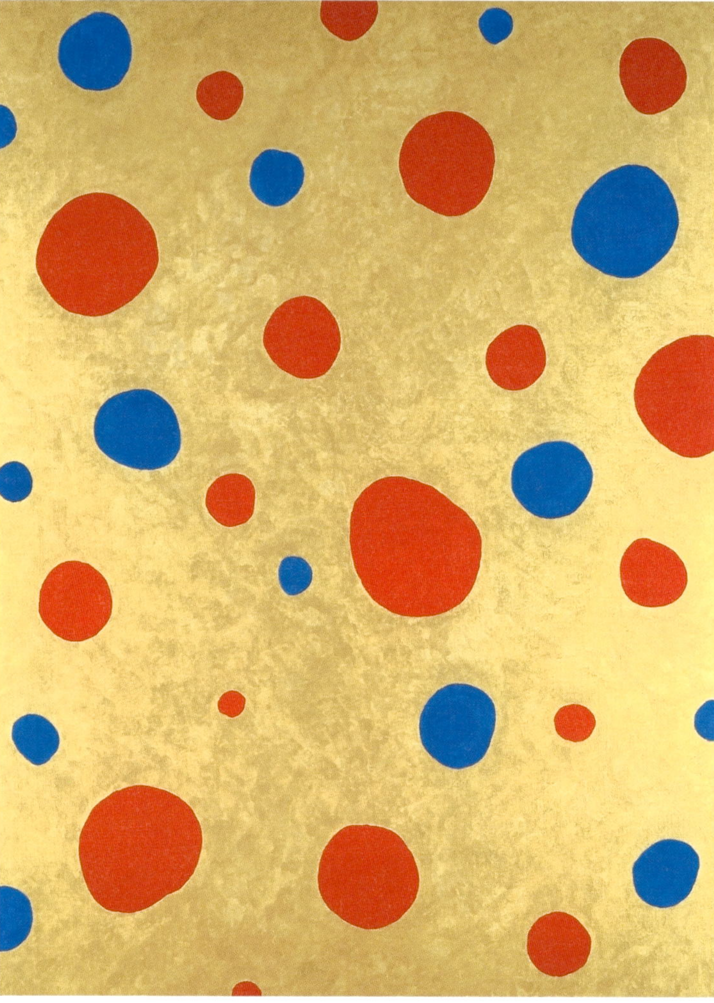

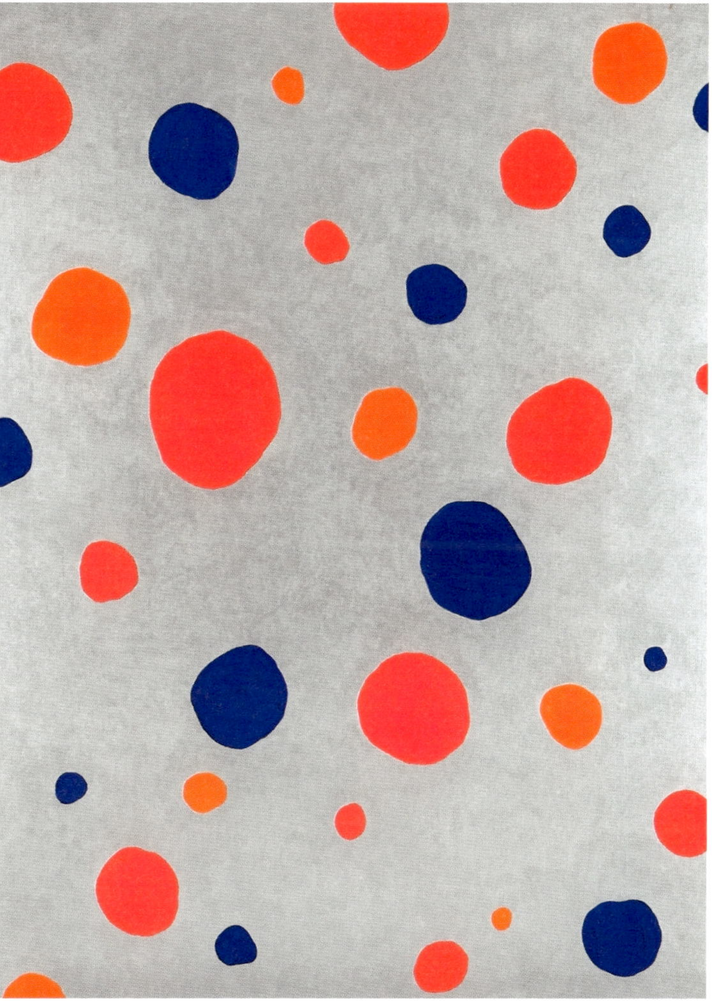

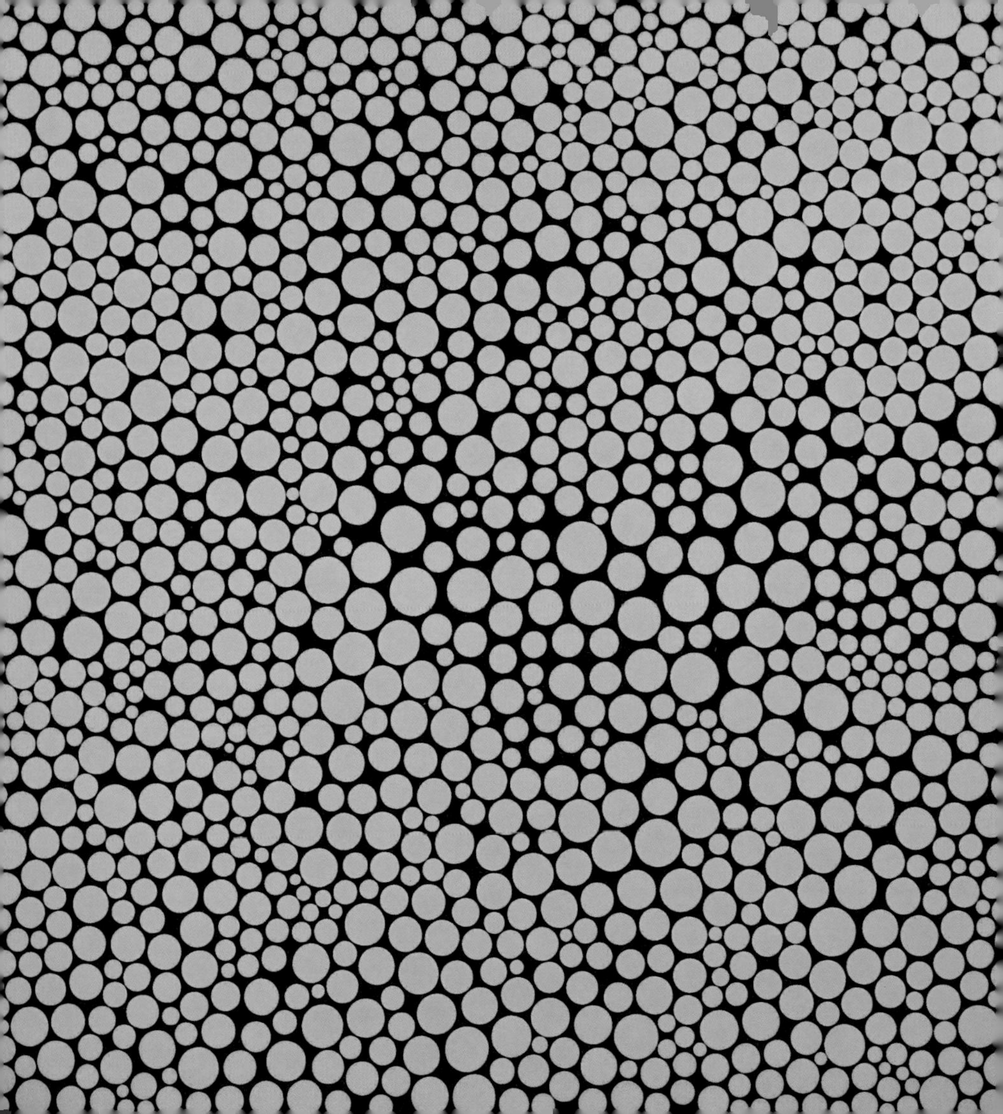

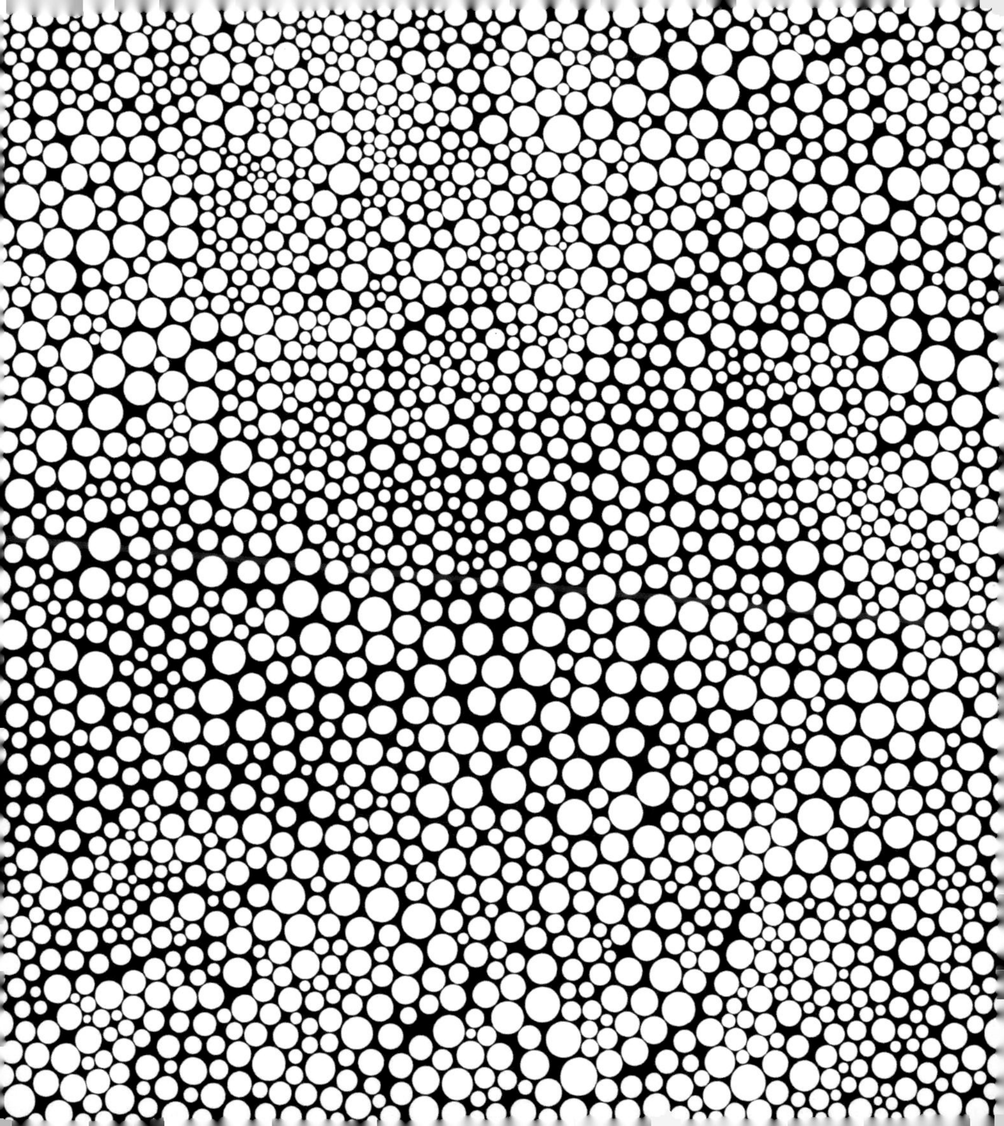

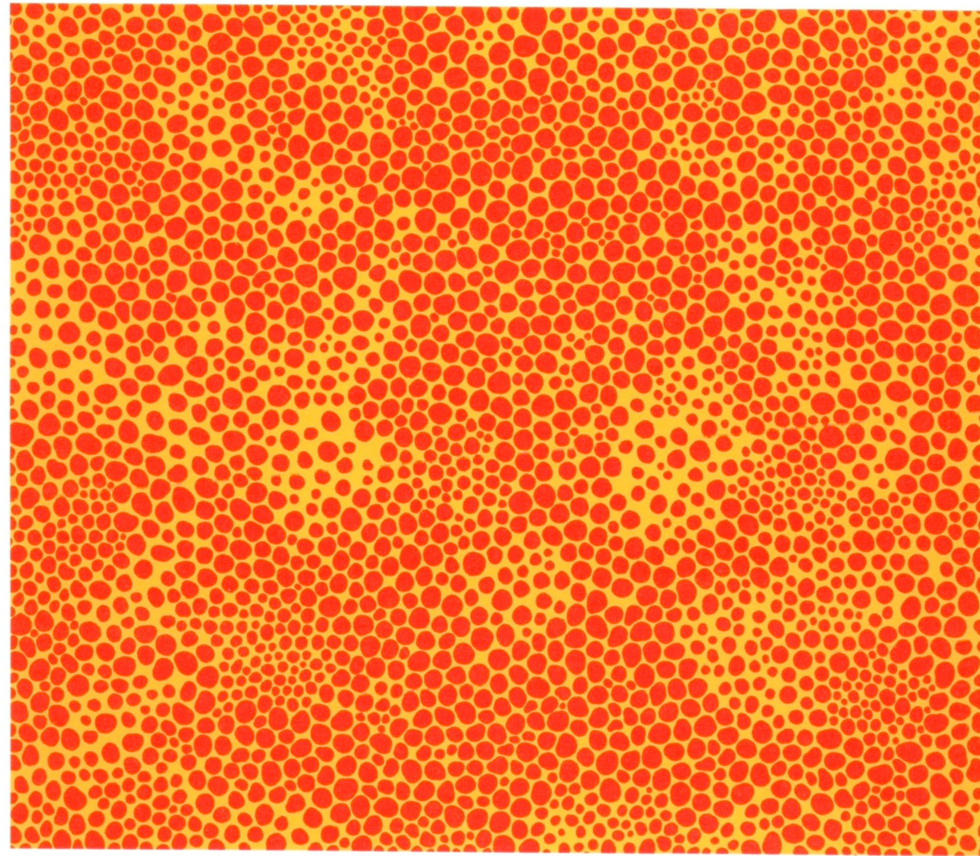

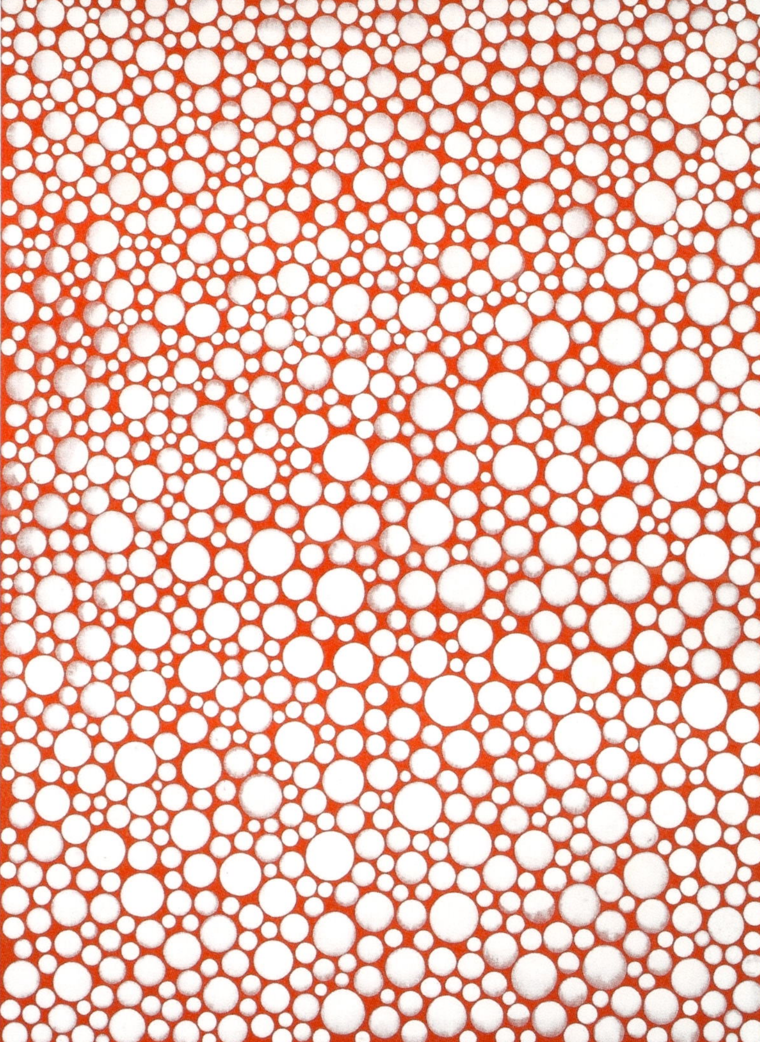

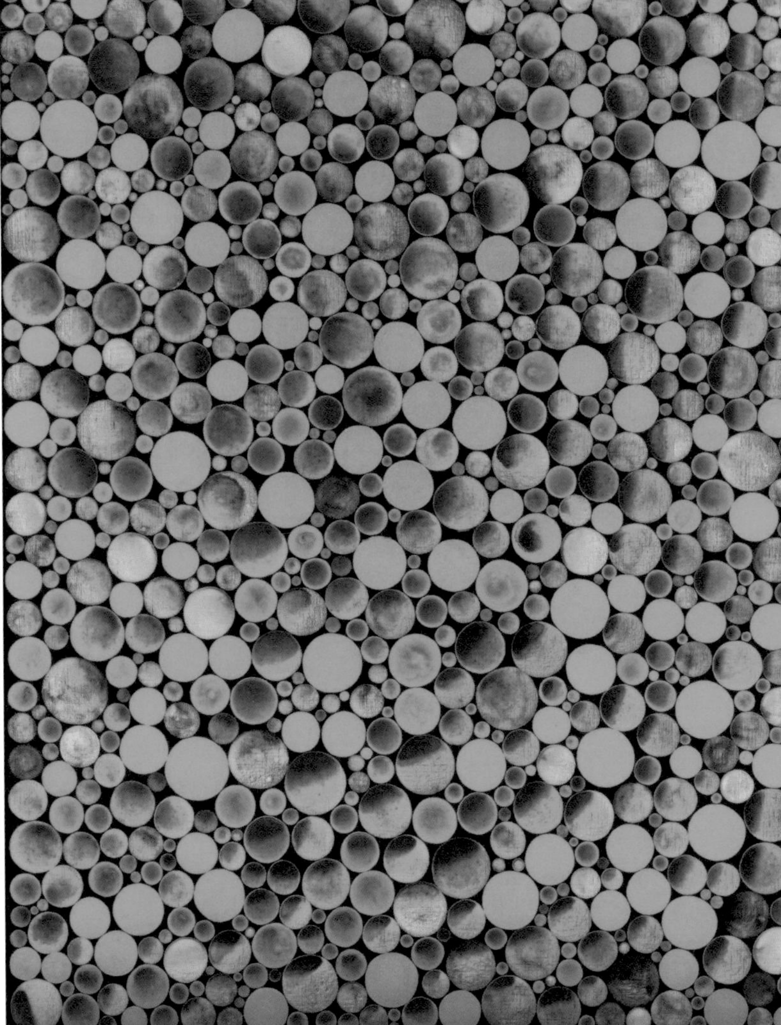

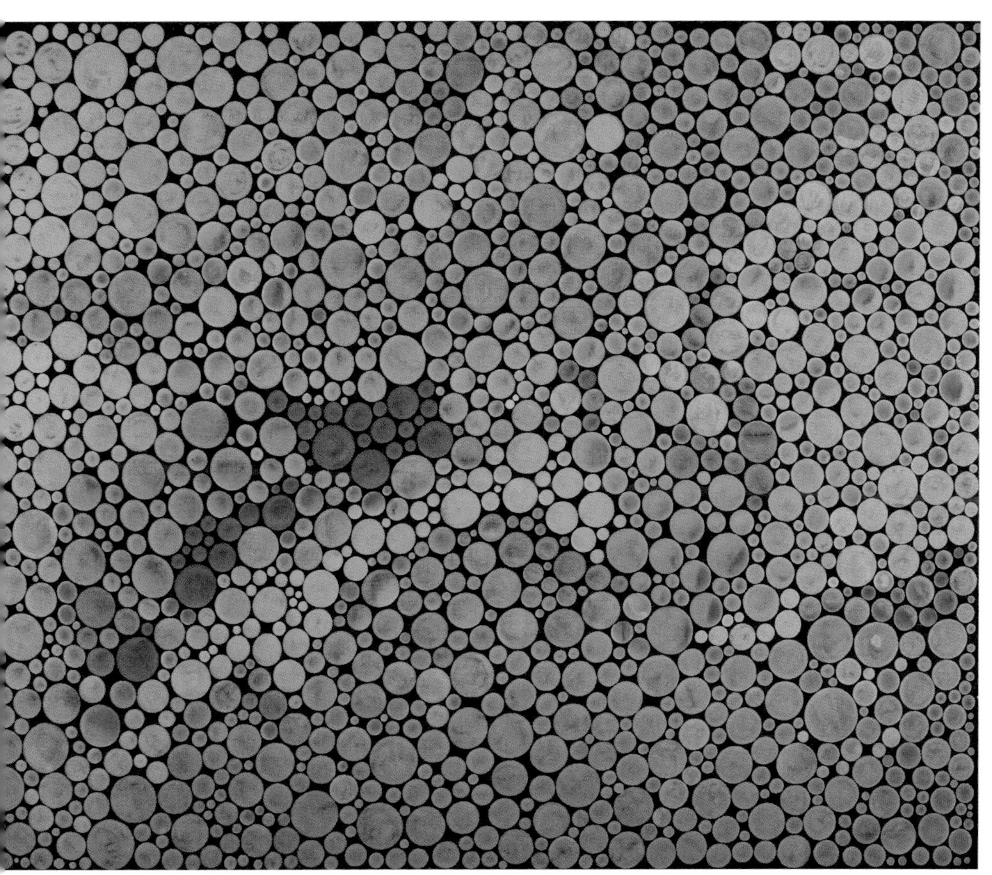

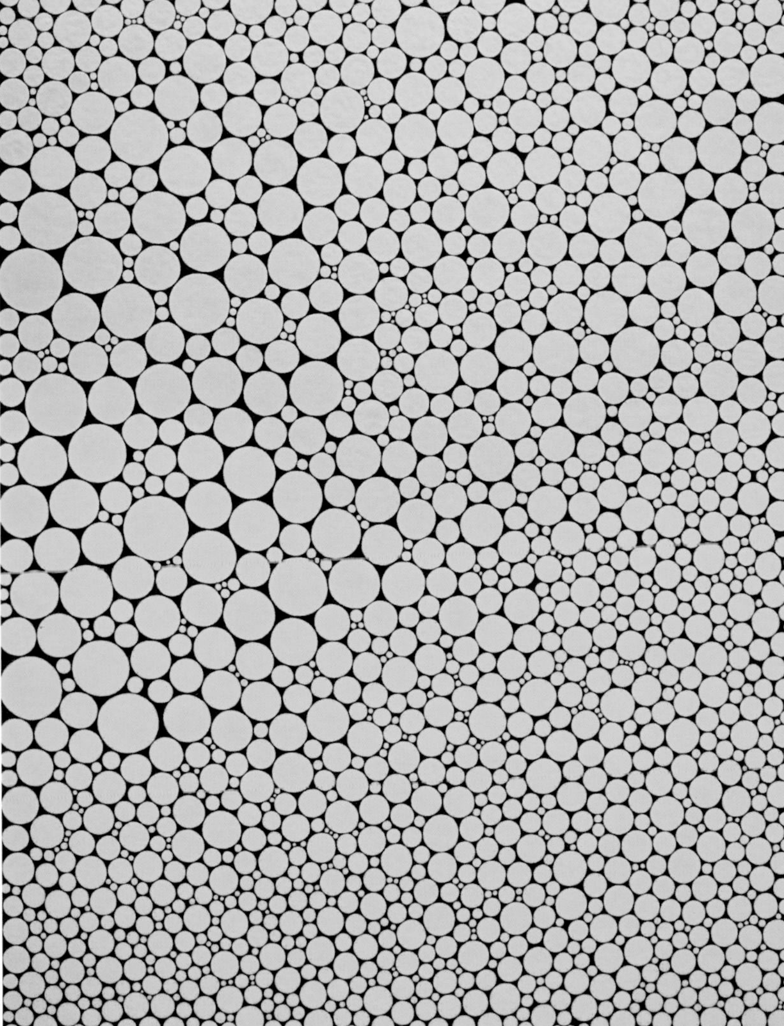

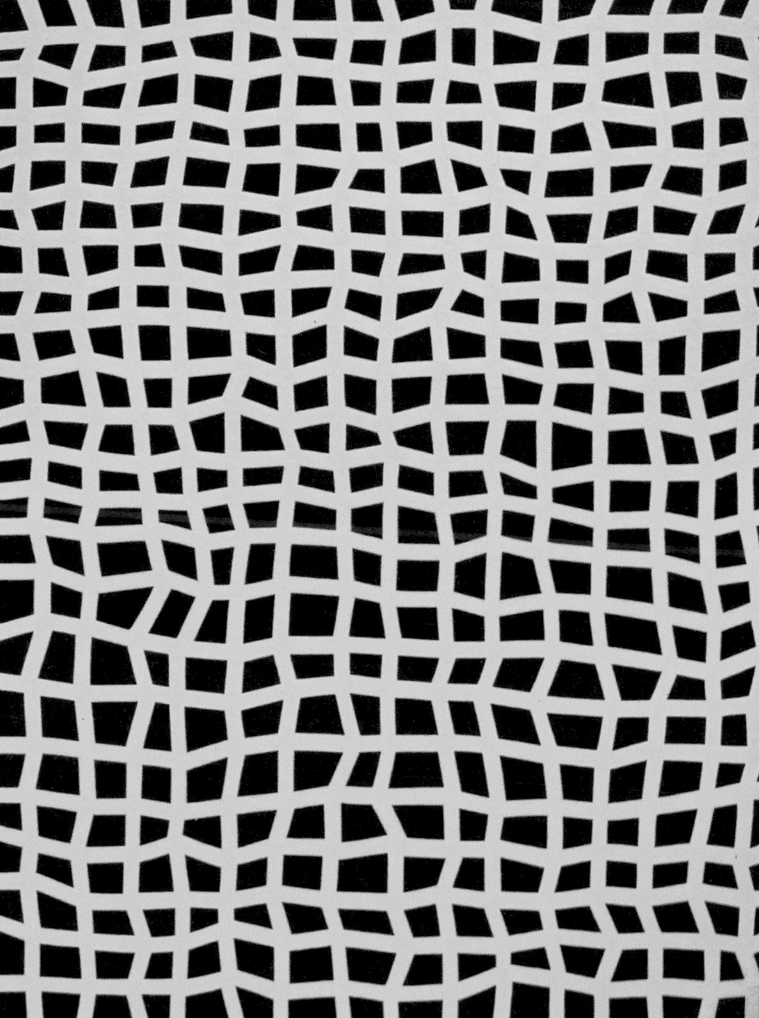

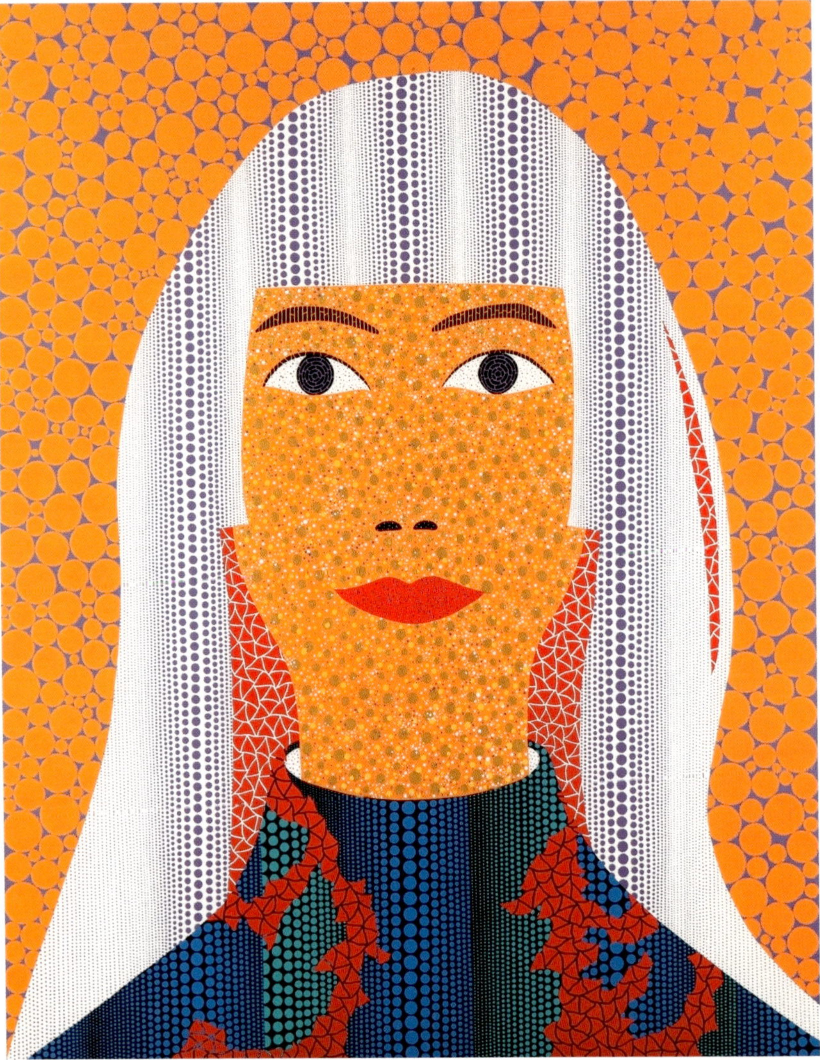

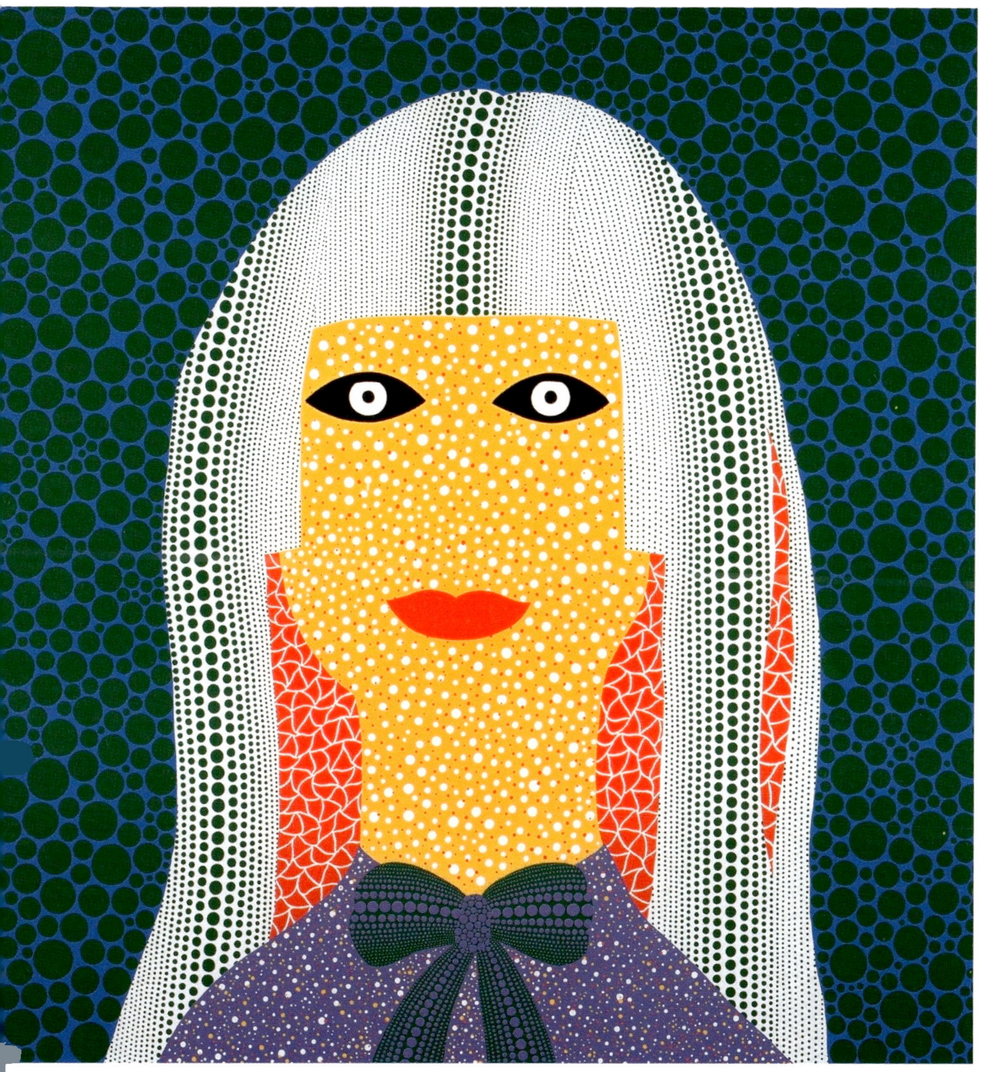

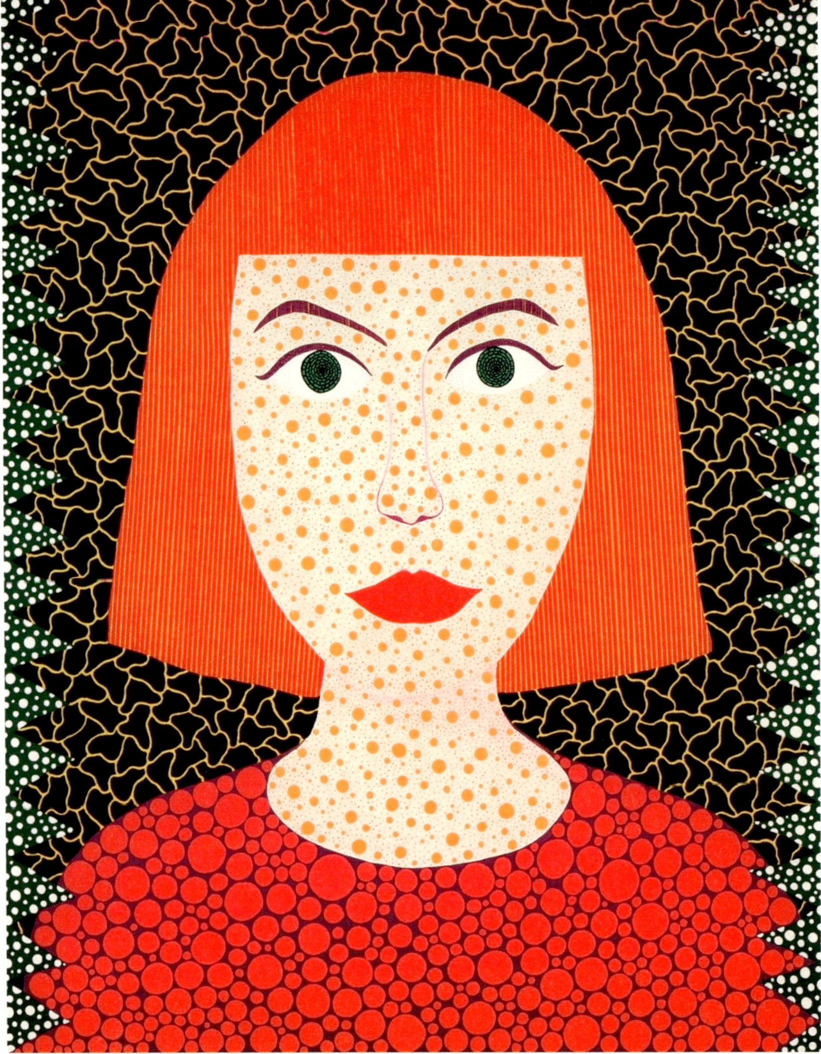

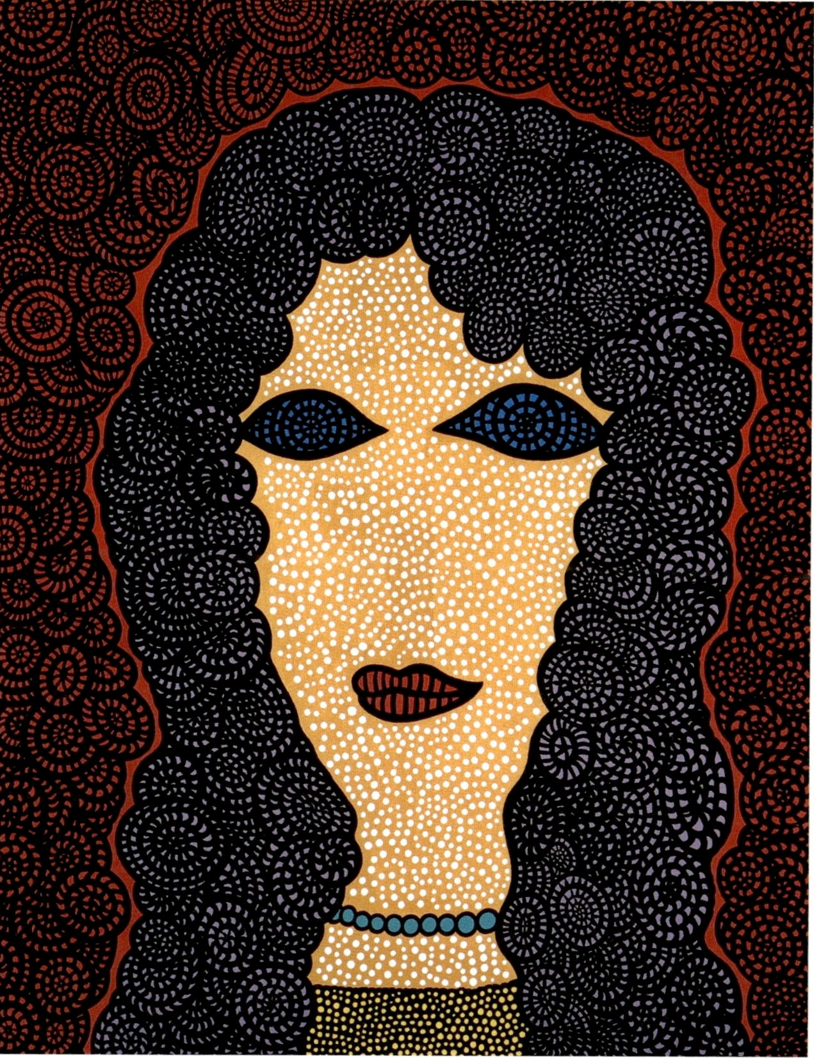

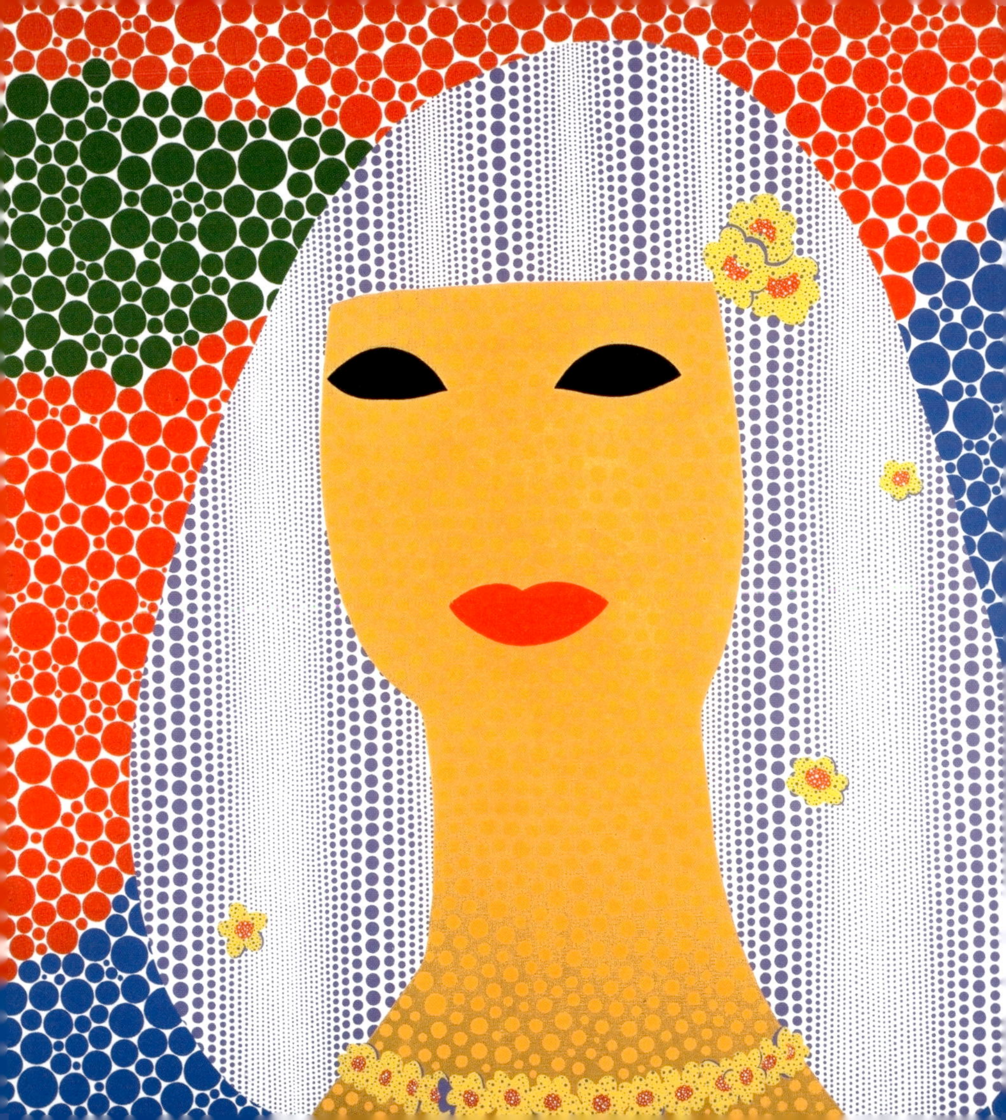

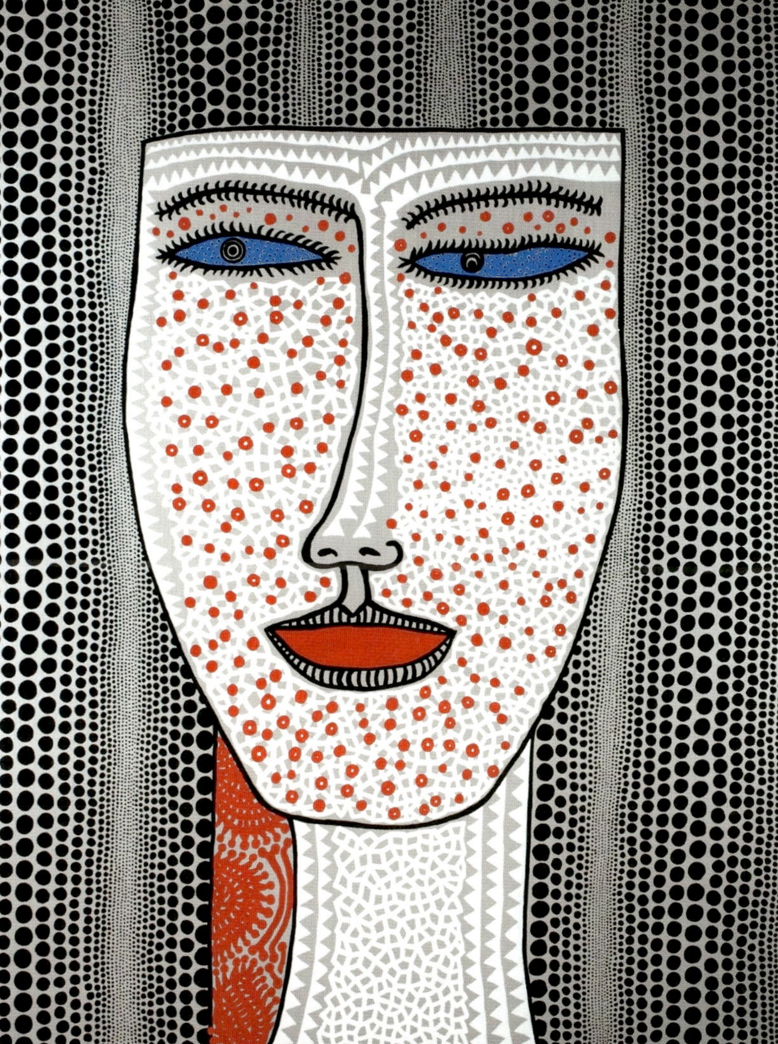

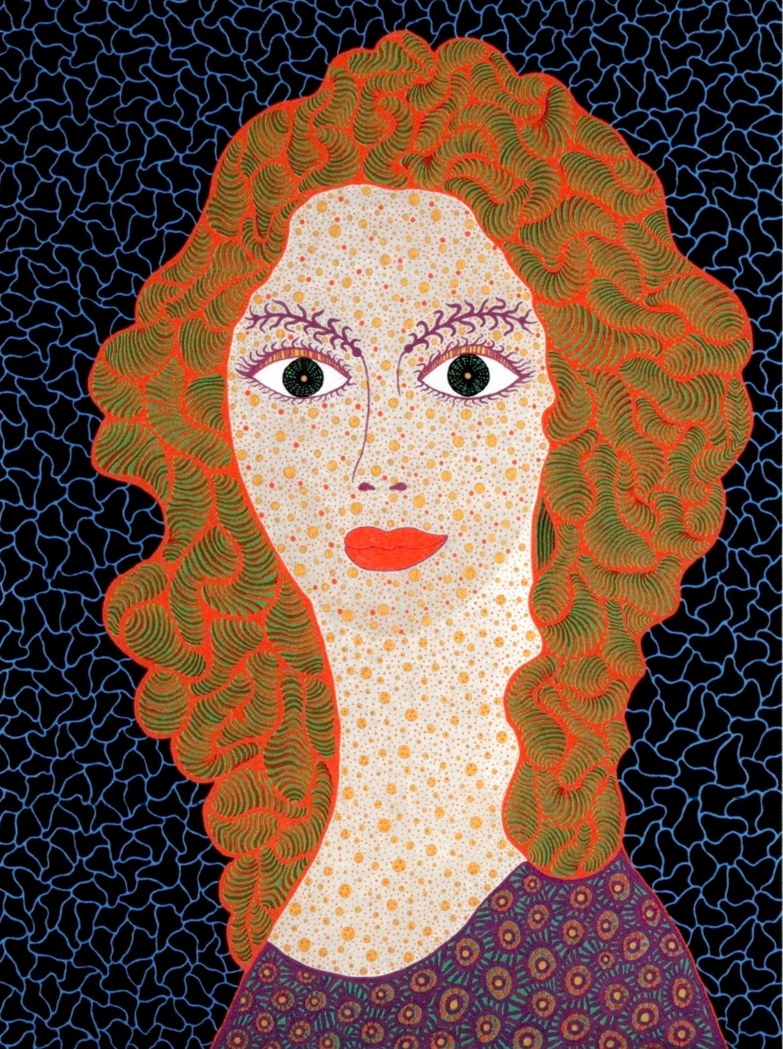

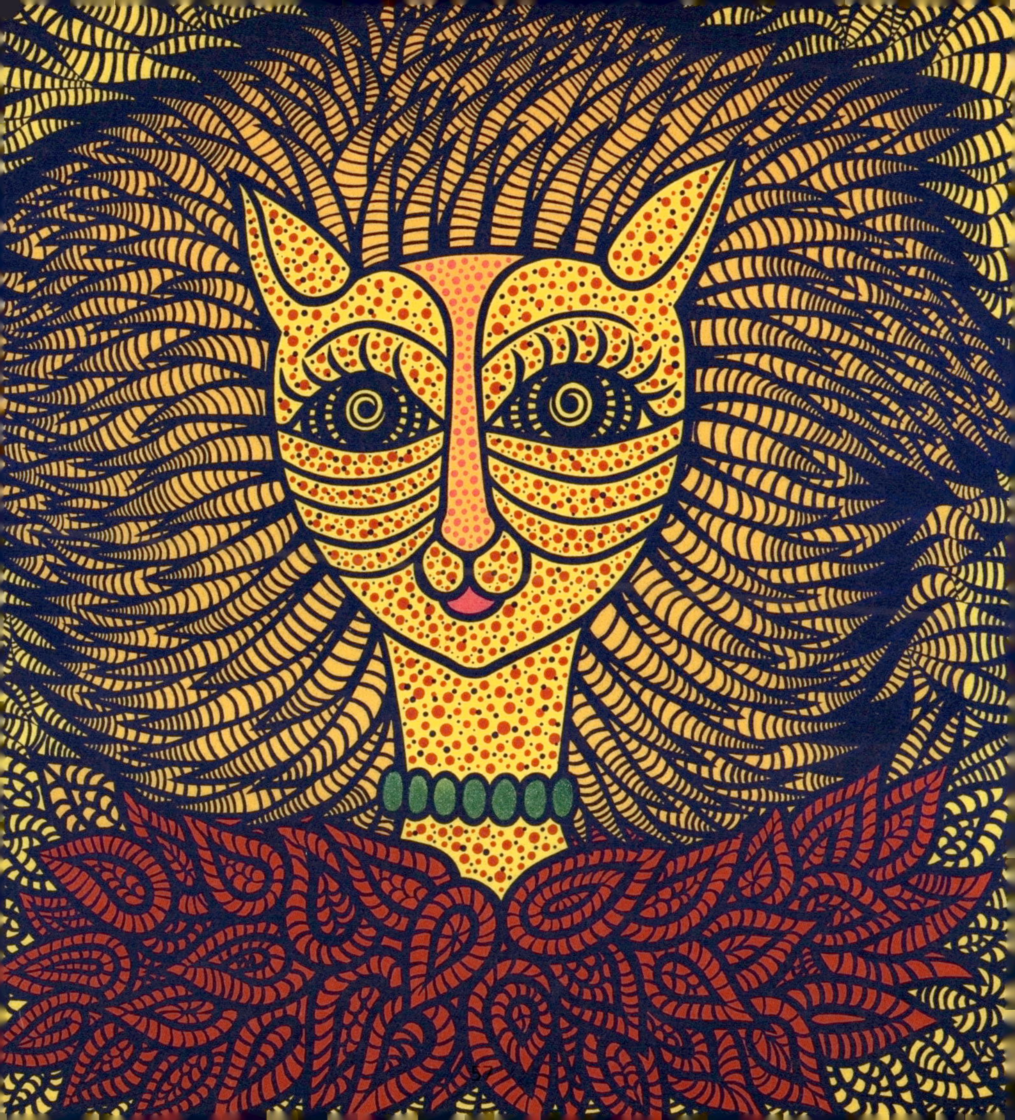

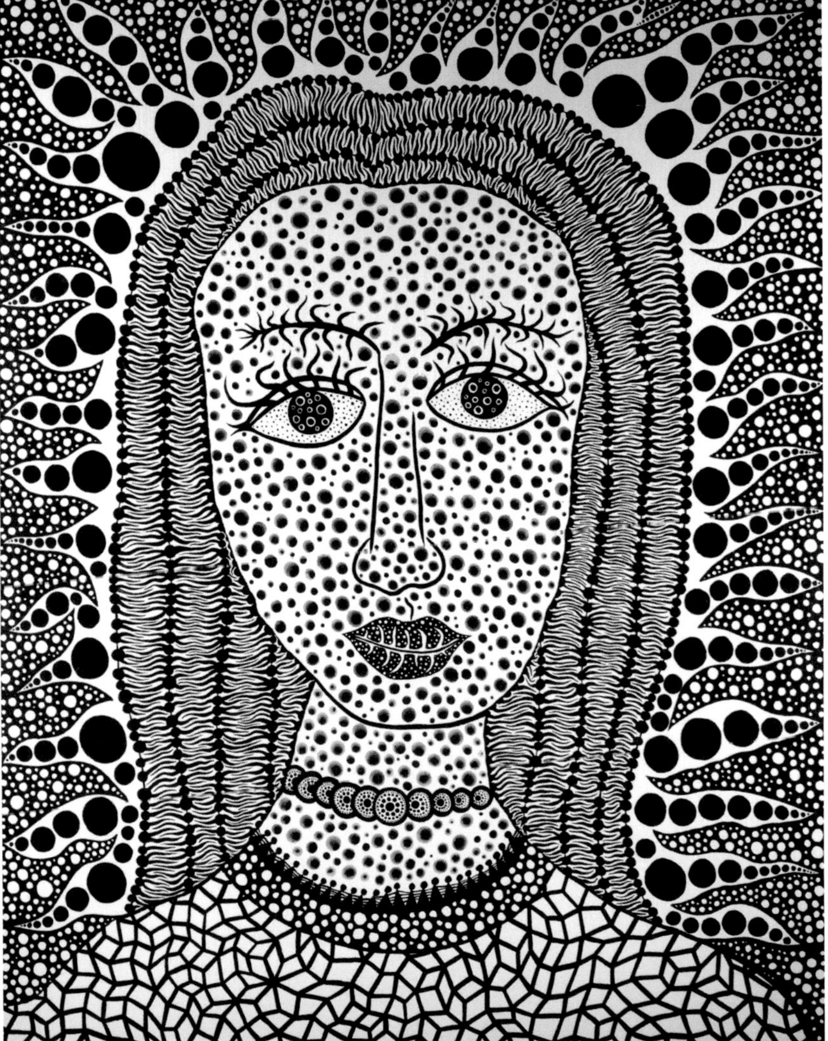

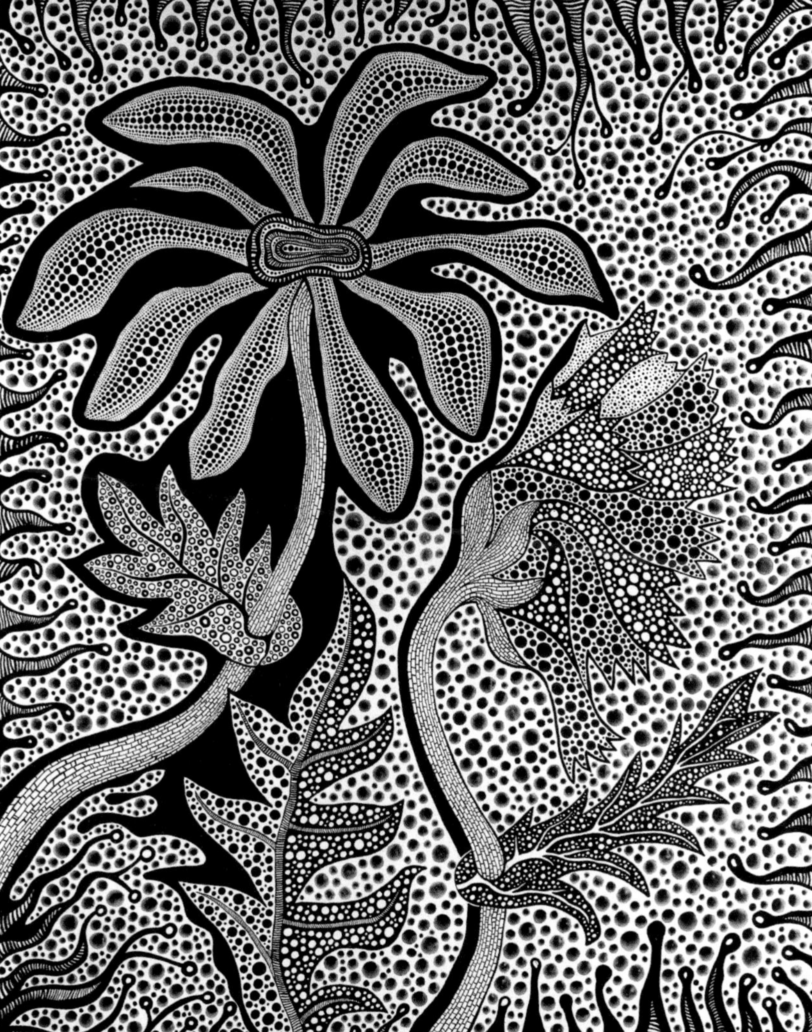

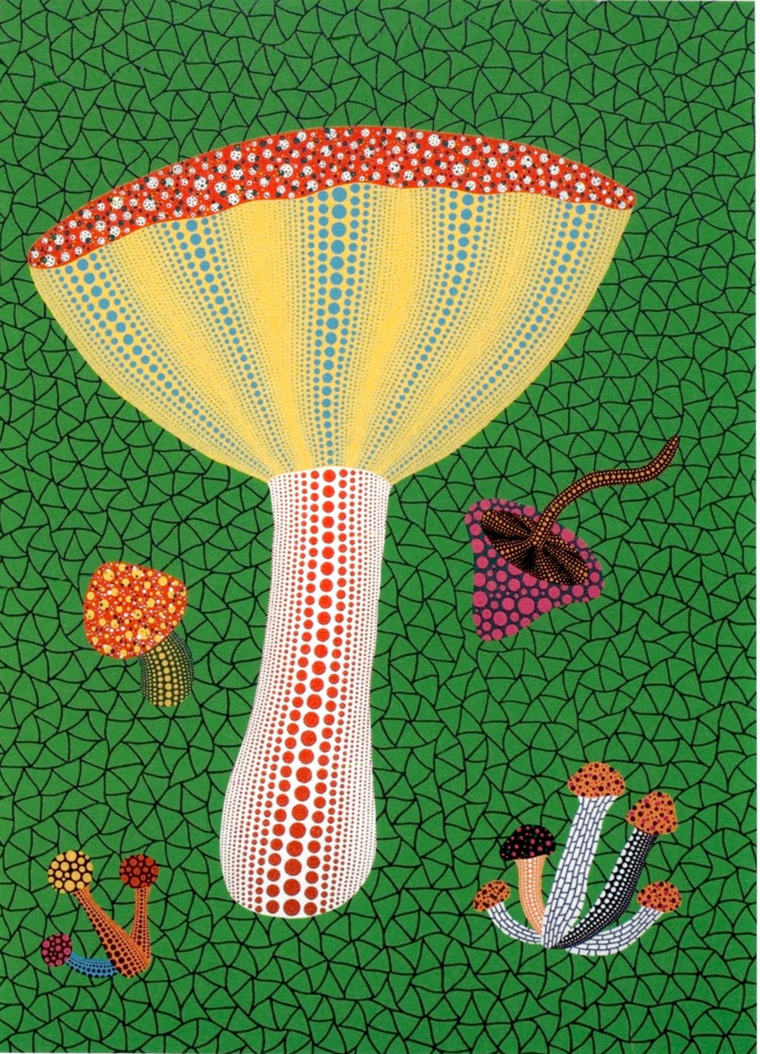

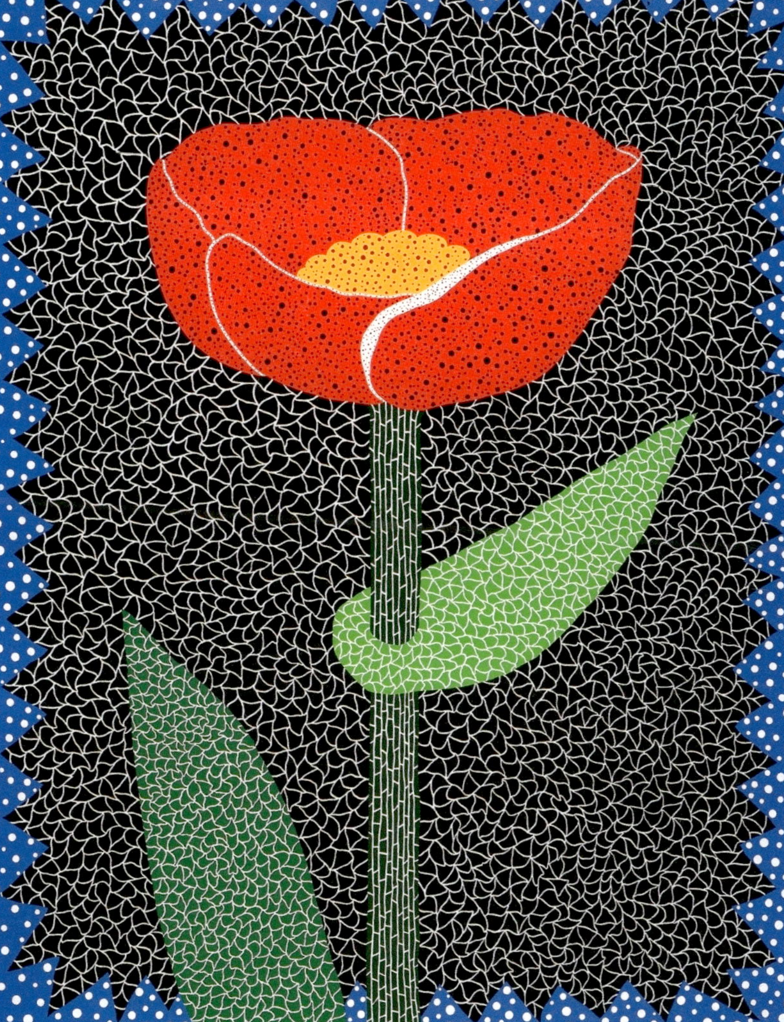

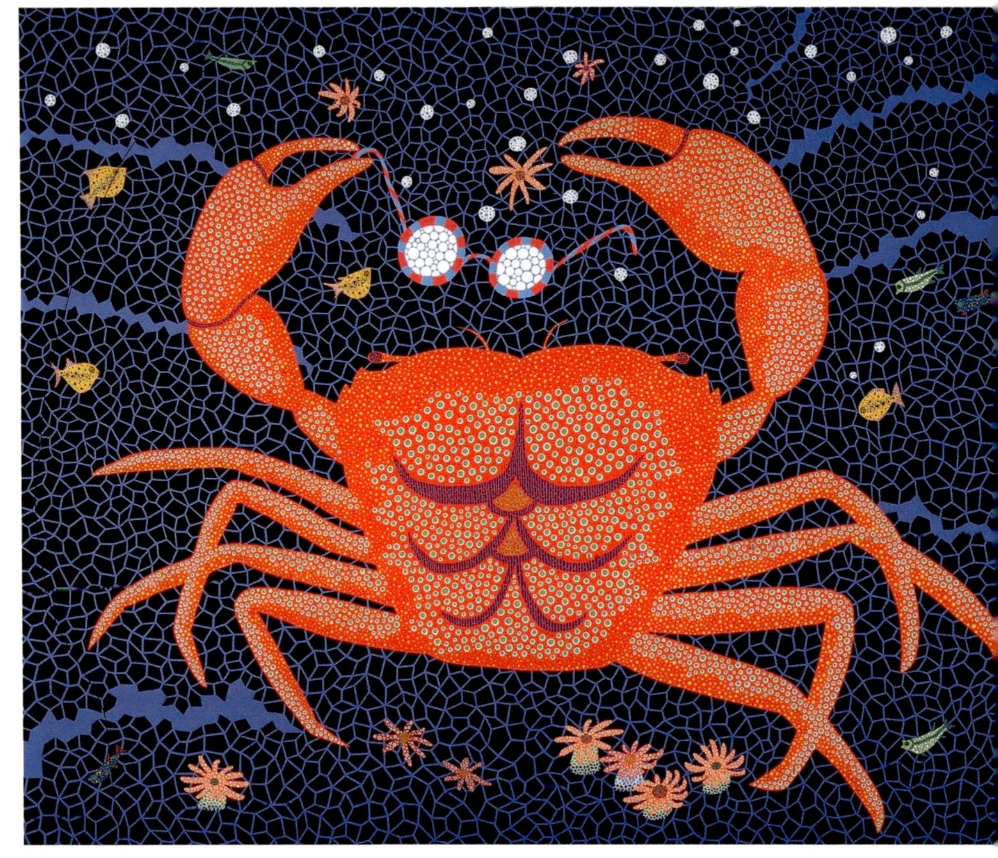

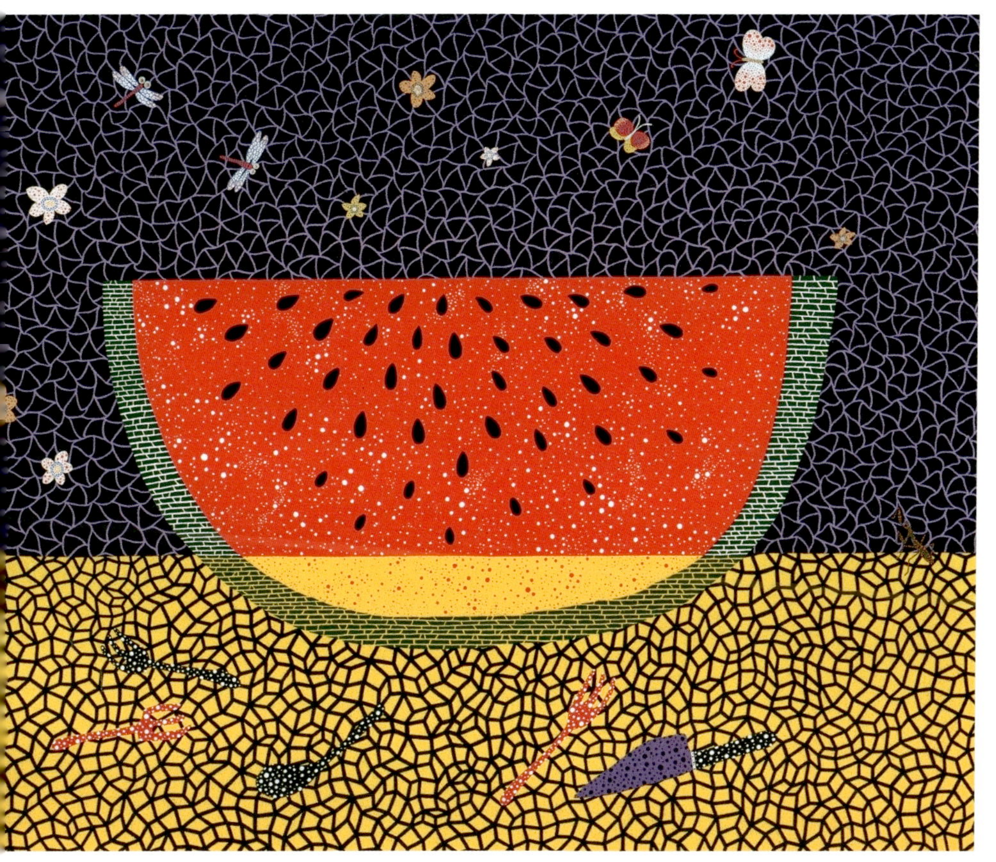

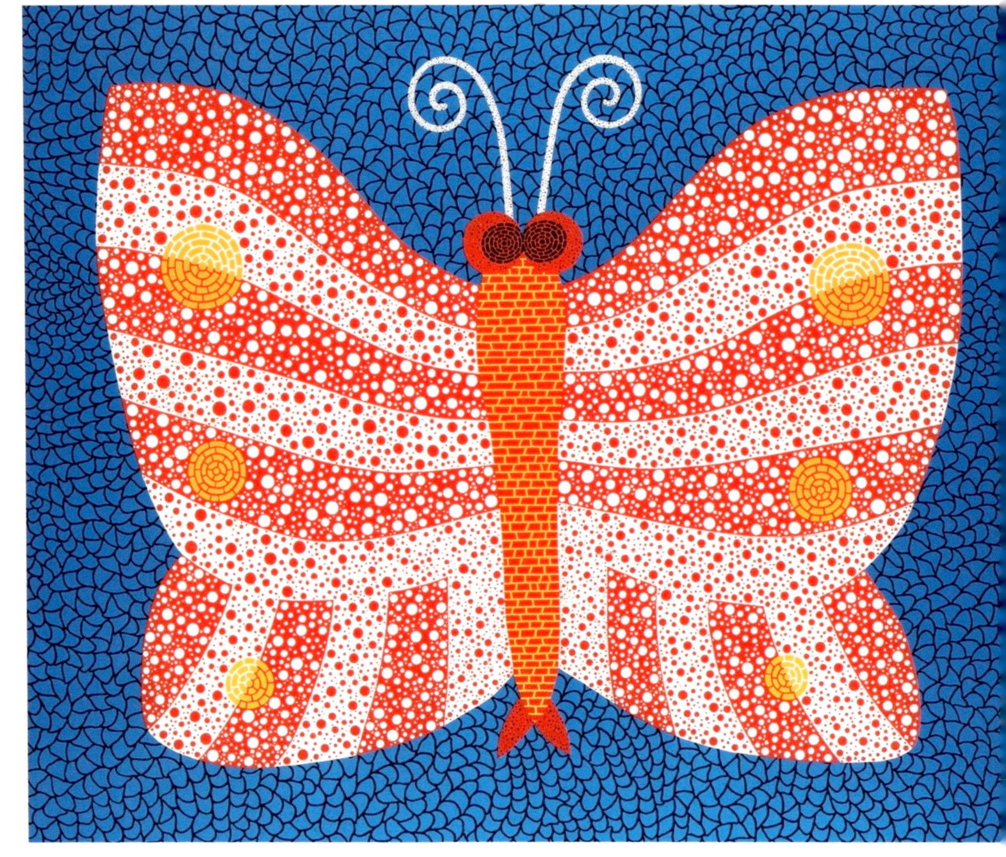

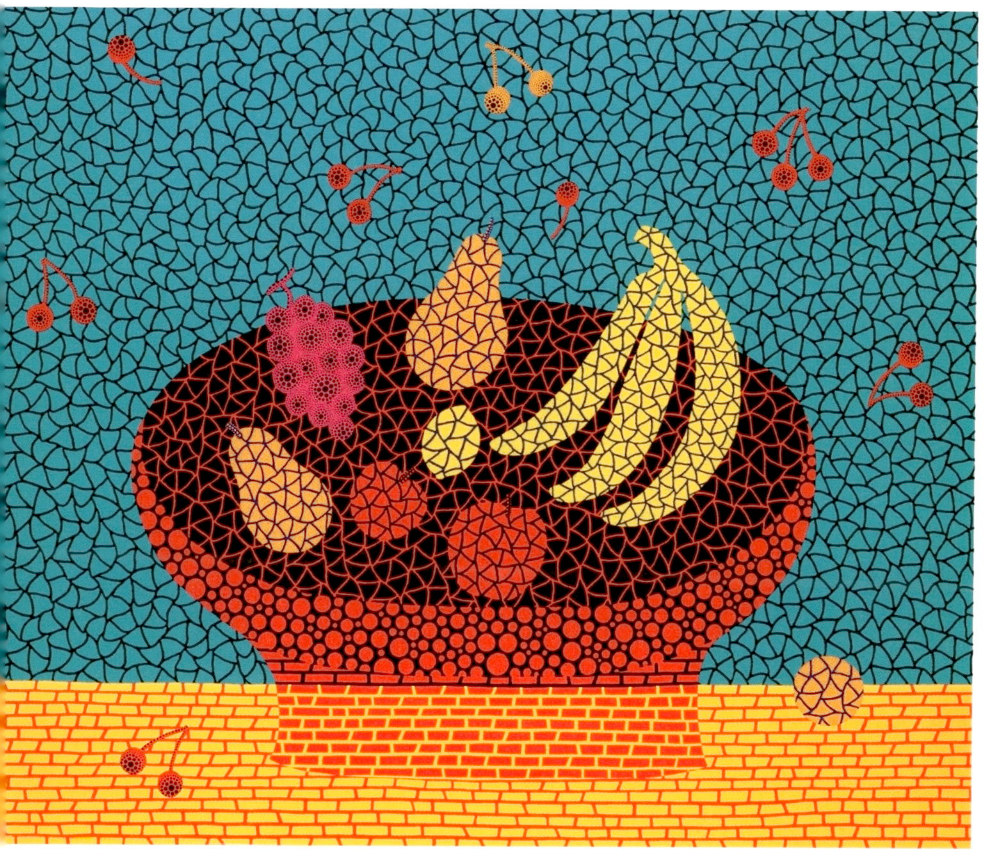

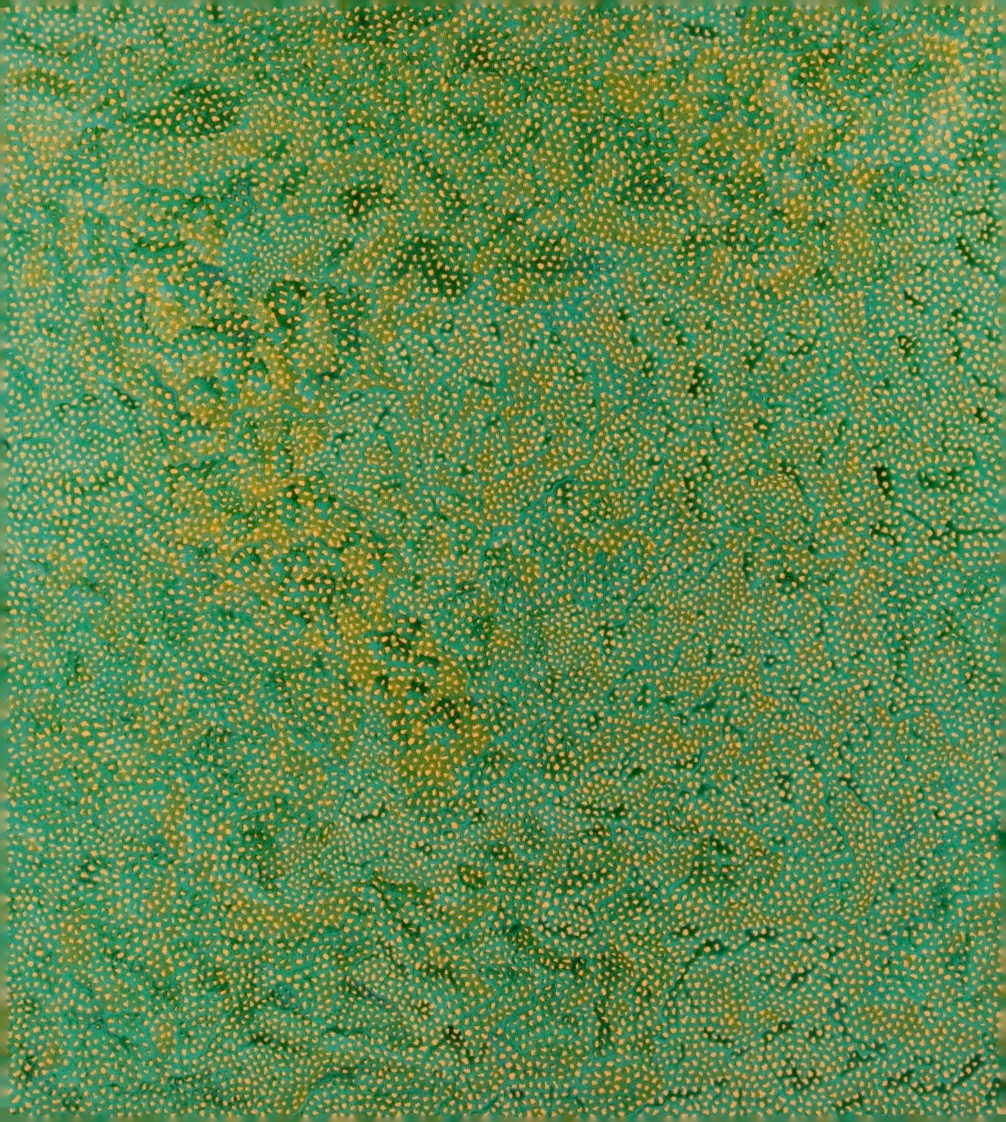

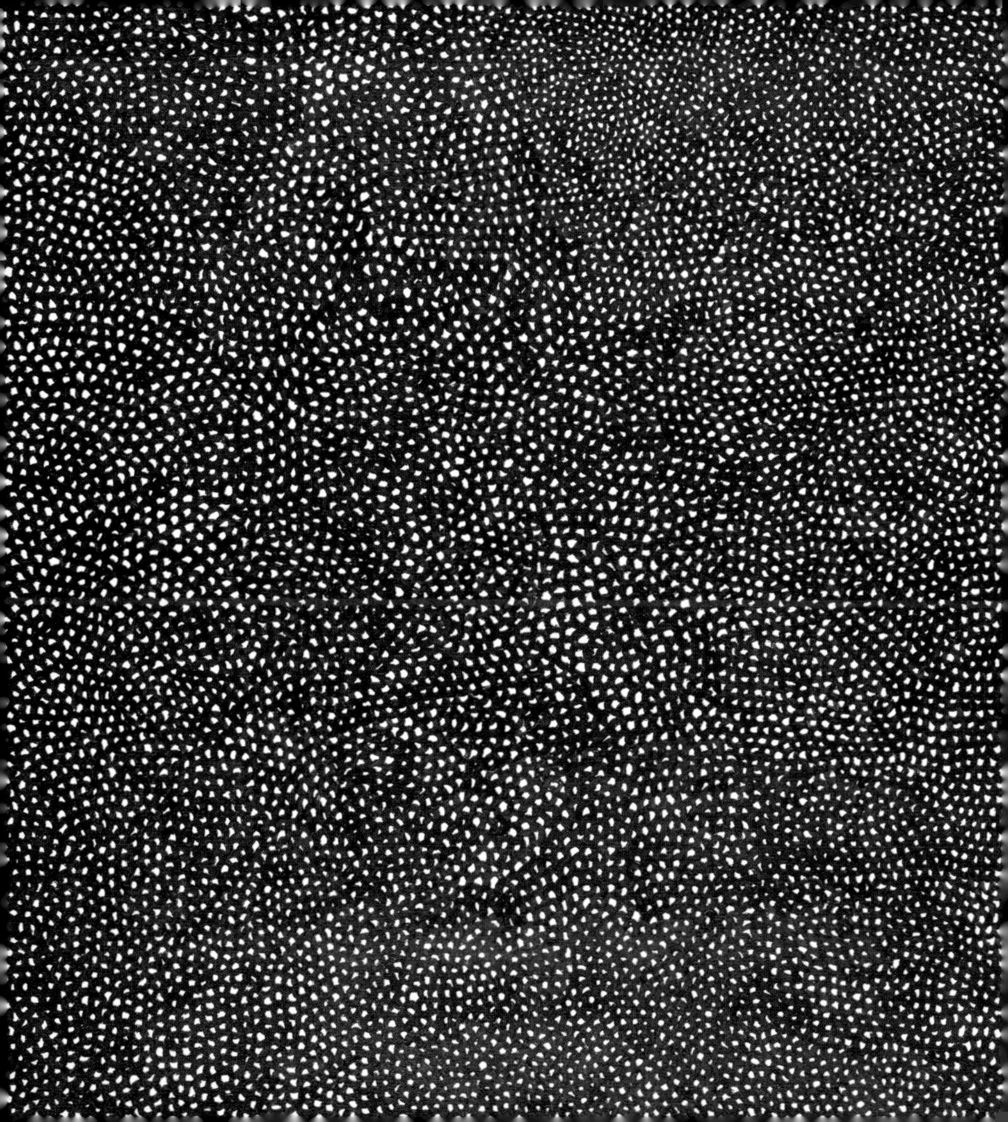

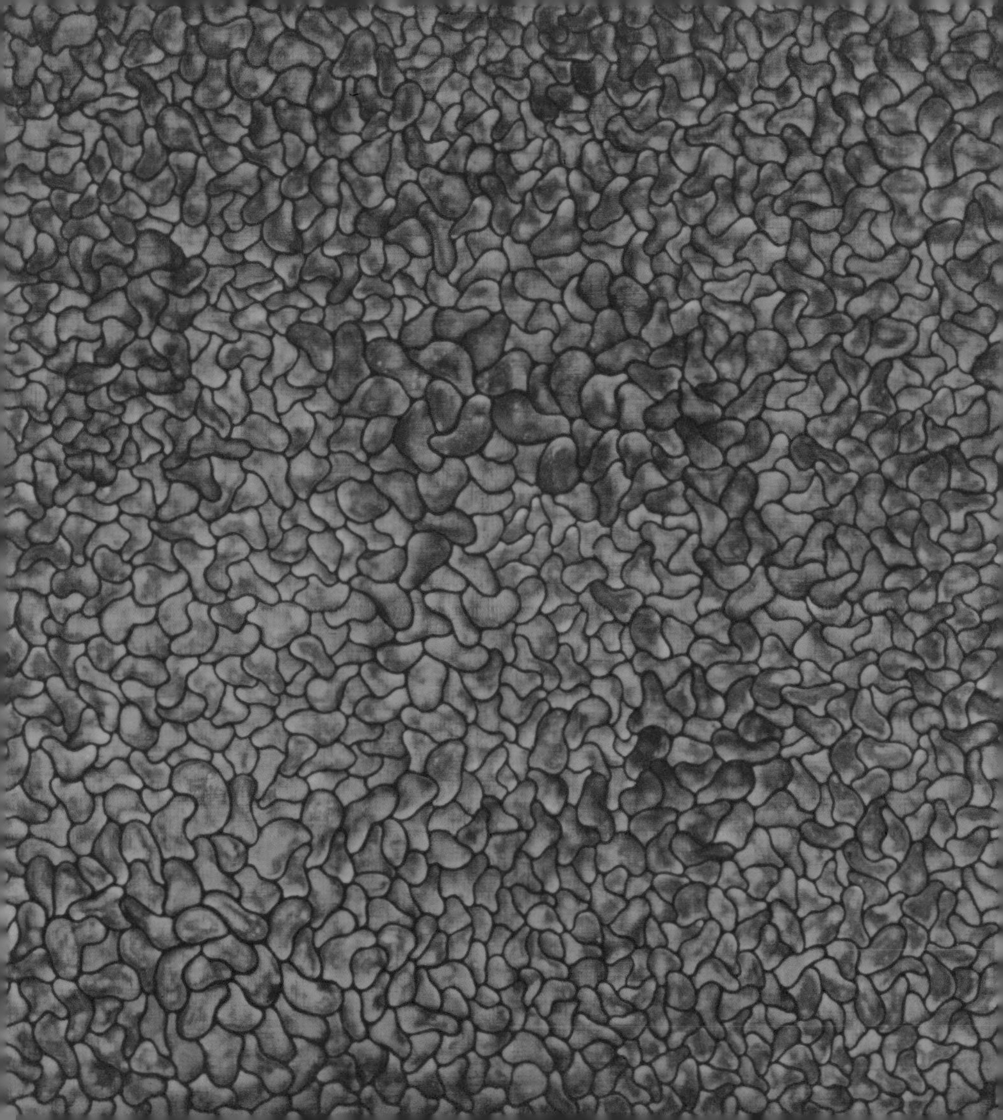

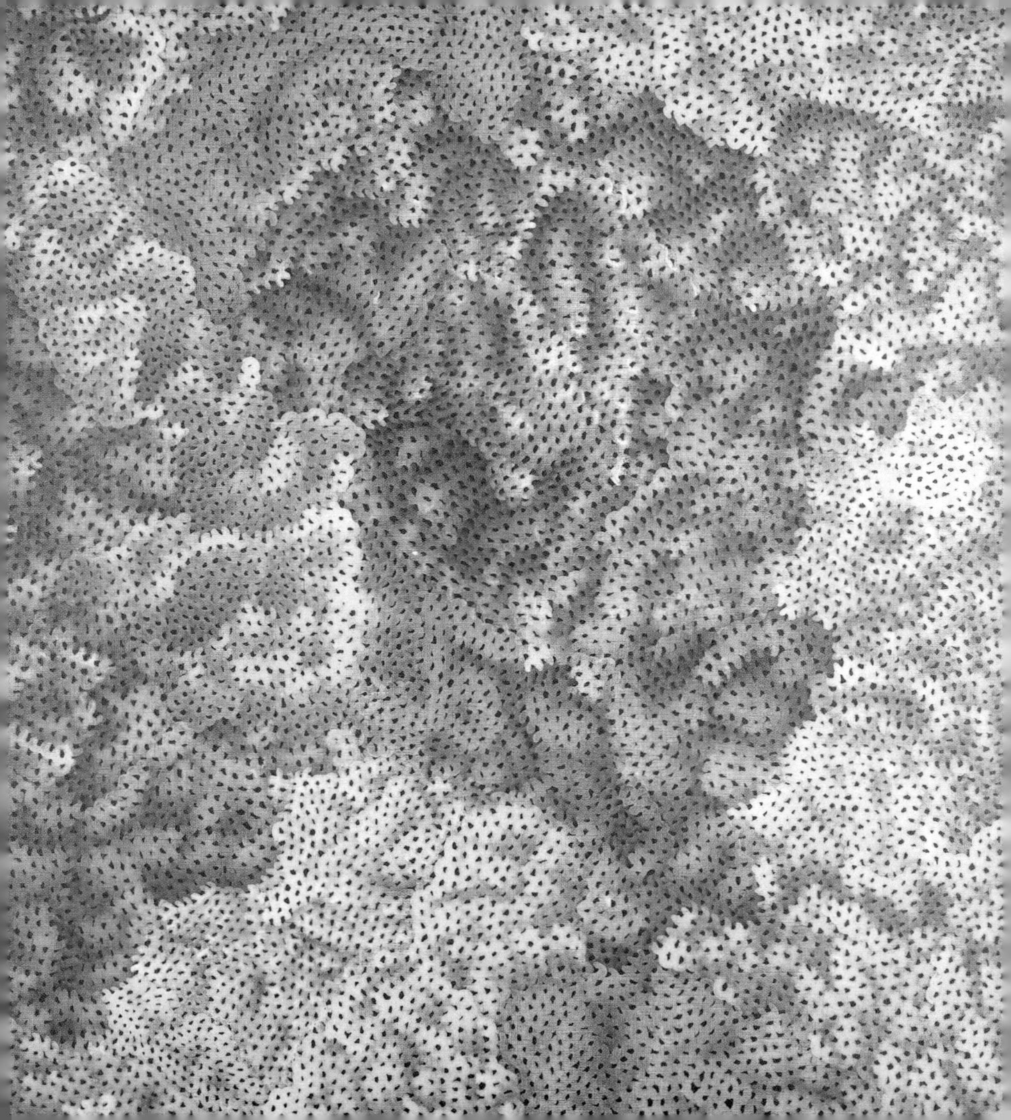

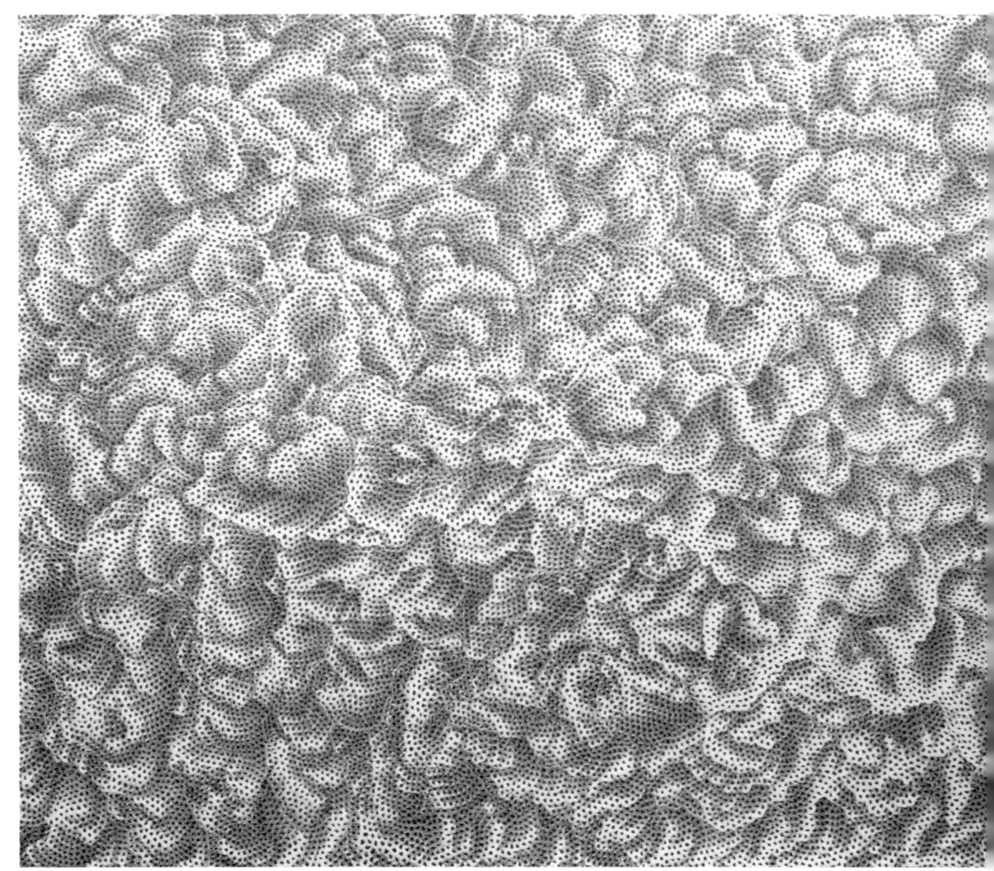

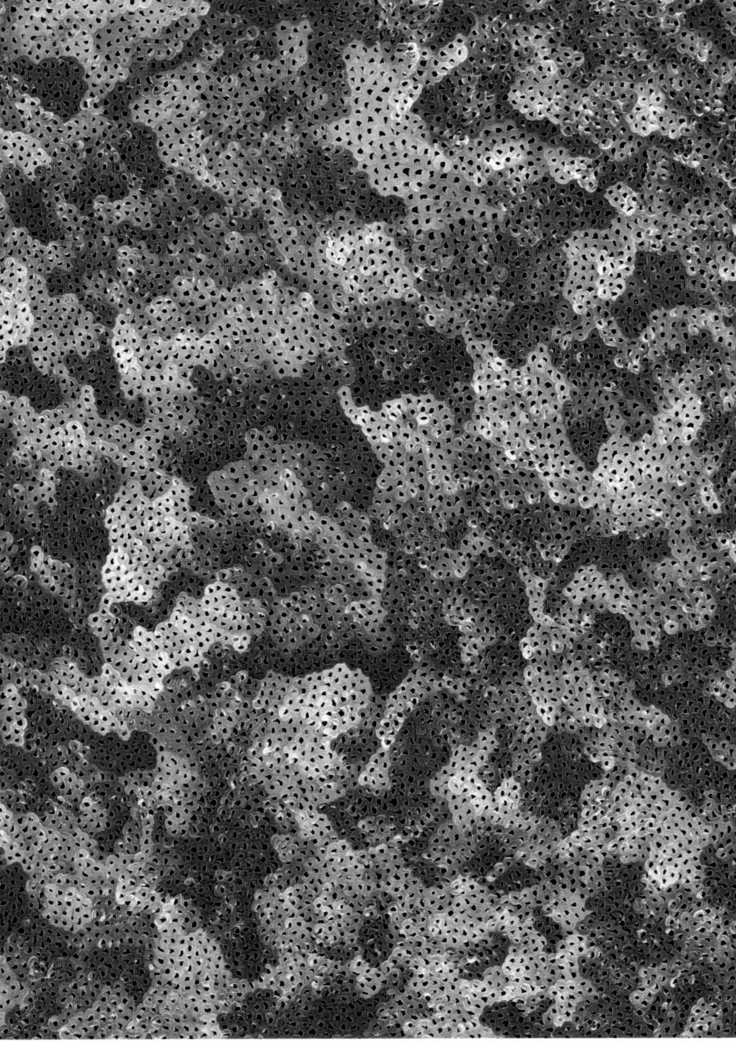

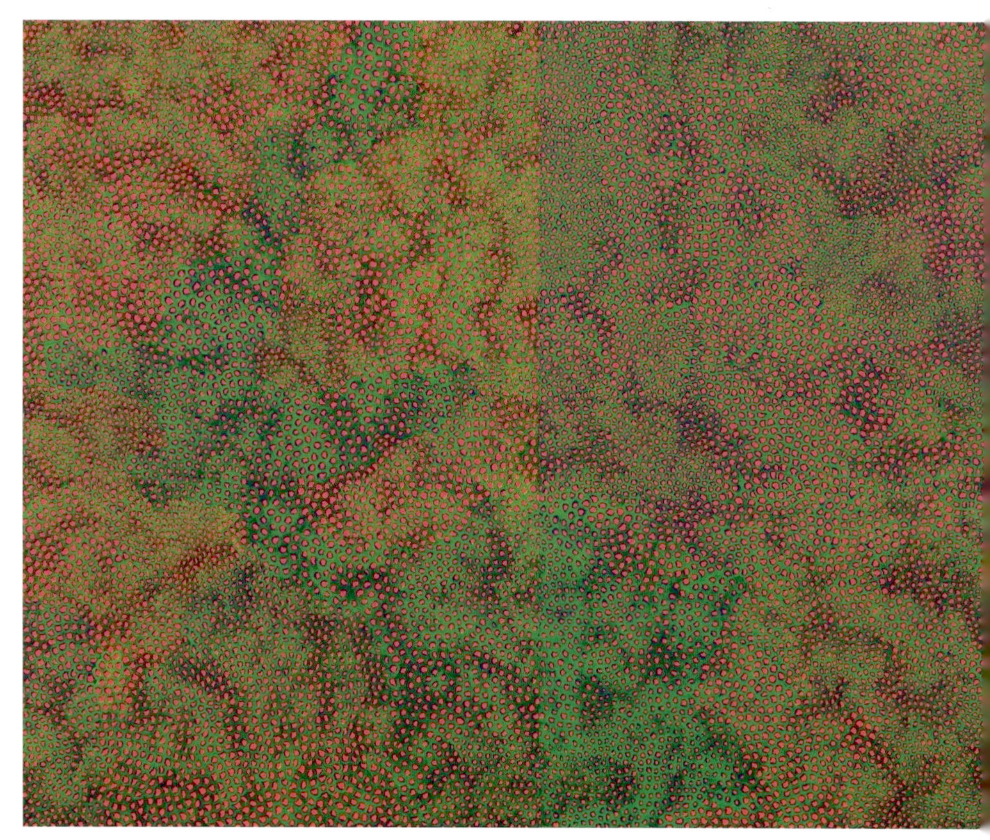

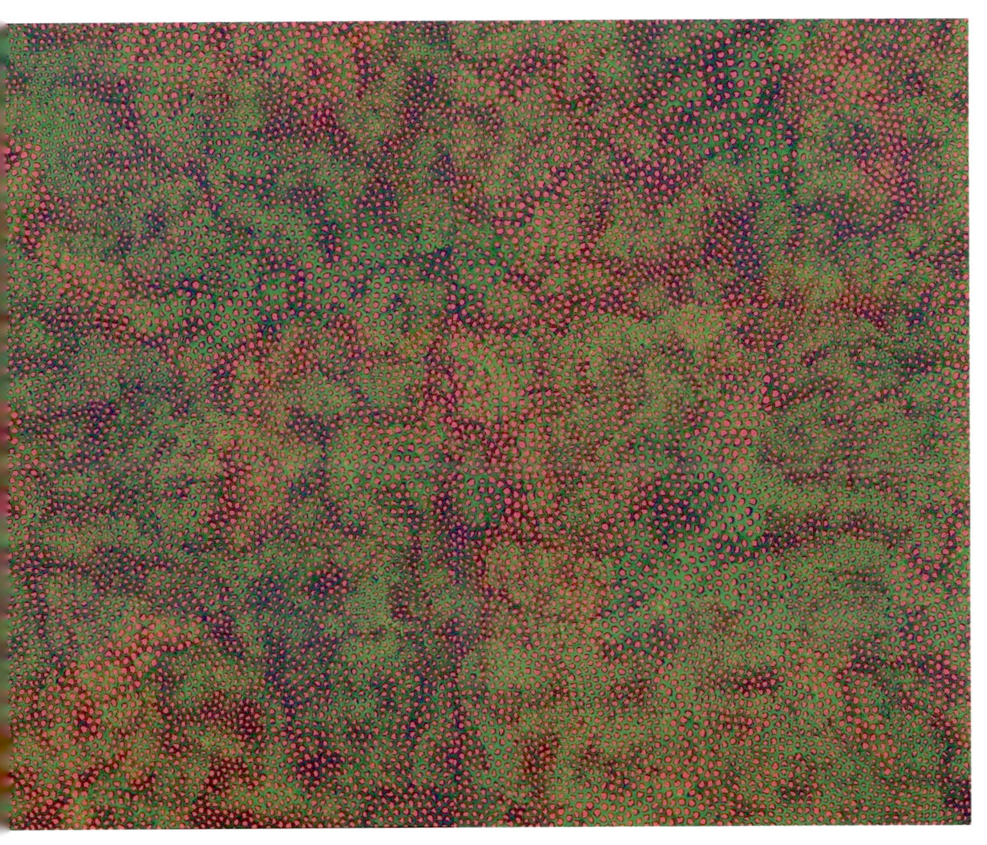

私は今もなお、いや、時とともにますます、

芸術の敵でありそれ以上に戦友である悪魔と闘いつづけている。

私は一度たりとも、すべて決定されたものの中に身を置いたことはなく、

常に自由の中にのみ生きているからだ。

I still battle, increasingly so with the passage of time,
against the devil who is both an enemy, yet also an even greater ally of art.
This is because not once have I placed myself in a position
where everything is predetermined, I only ever live in freedom.

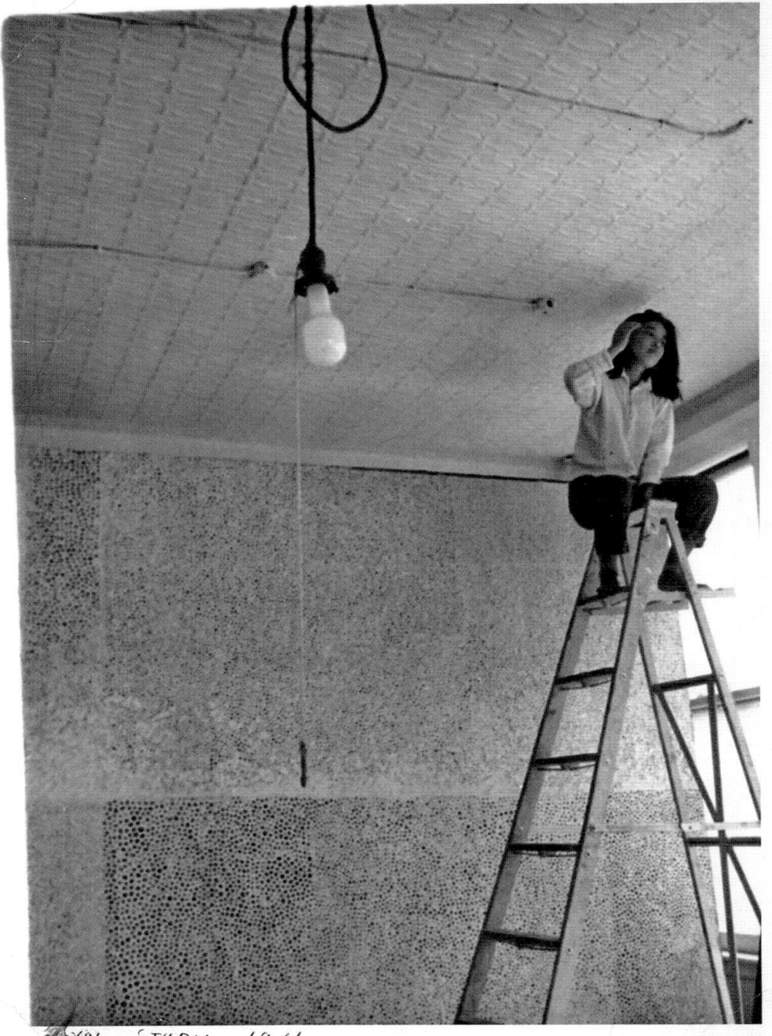
STUDIO 1961

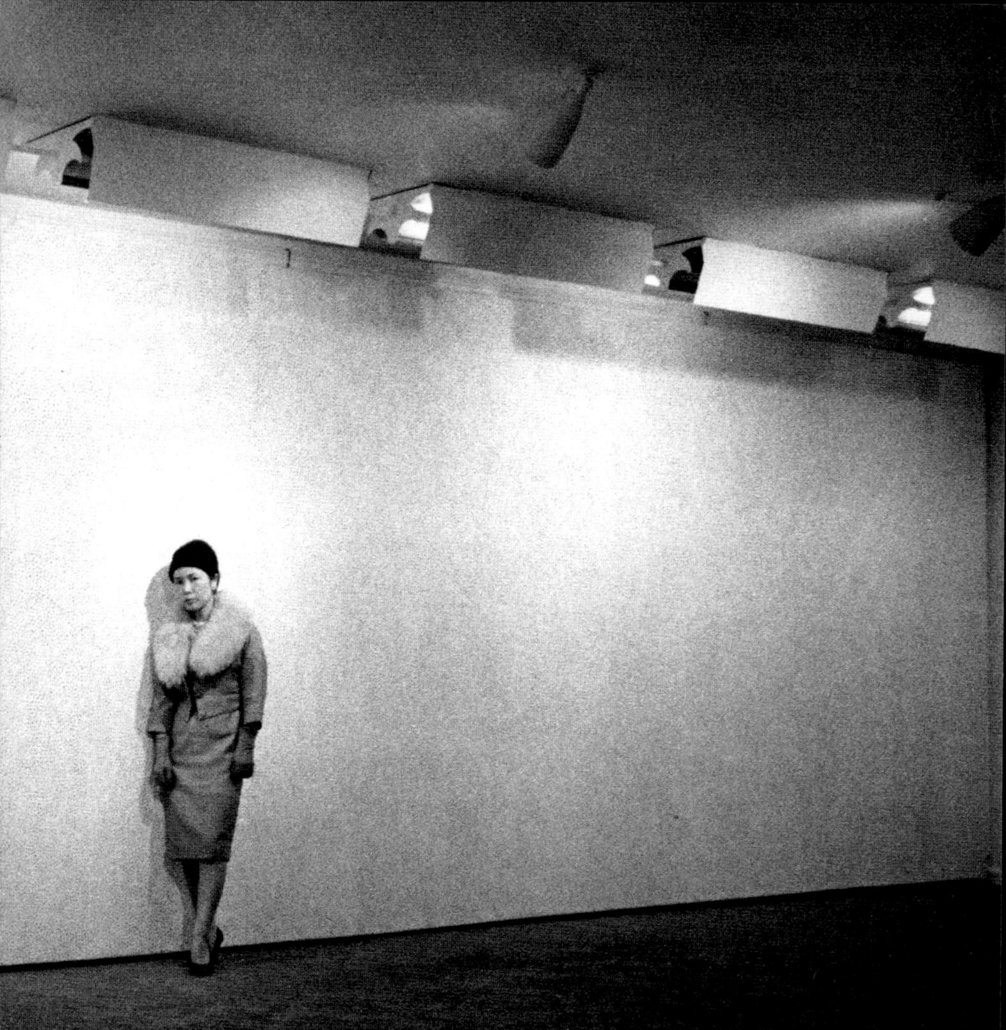

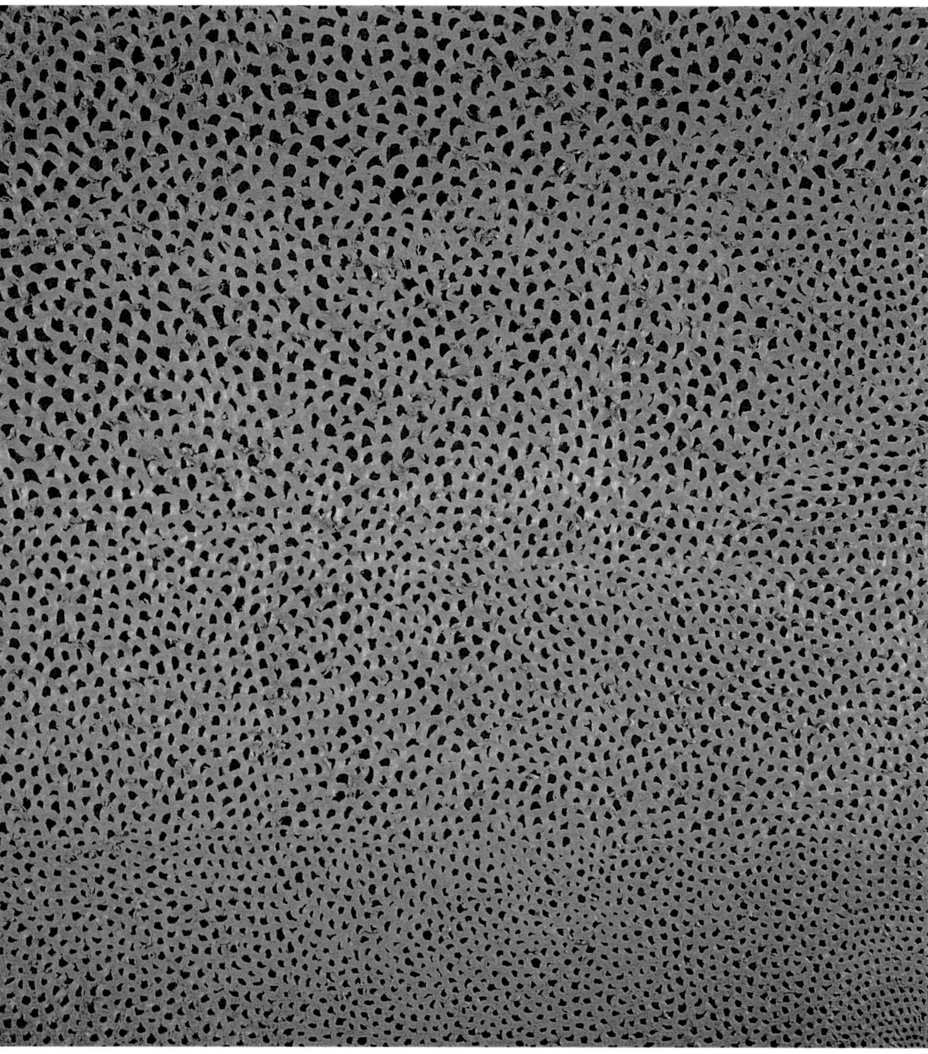

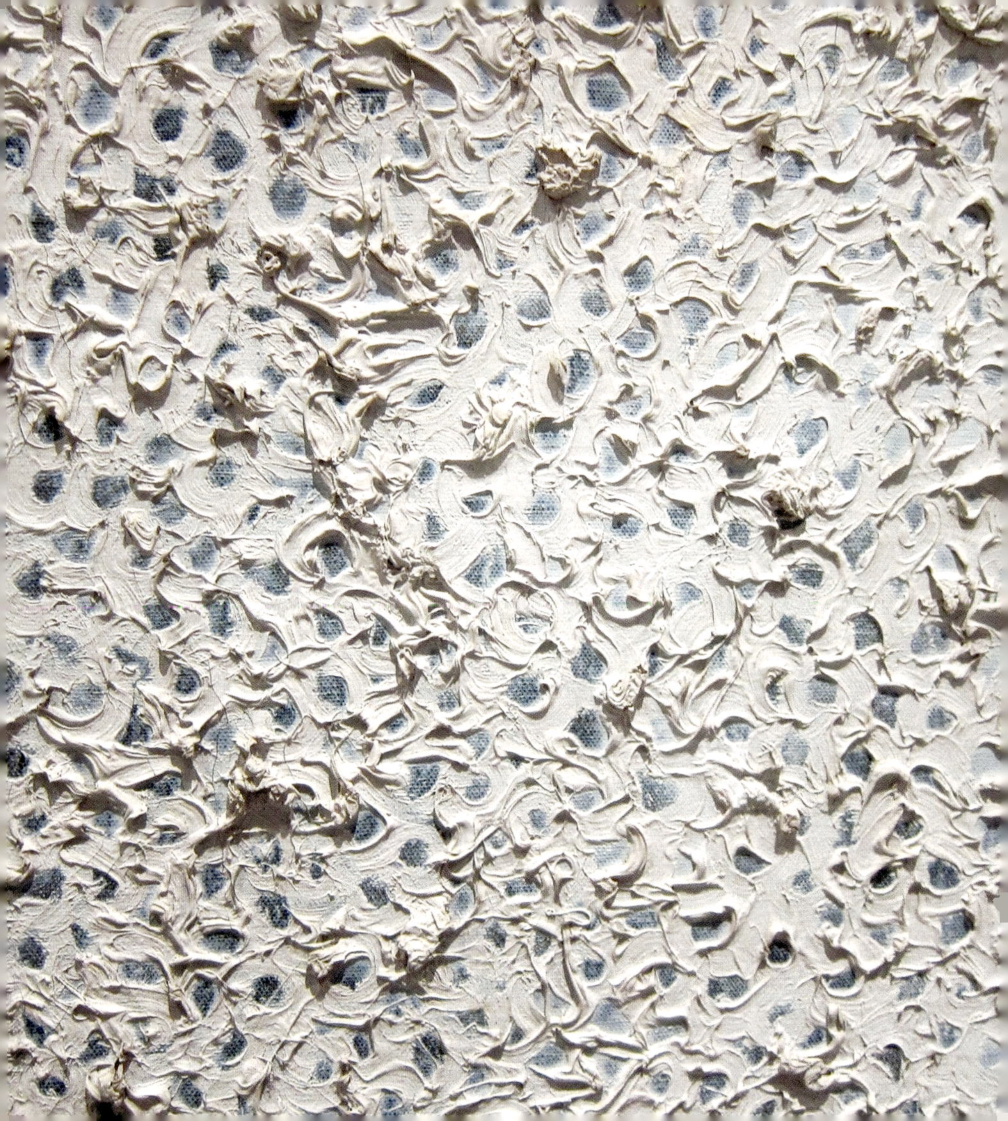

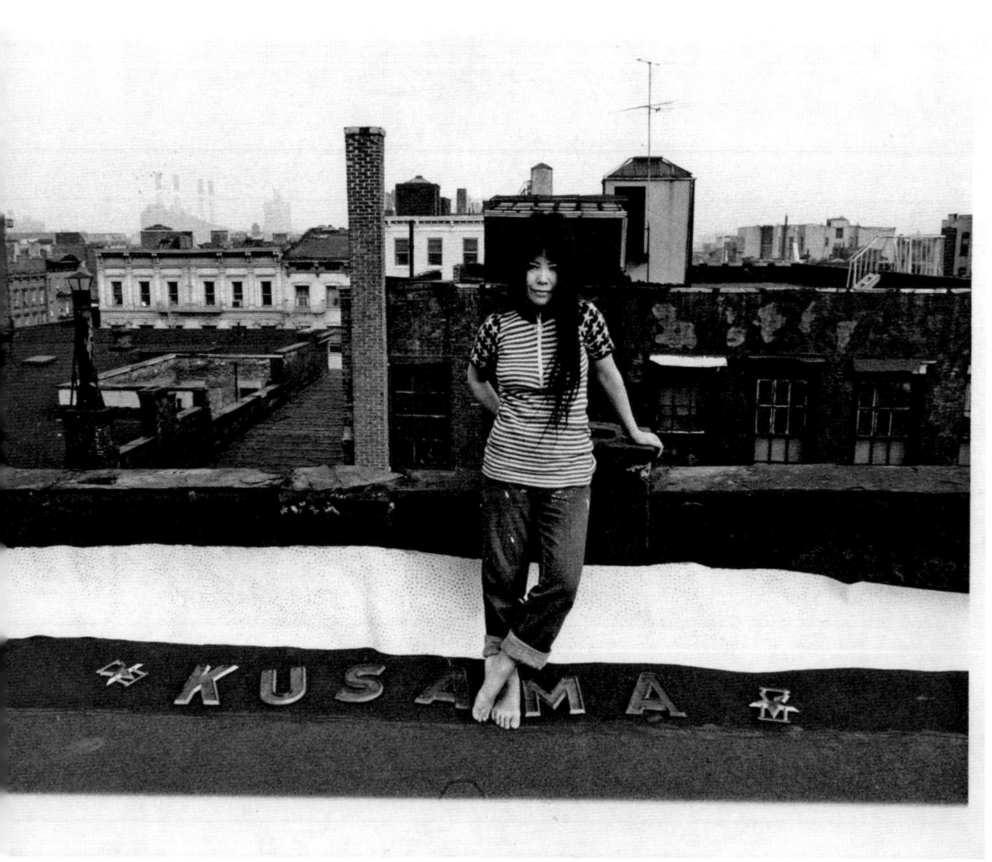
KUSAMA

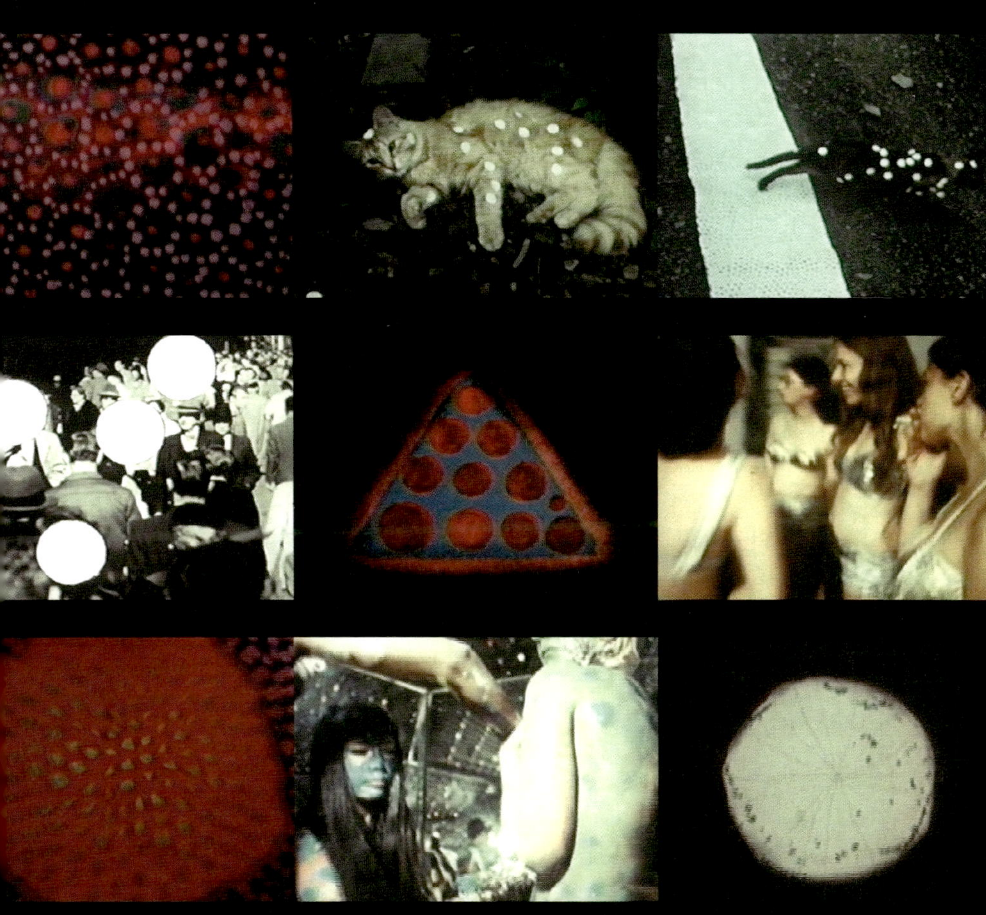

AGGREGATION: ONE THOUSAND BOATS SHOW

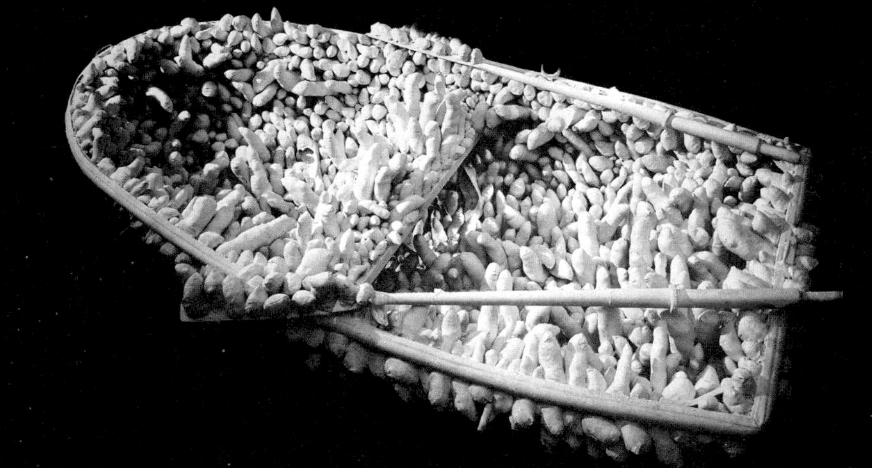

KUSAMA

DECEMBER 17 – JANUARY 11, 1964

GALLERY: GERTRUDE STEIN 24 E. 81 ST. N.Y. 28

OPENING TUESDAY DECEMBER 17, 5–7 · TUESDAY – SATURDAY 11–5 · LE 5·0600

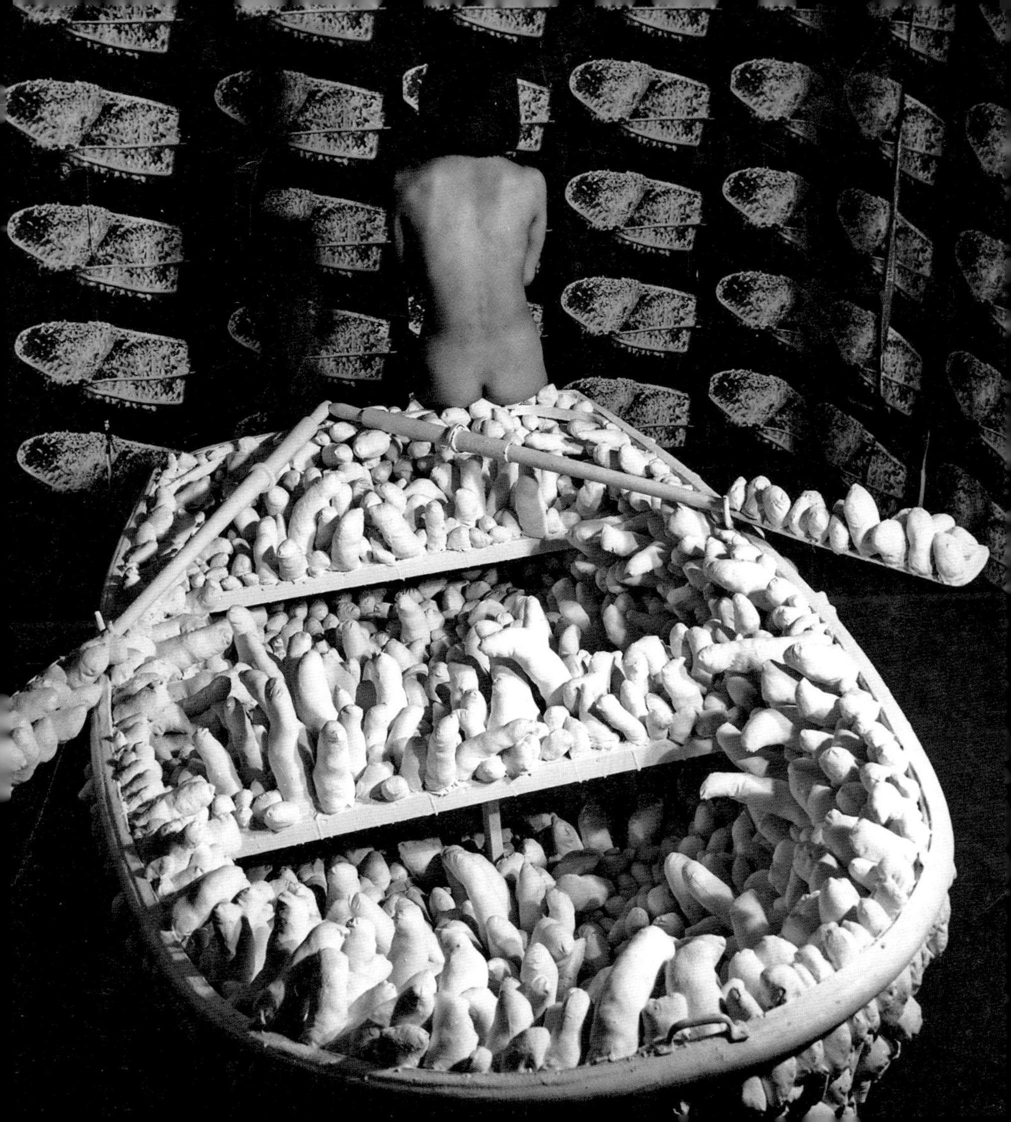

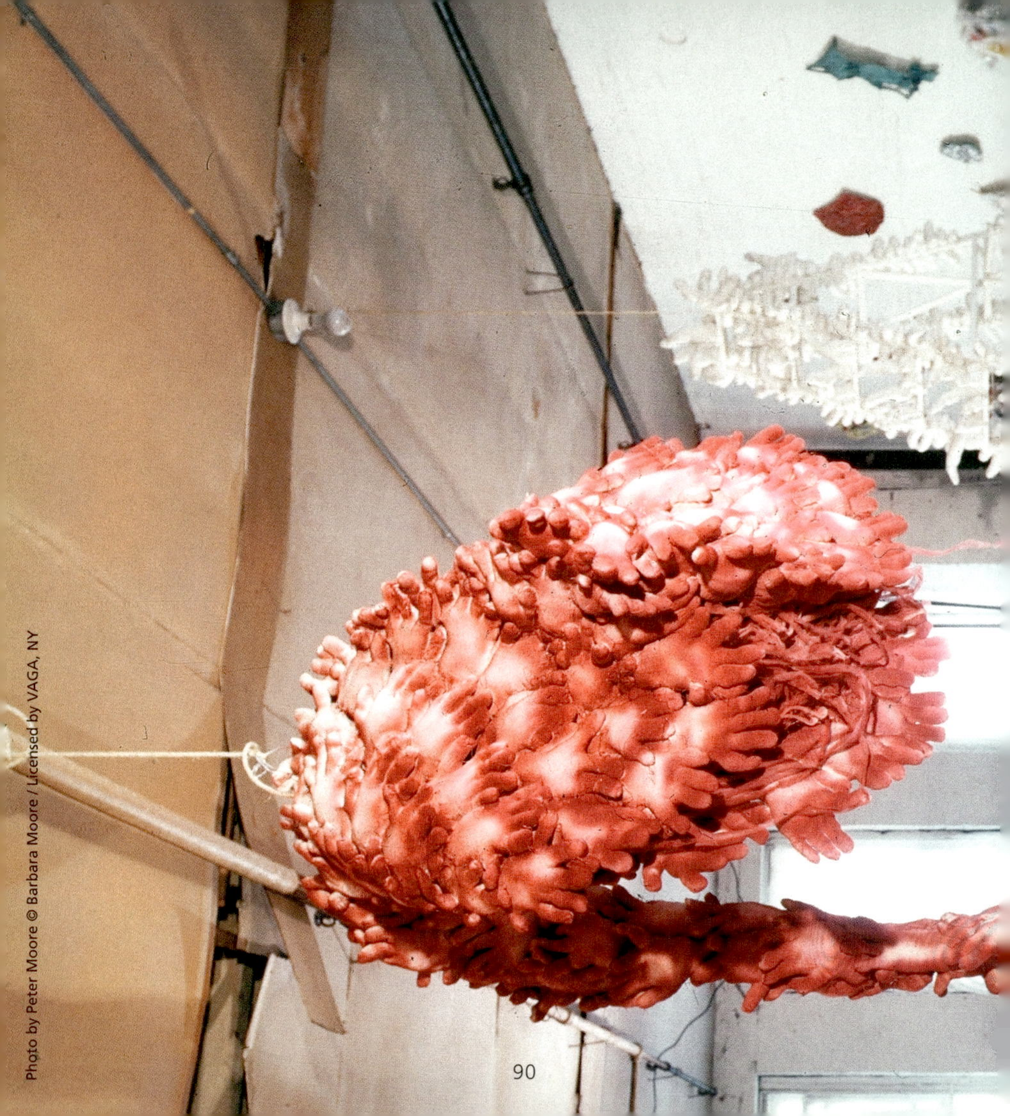

Photo by Peter Moore © Barbara Moore / Licensed by VAGA, NY

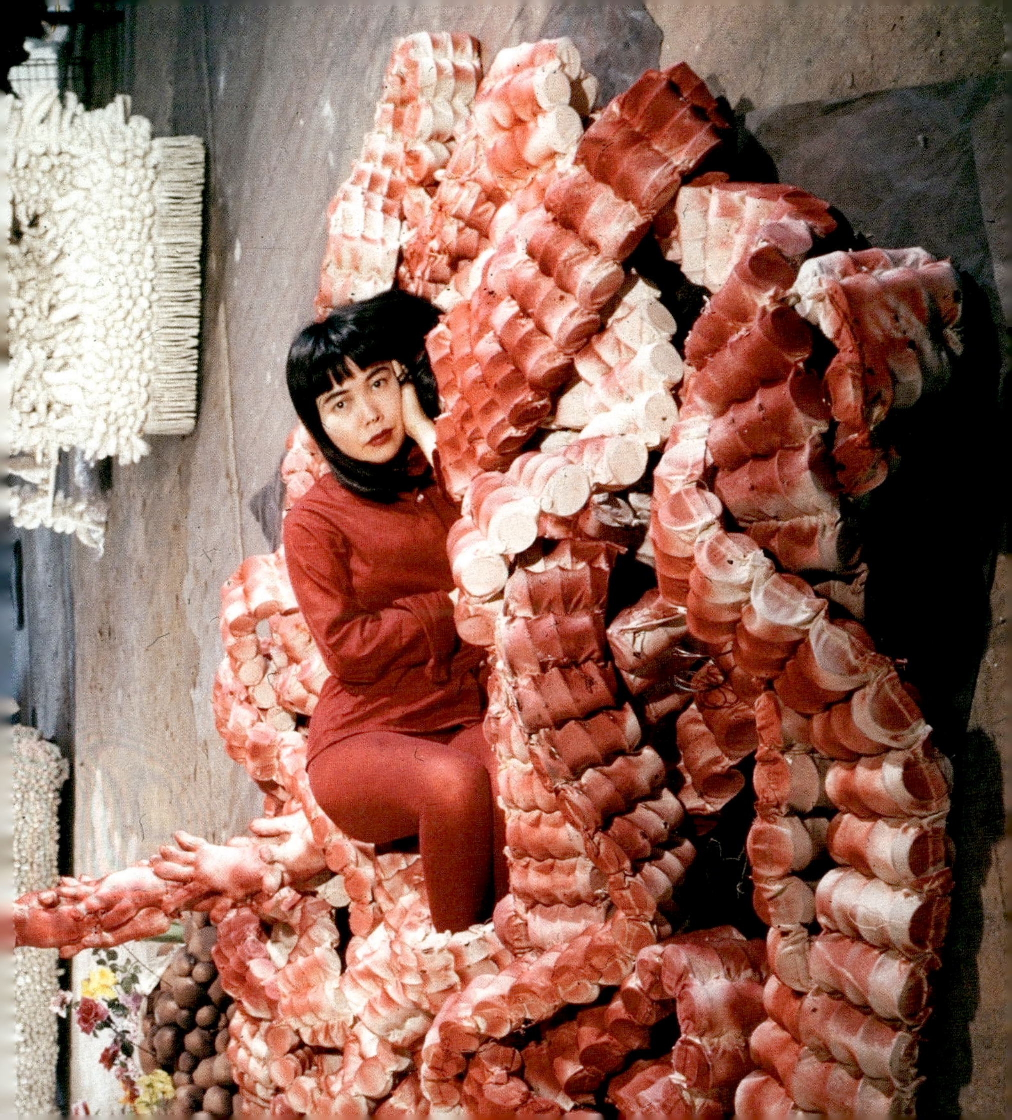

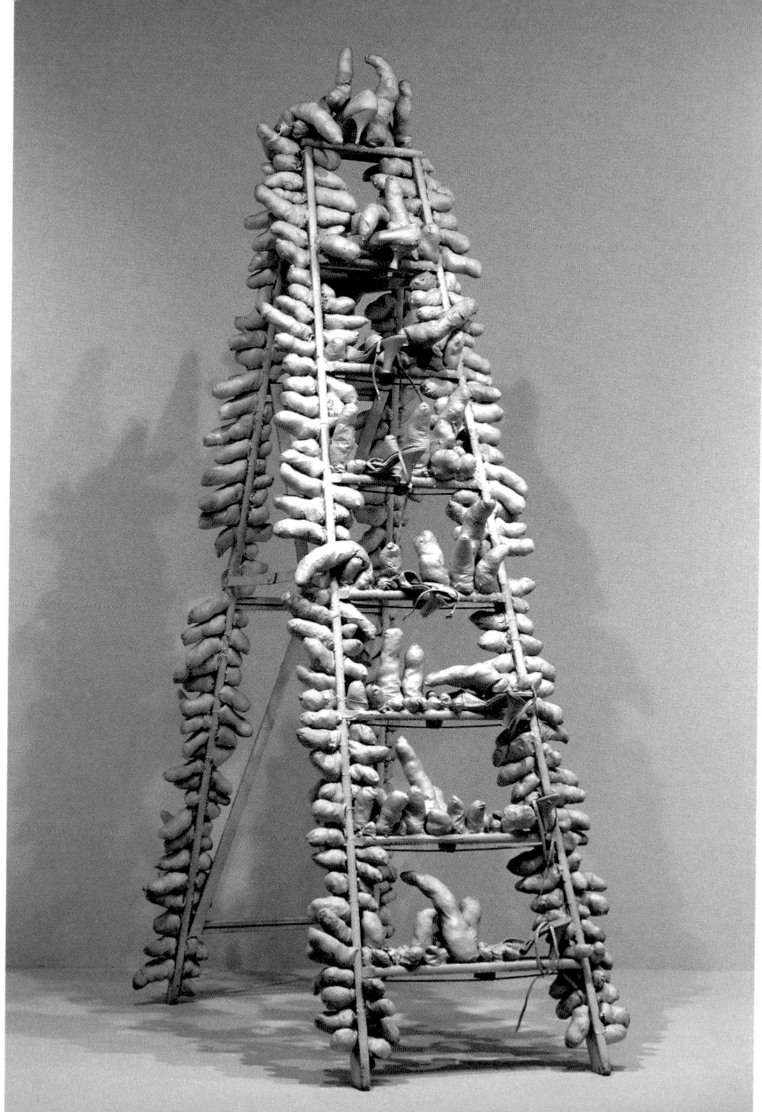

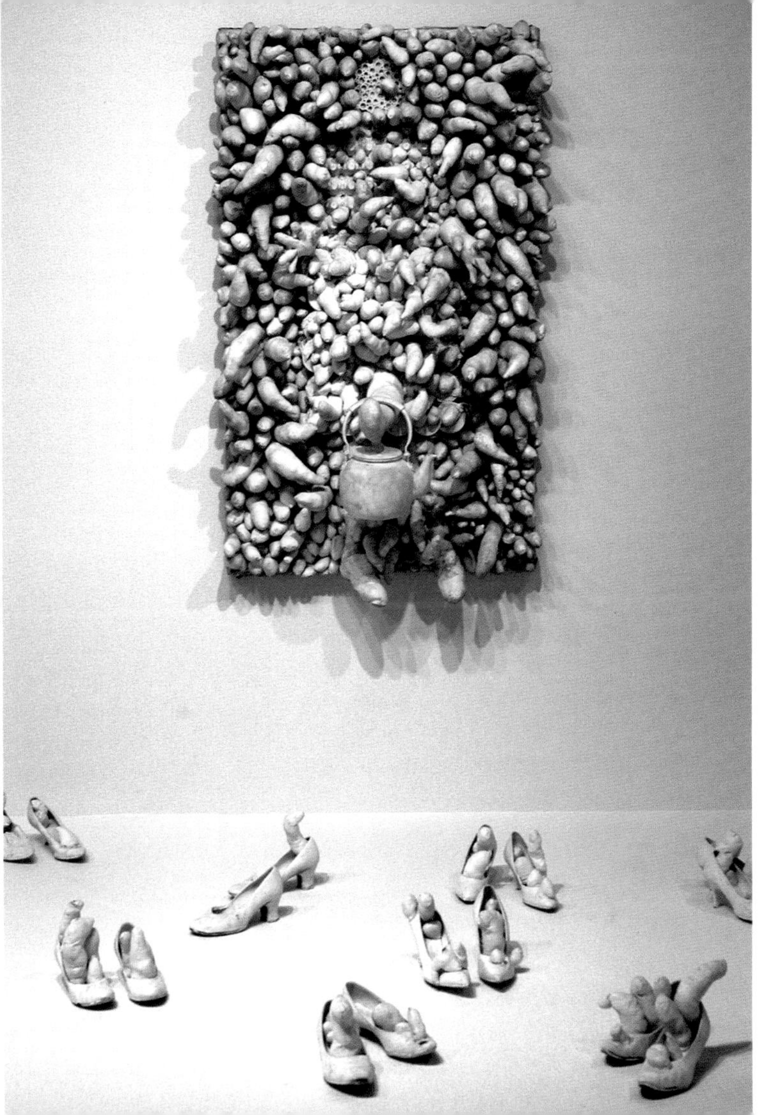

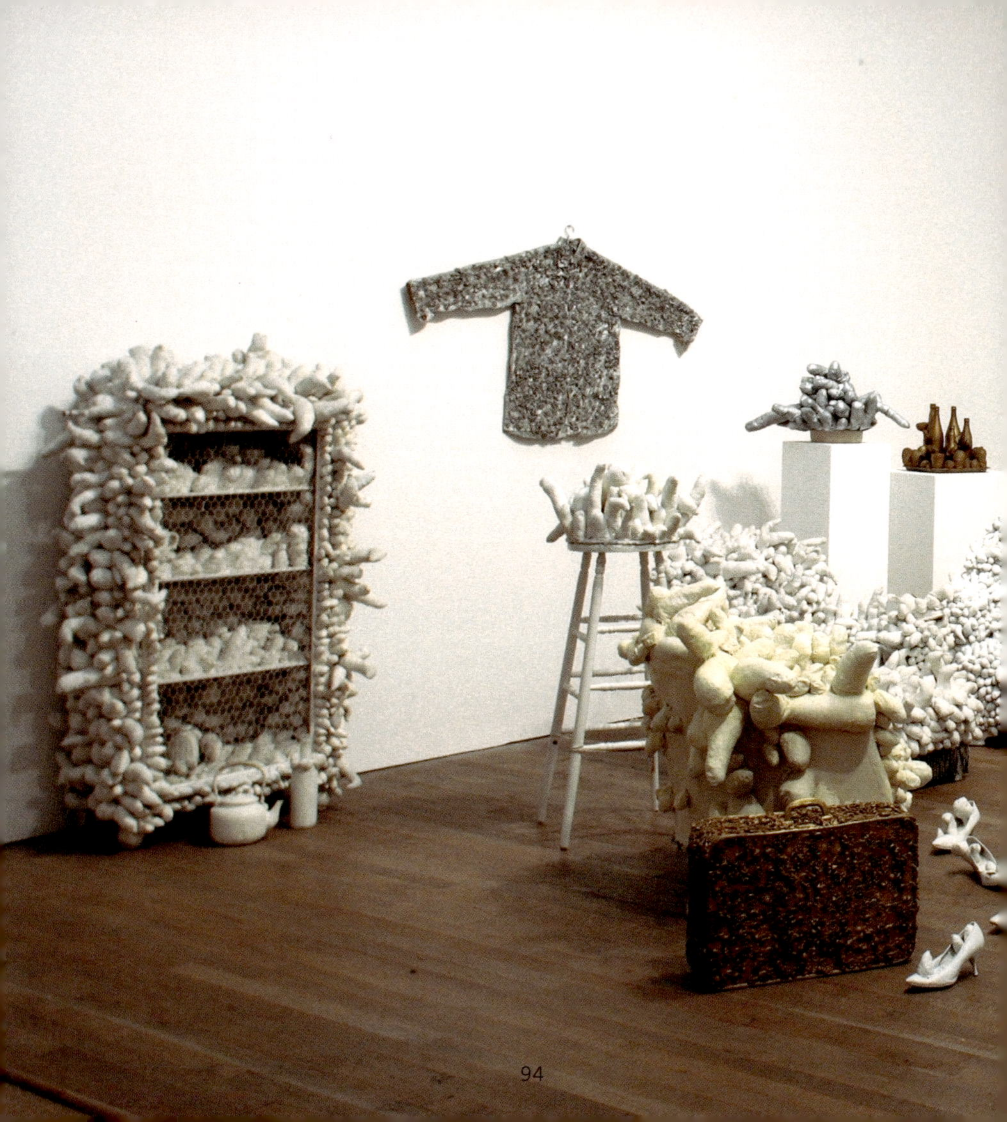

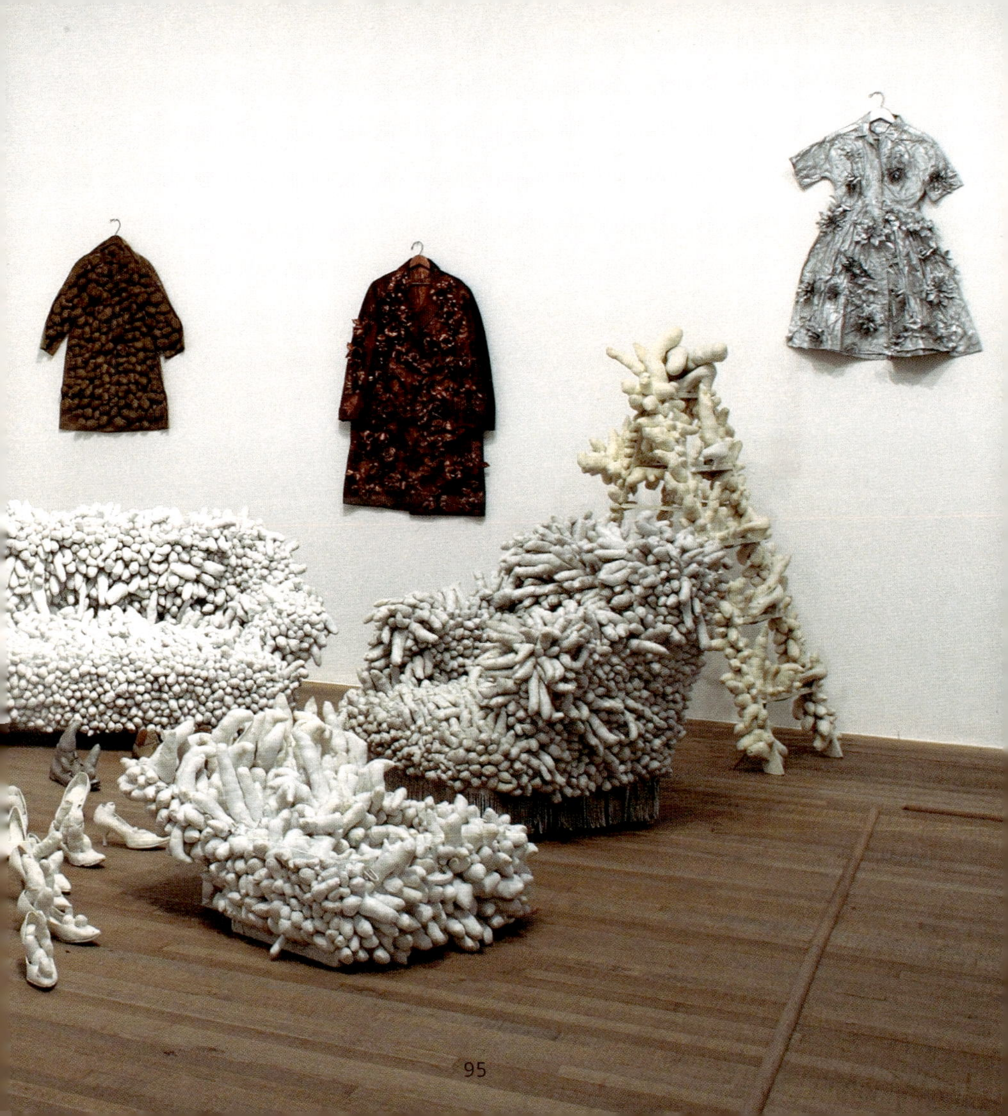

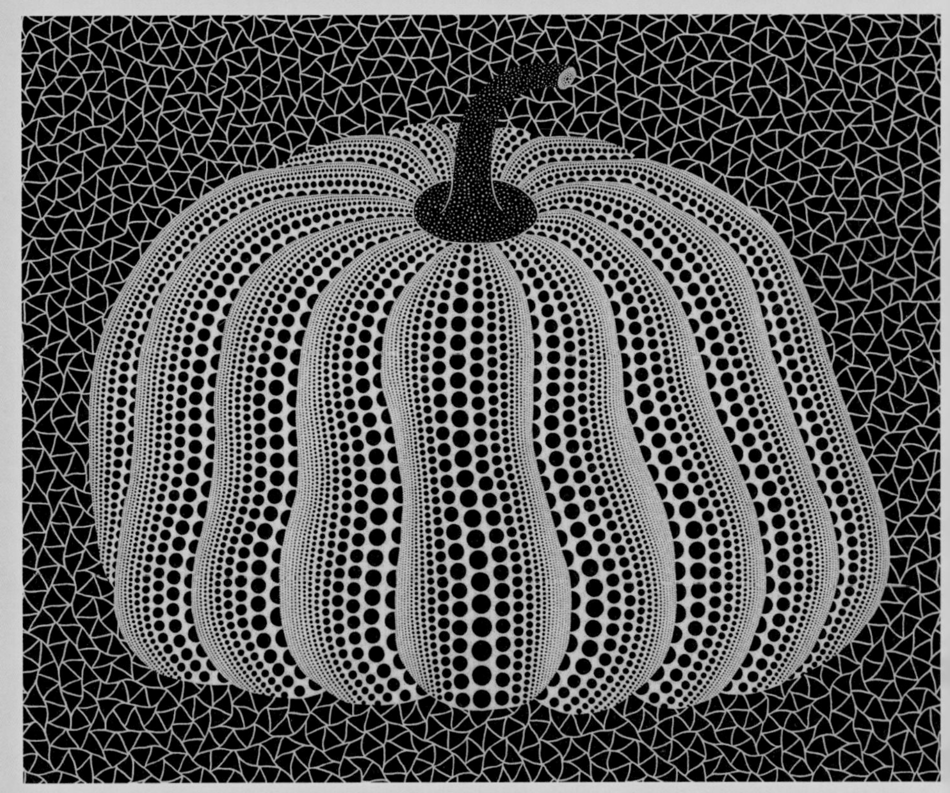

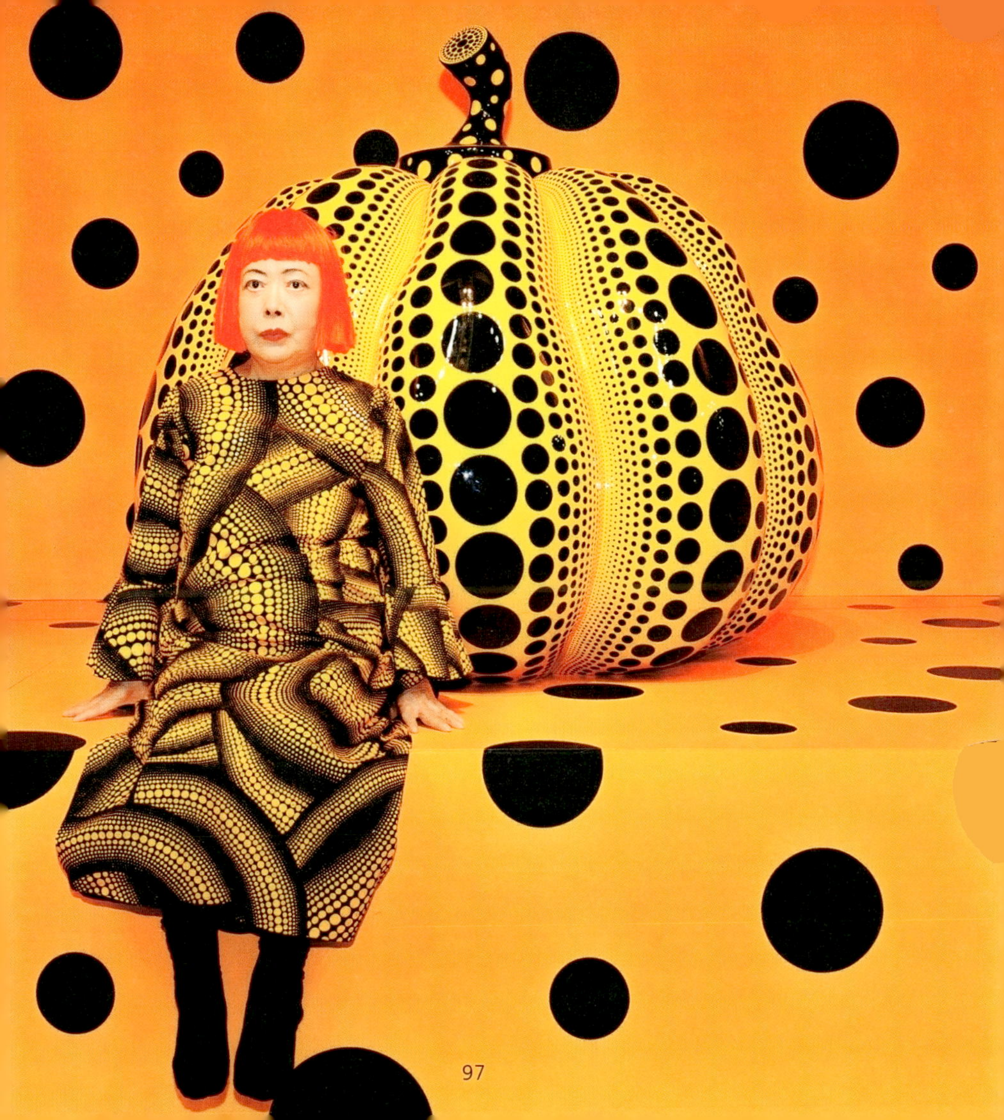

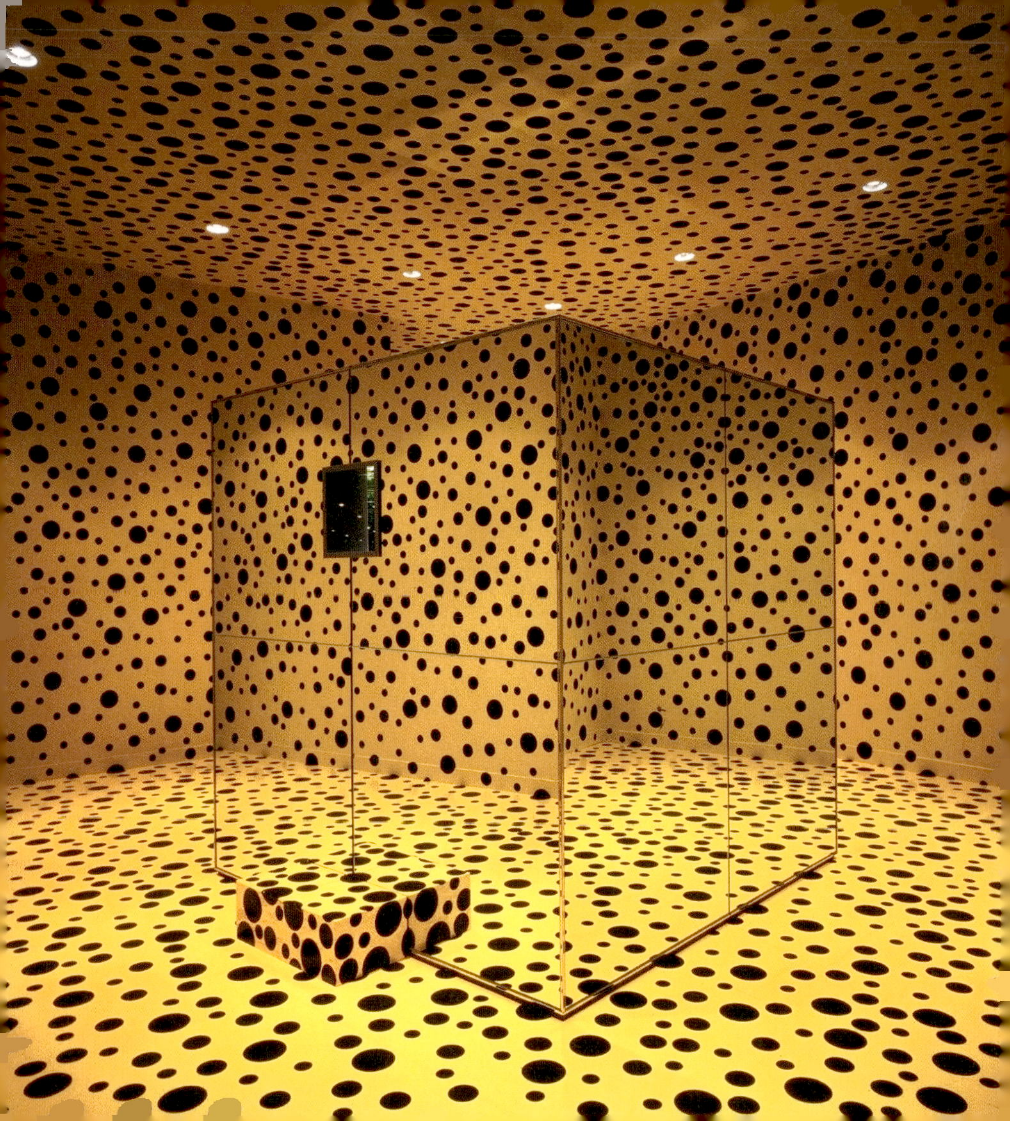

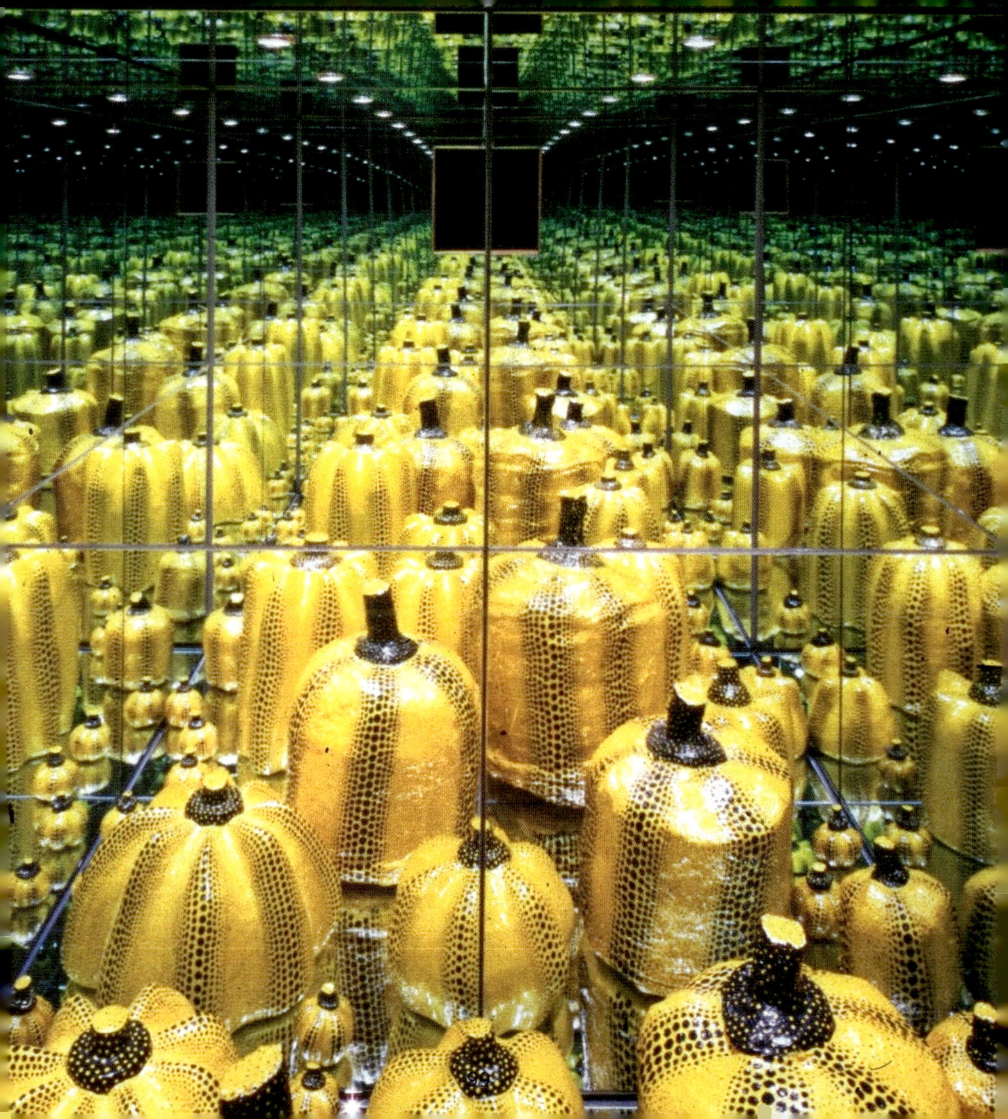

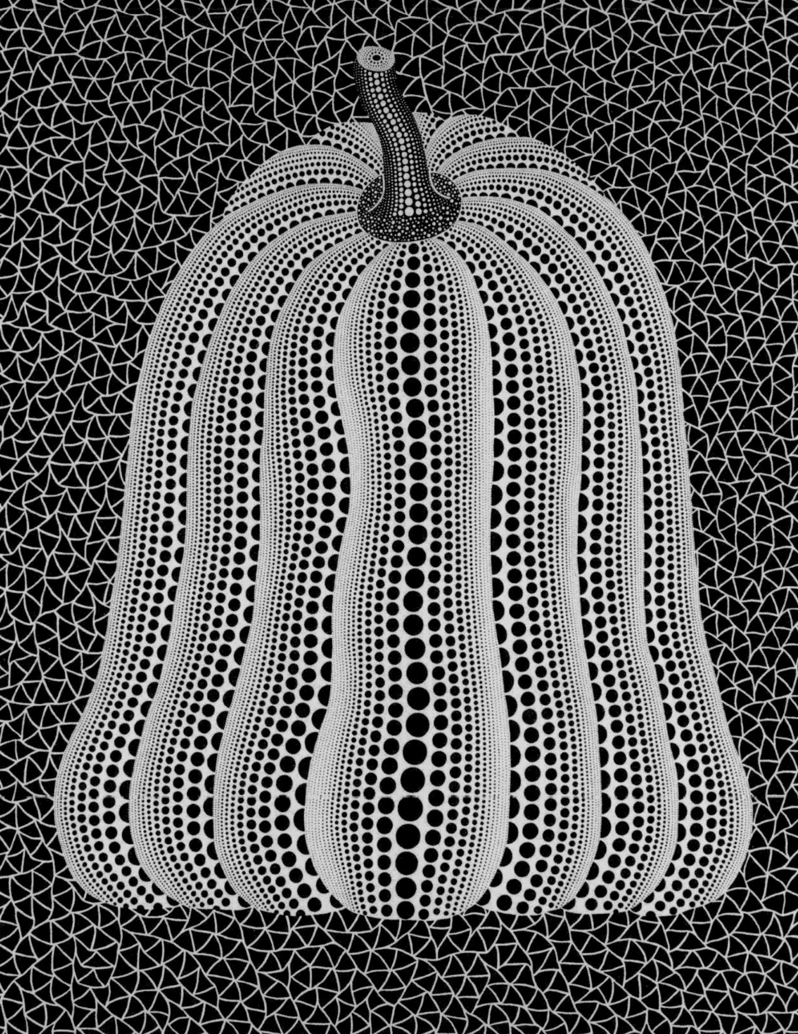

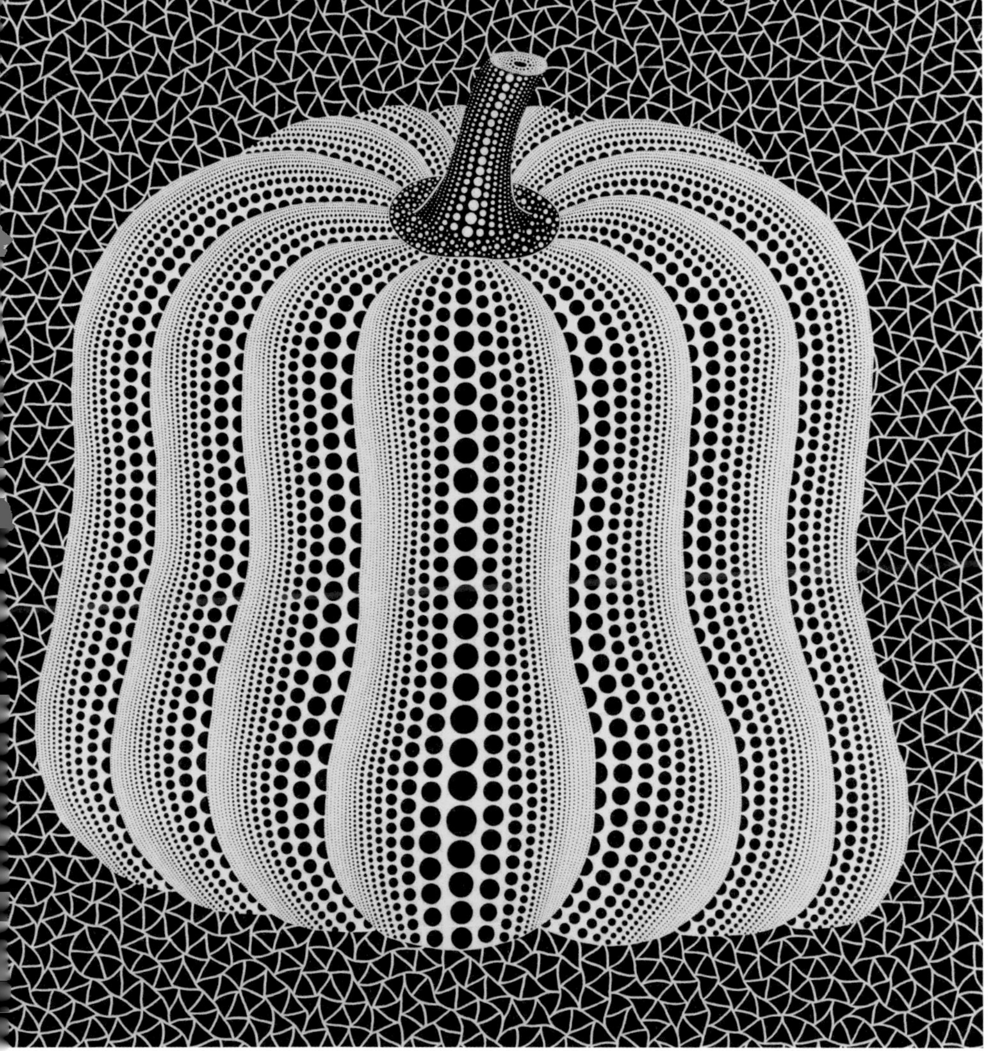

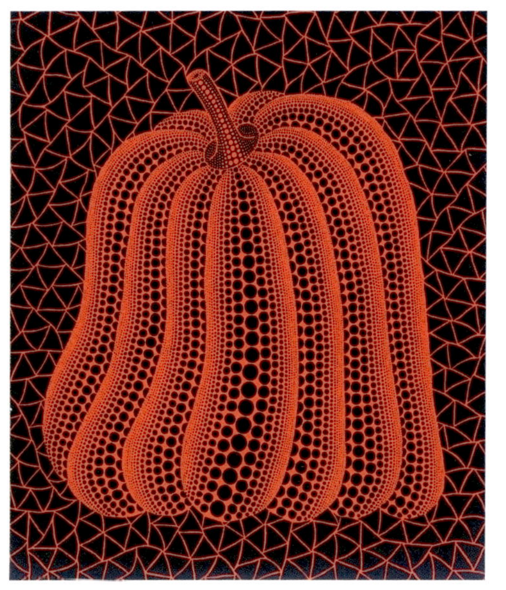

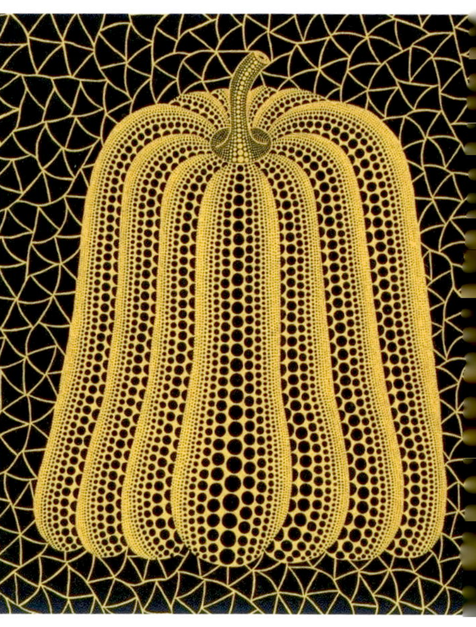

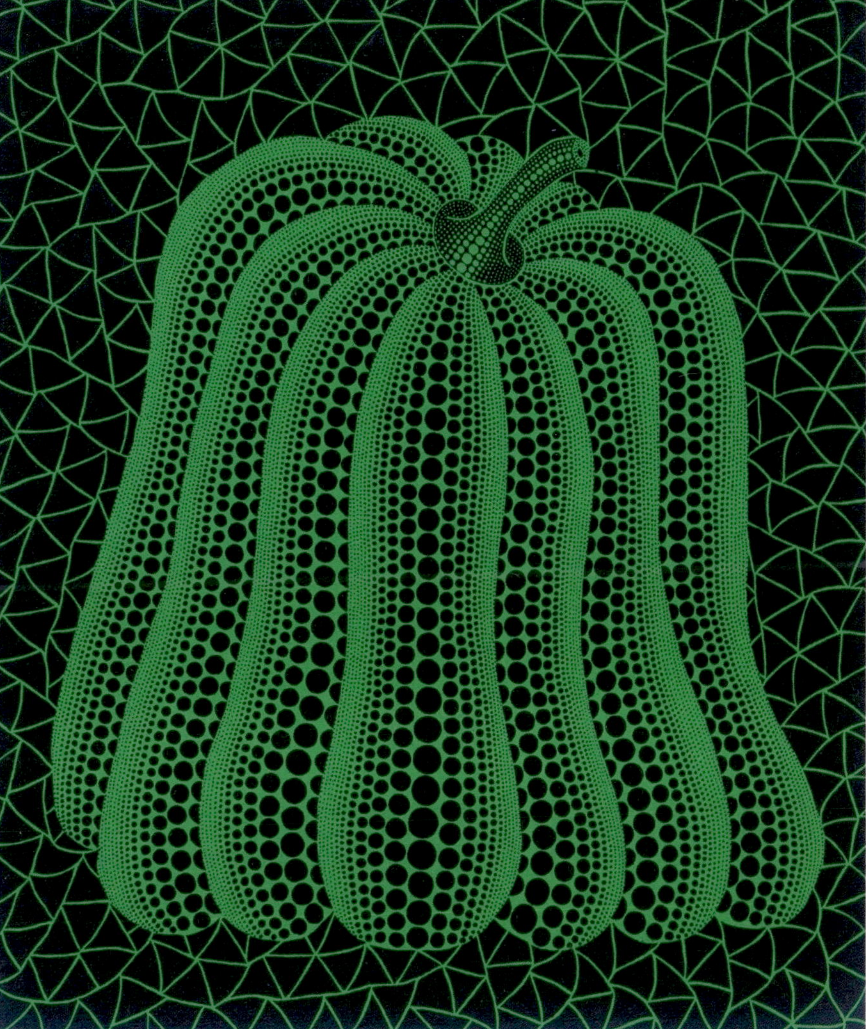

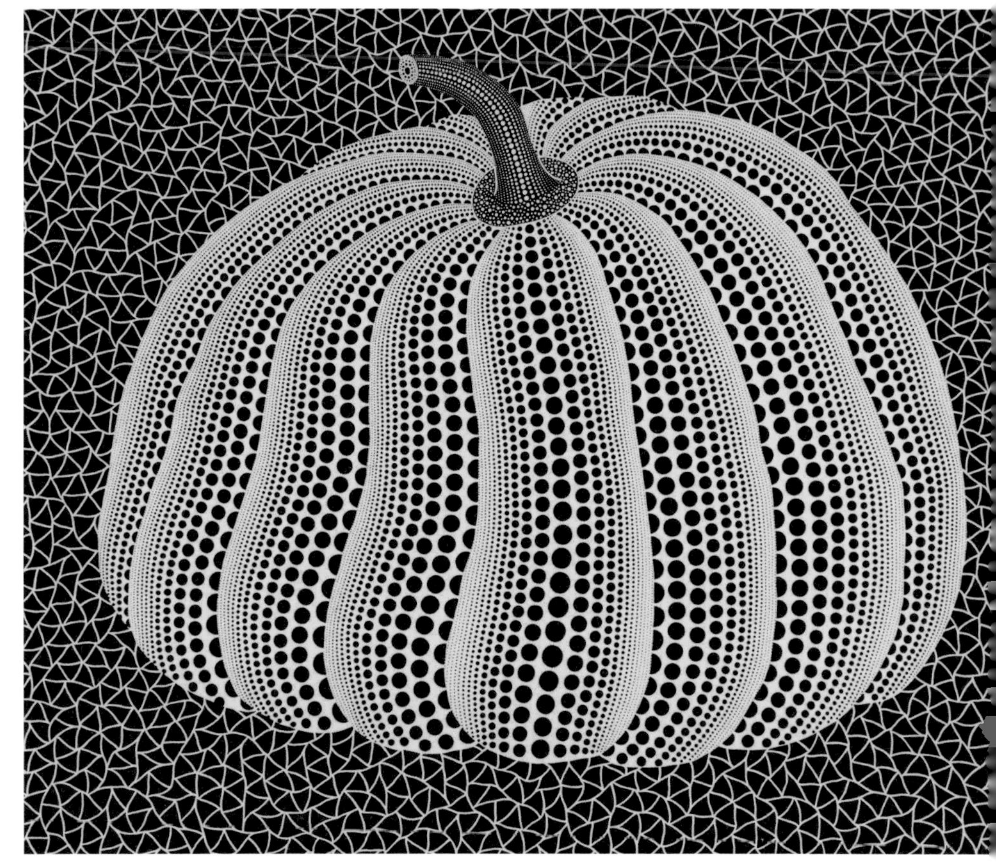

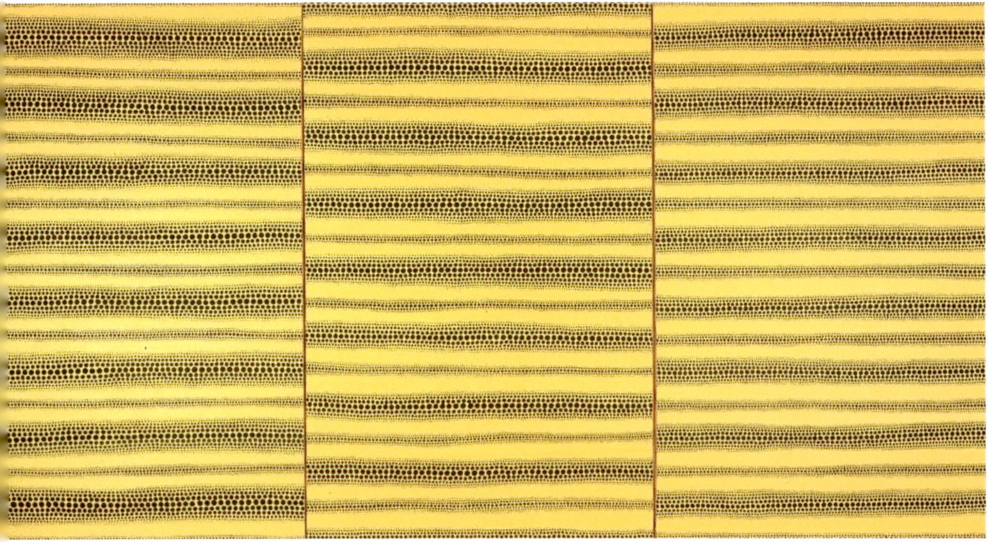

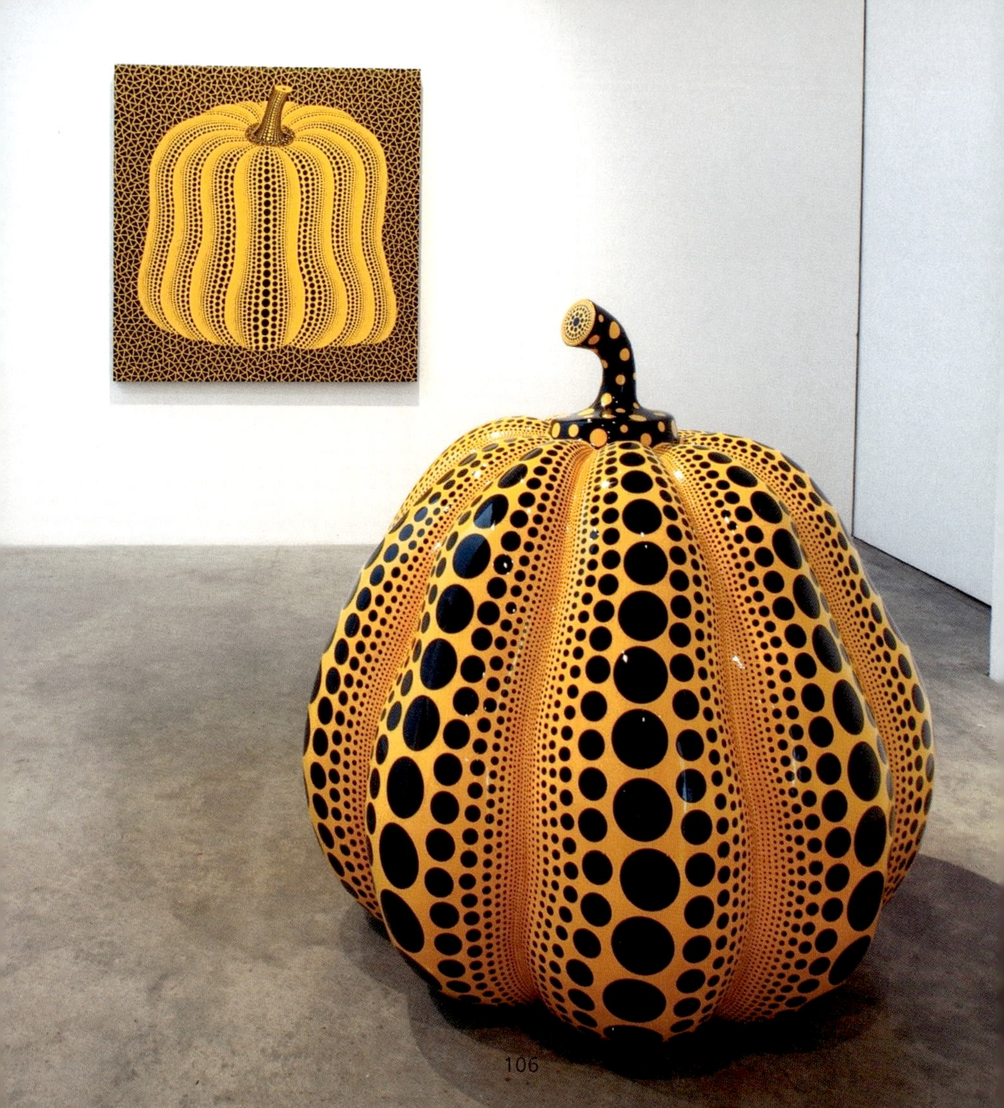

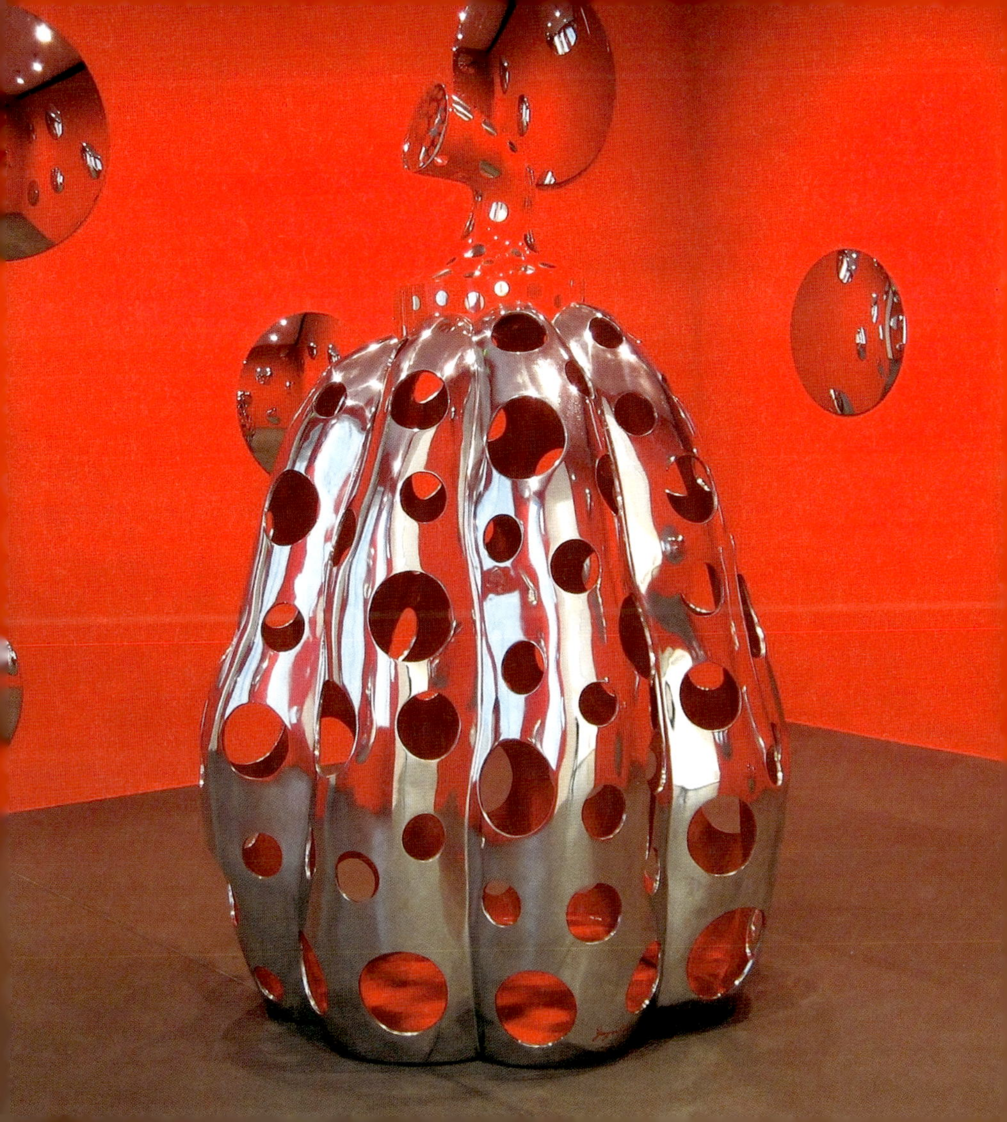

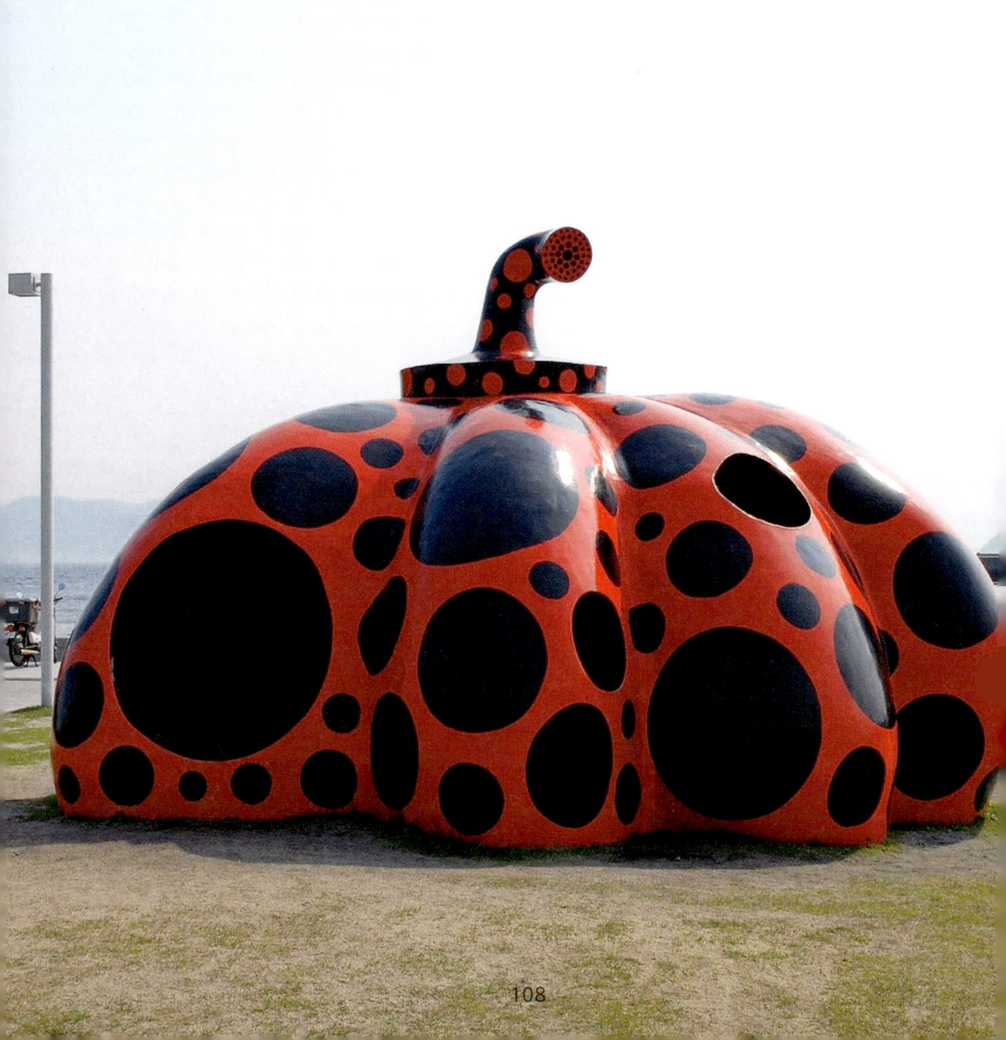

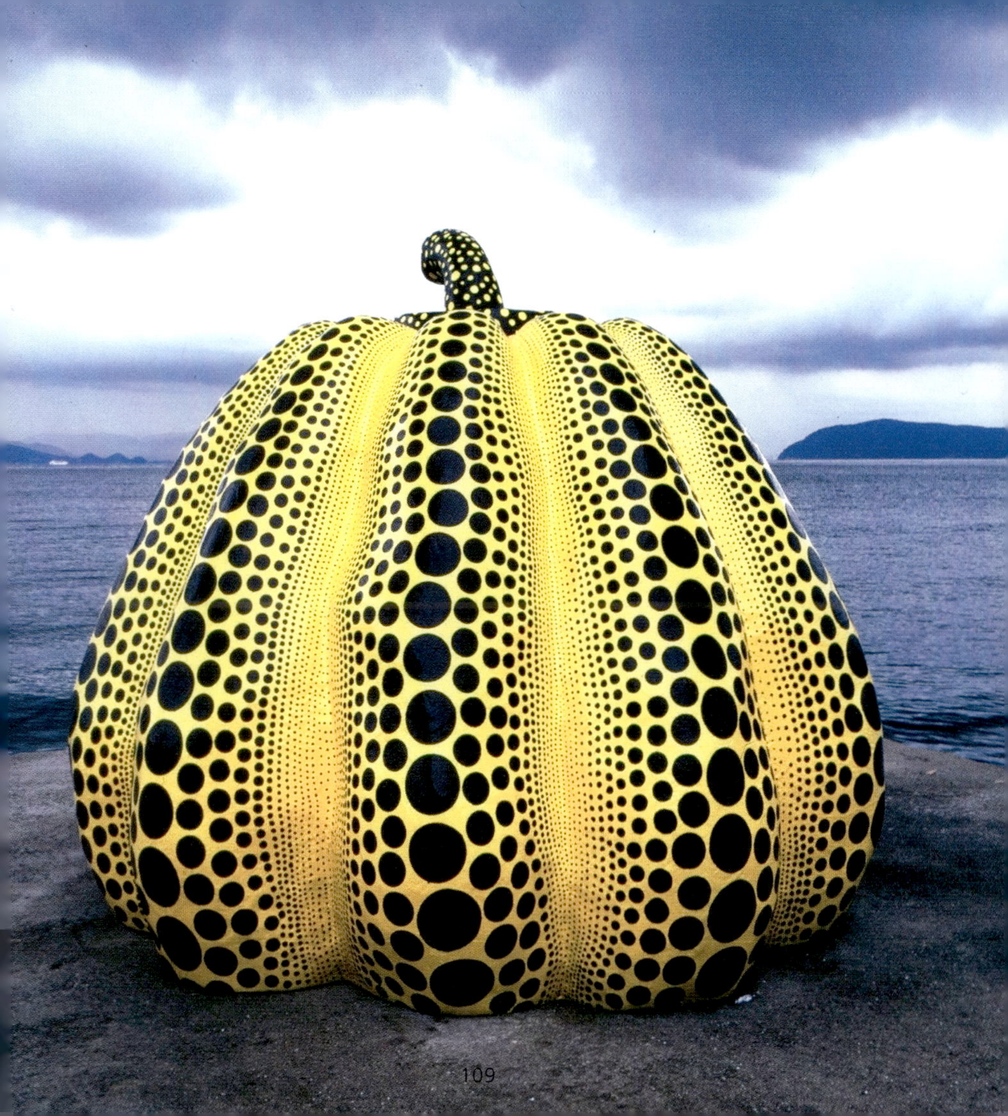

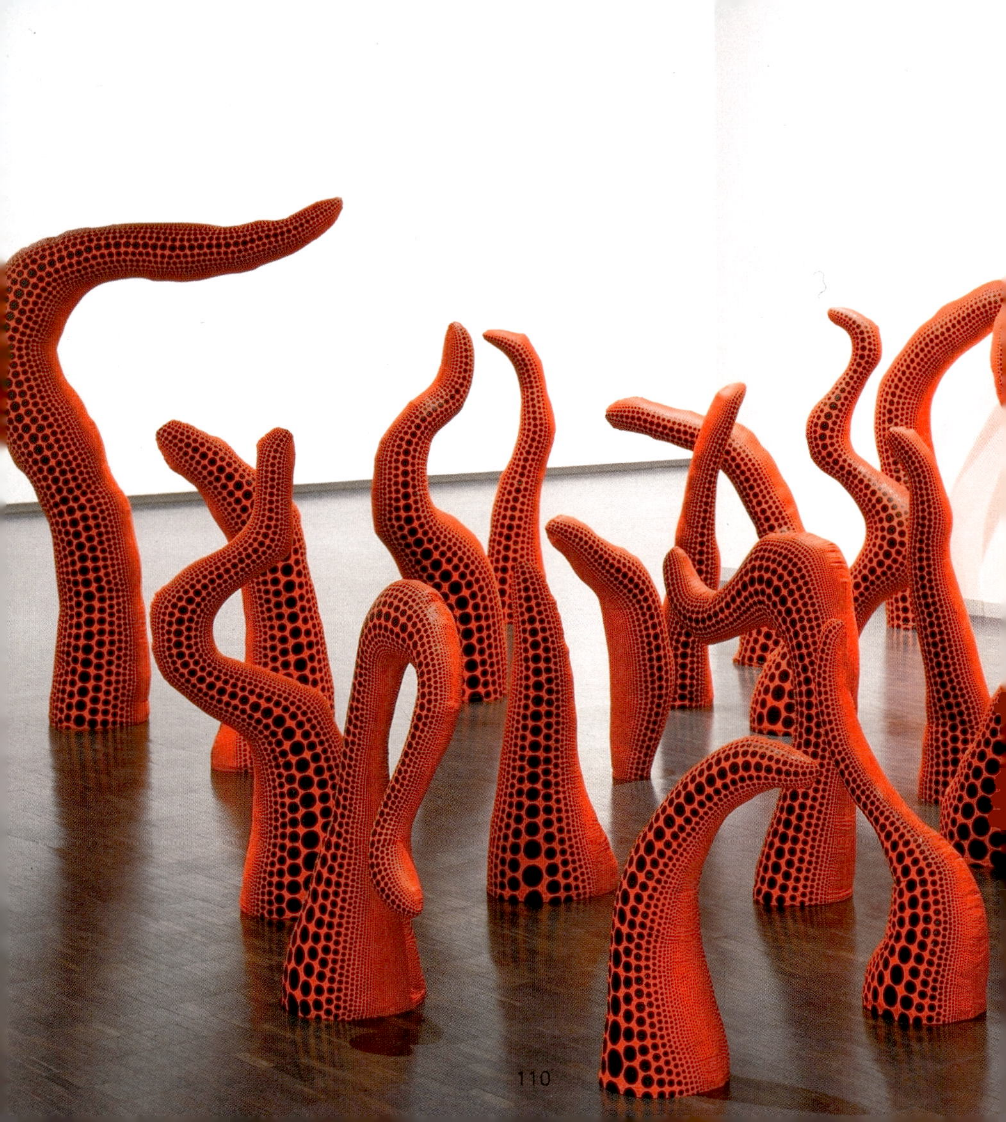

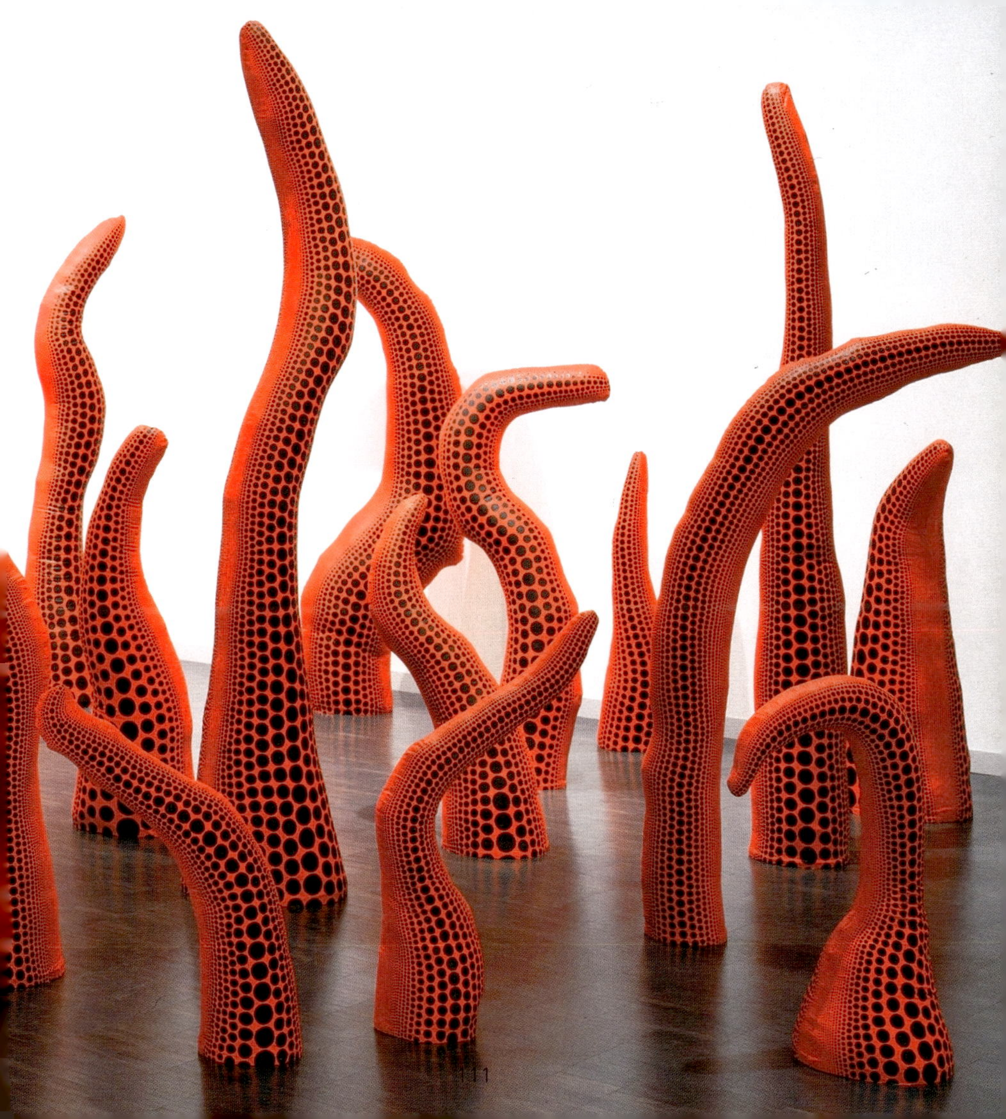

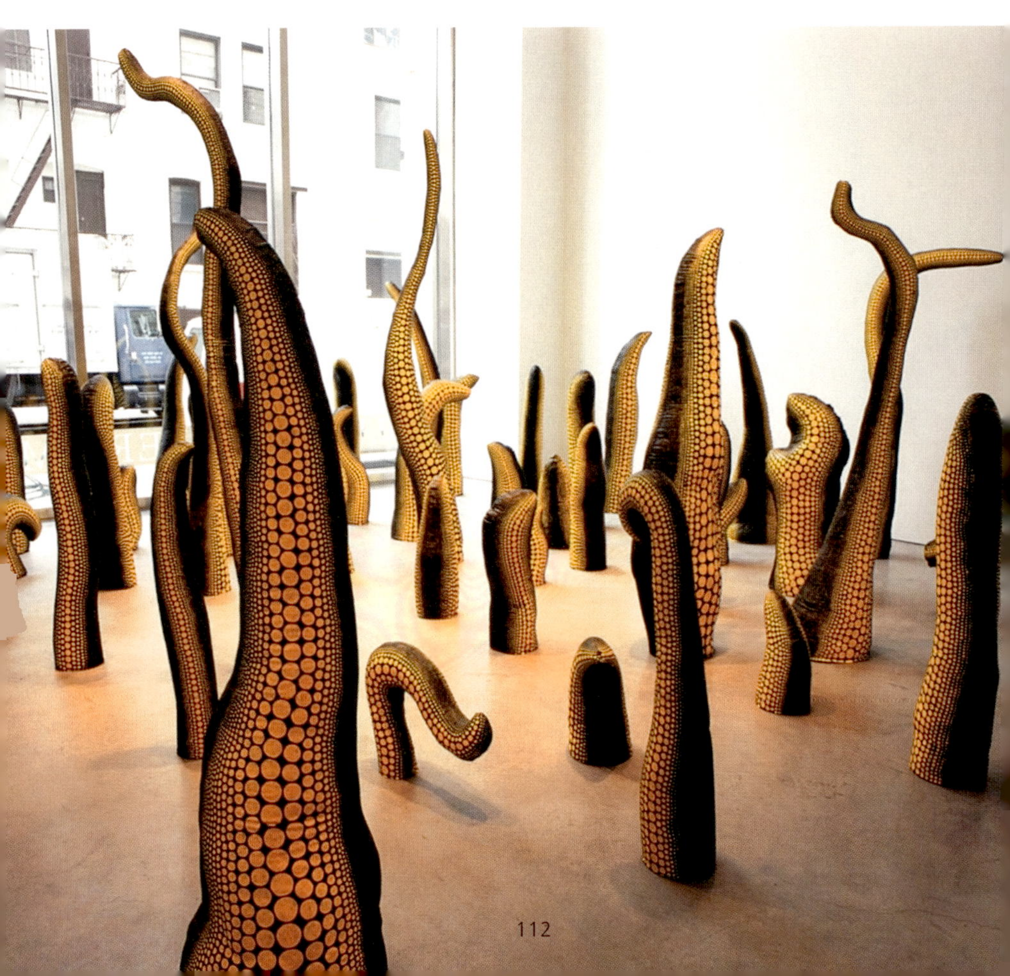

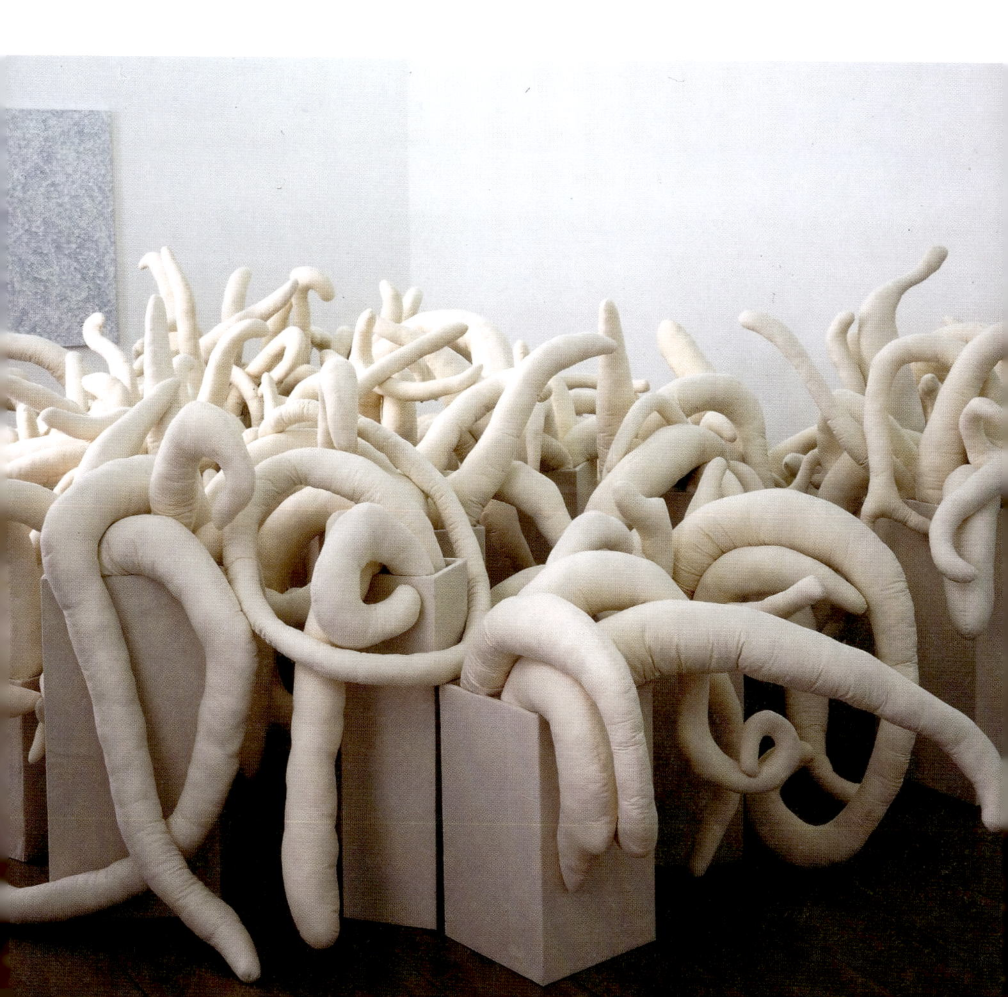

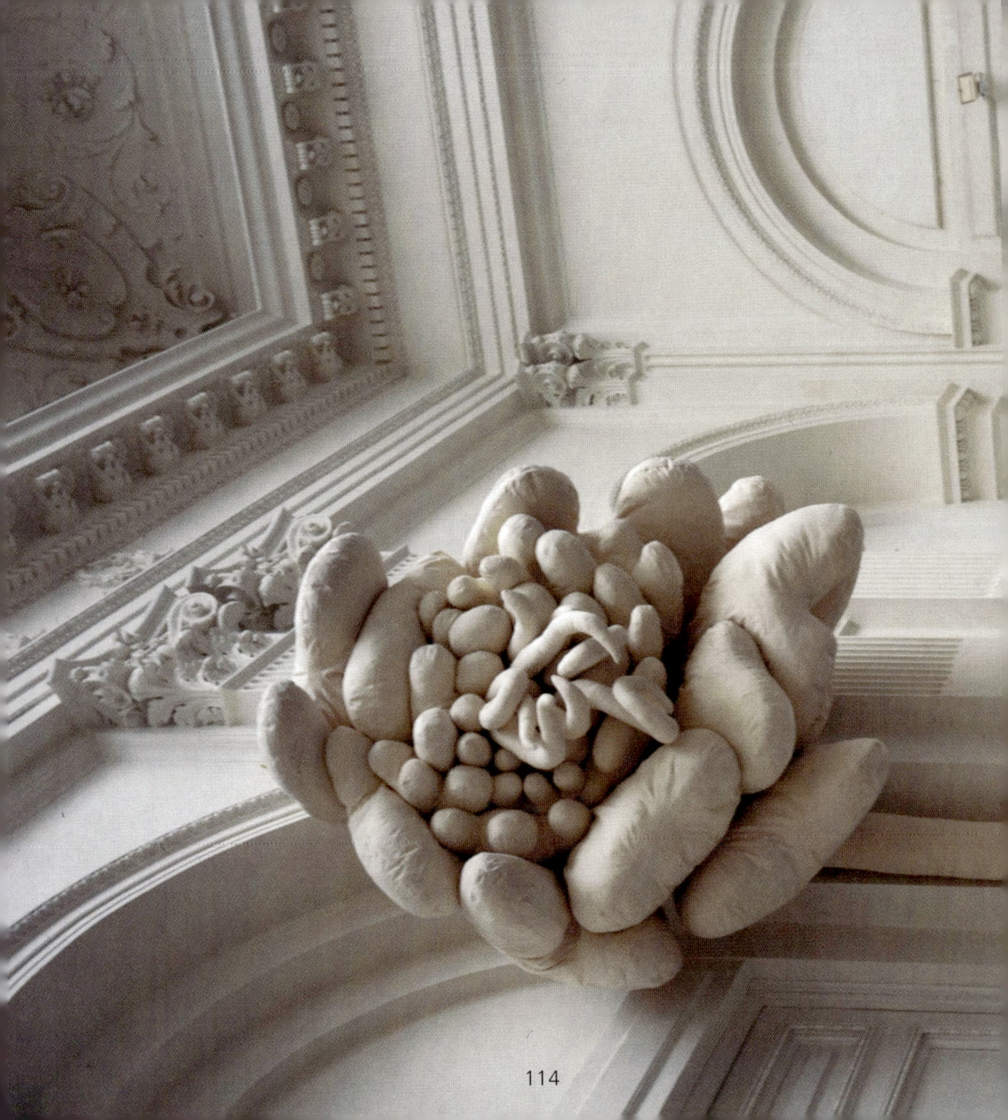

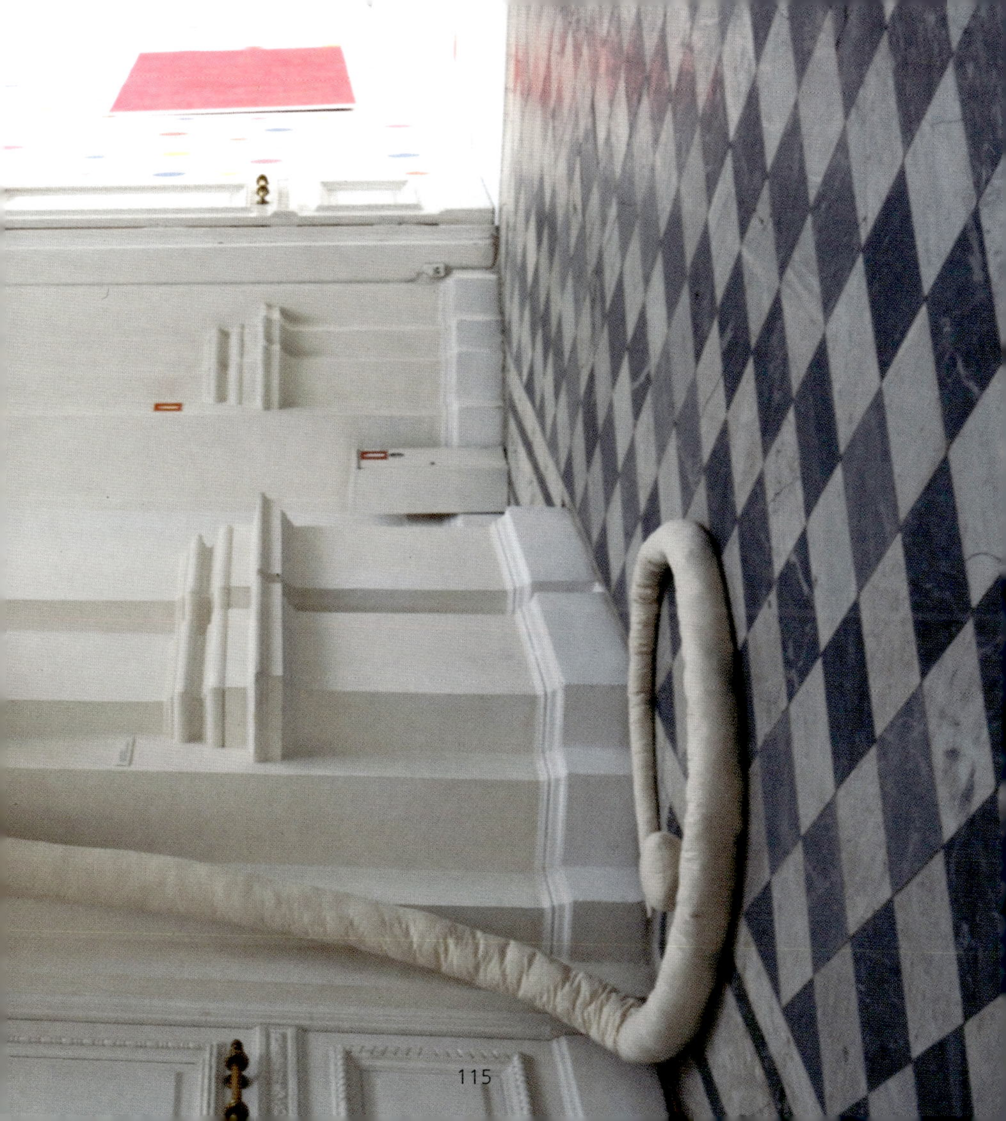

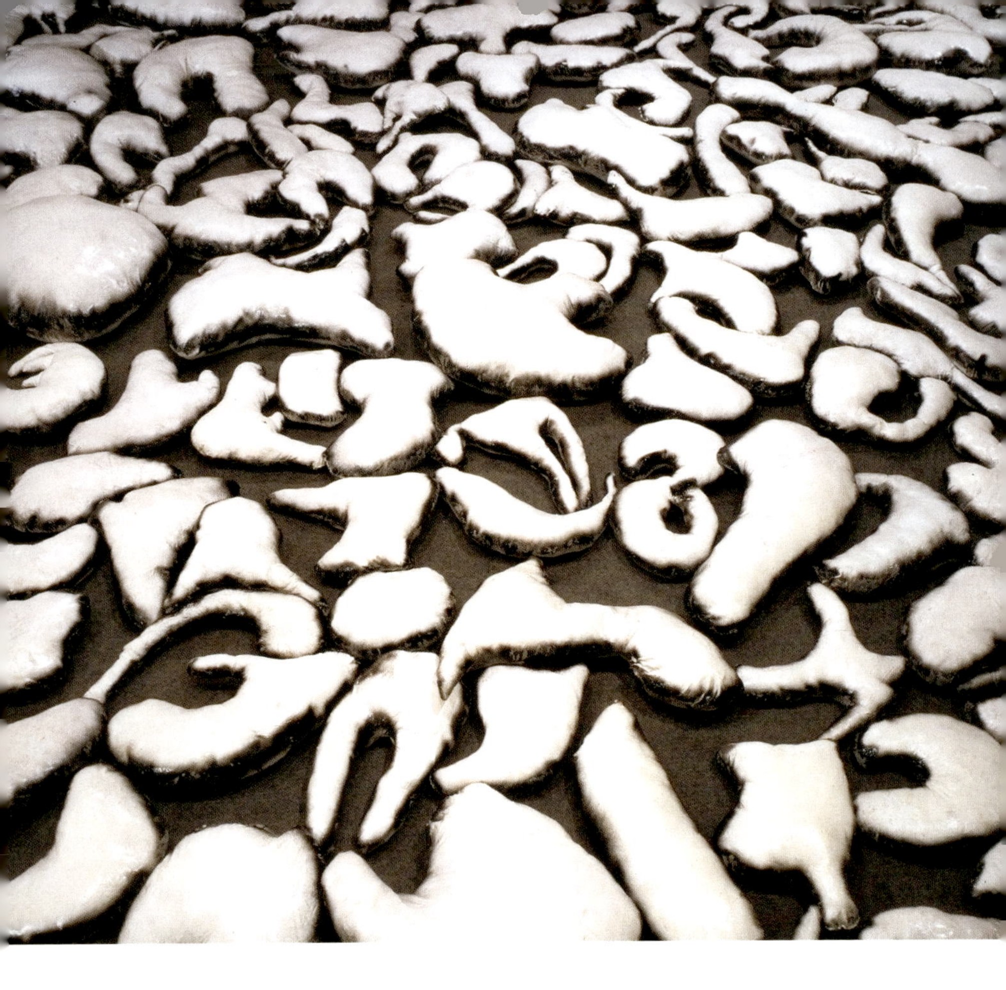

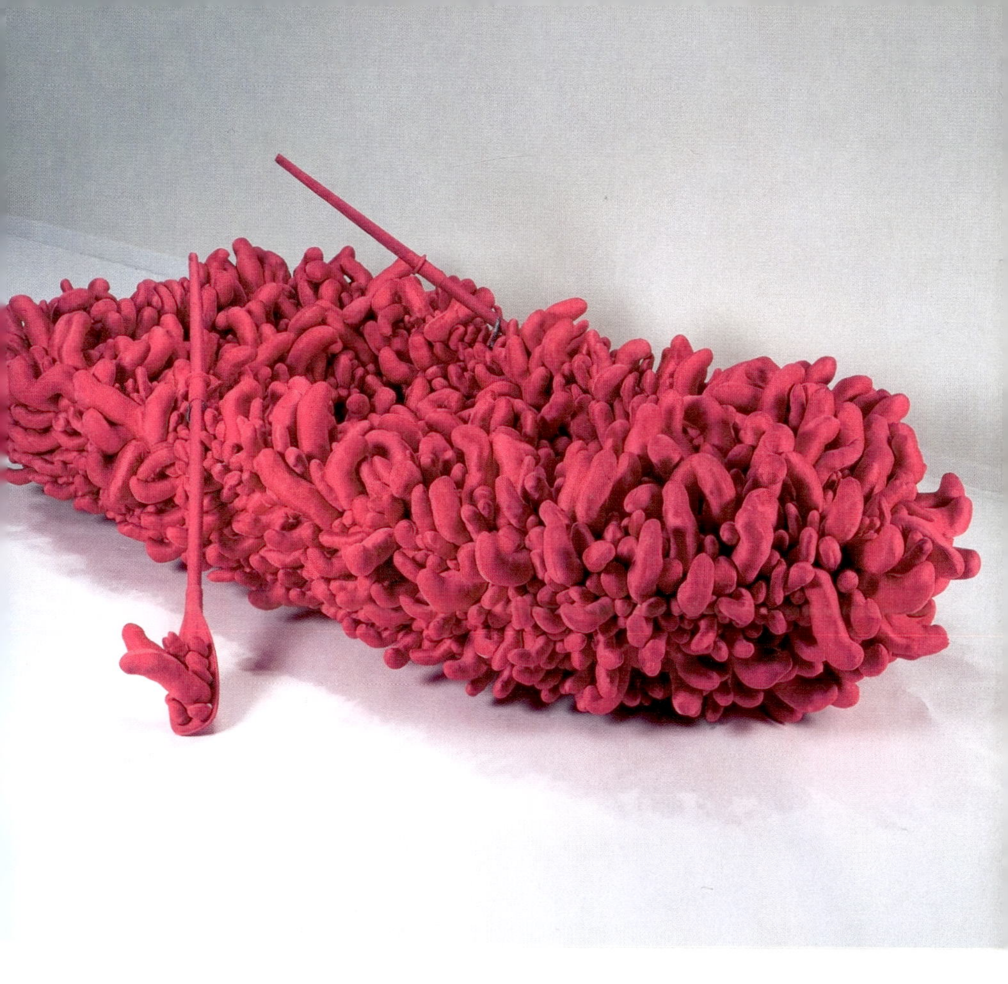

時よ、待ってくれ。

私はもっとよい仕事がしたいのだ。

もっと表現したいことが、絵や彫刻の中にいっぱいあるのだ。

Hey time, hold still awhile.
I want to do a better job.
There are so many things in painting and sculpture that I wish to express.

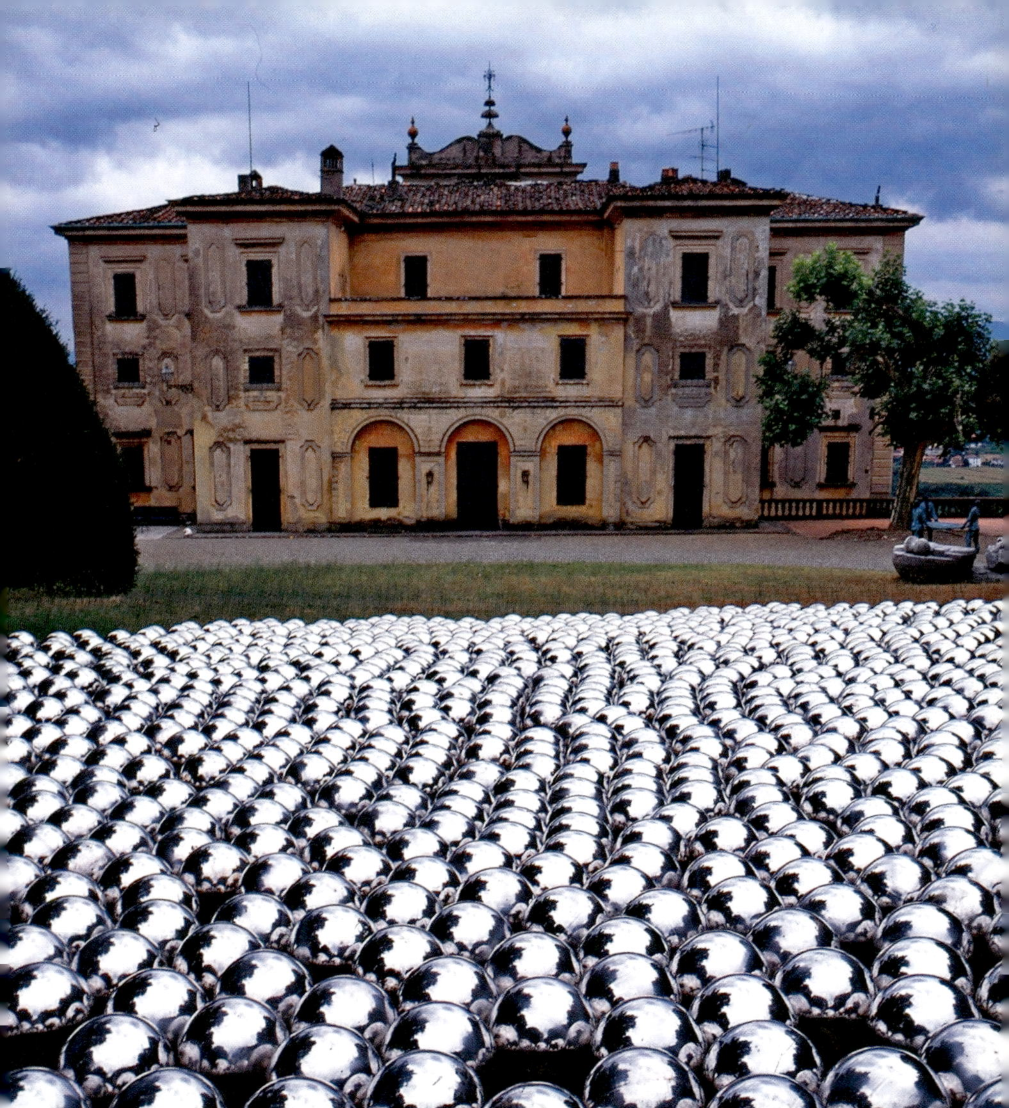

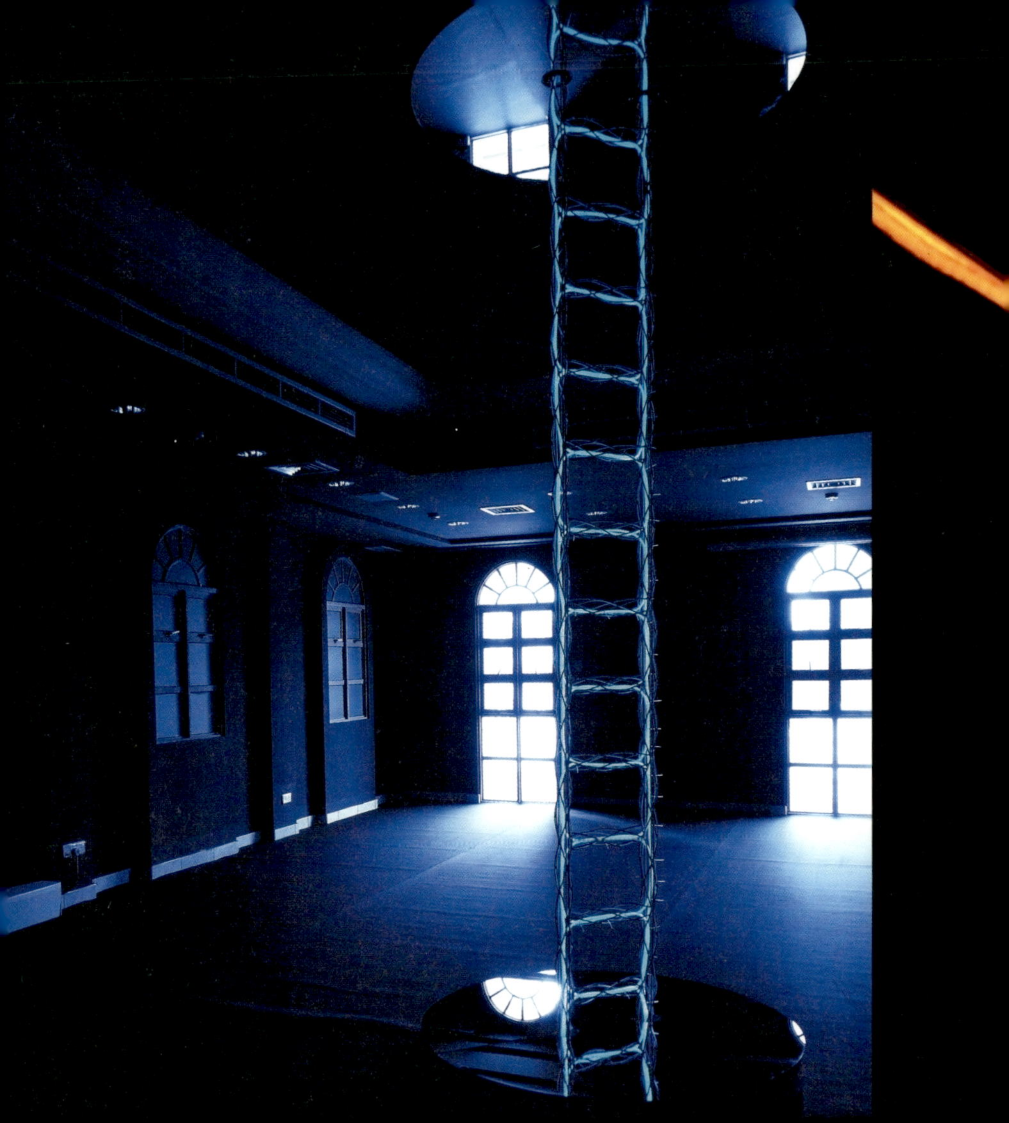

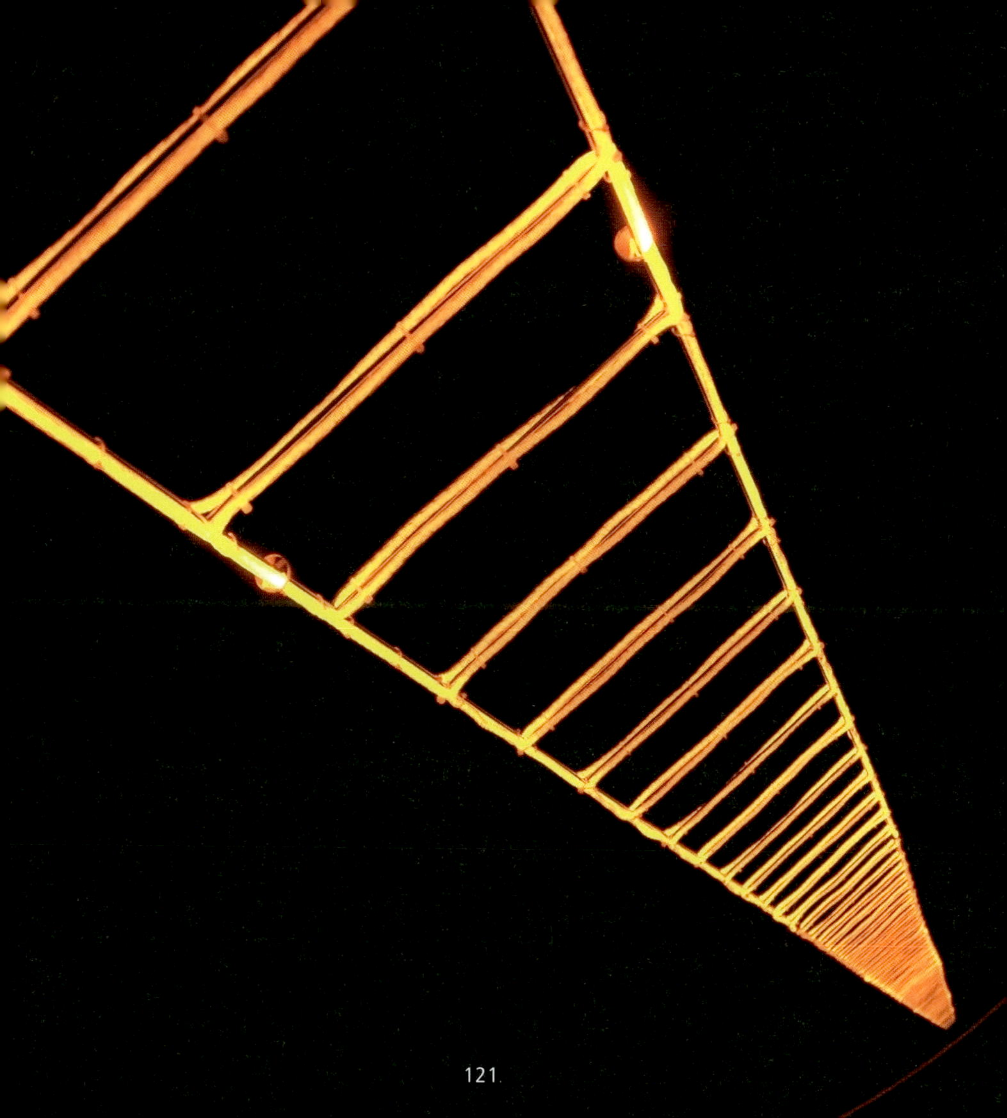

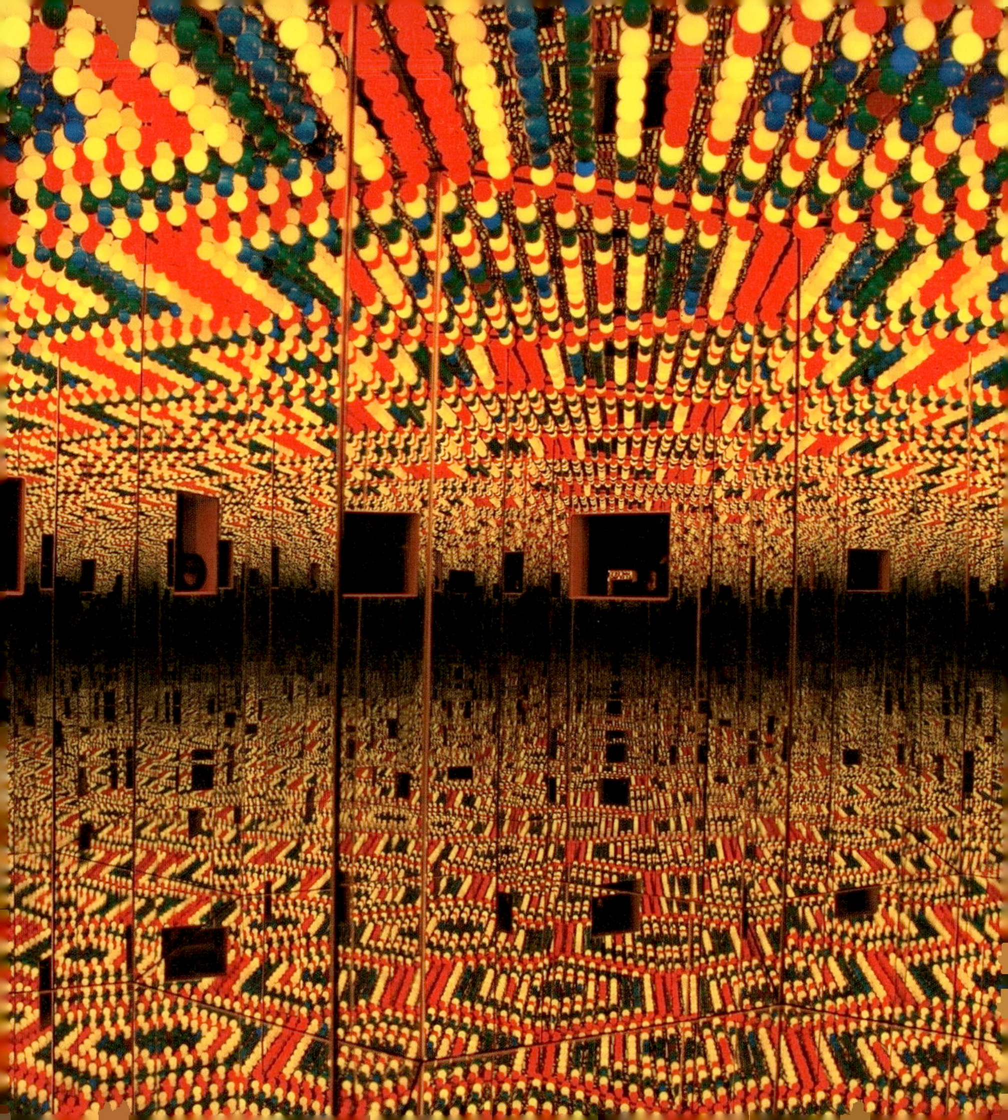

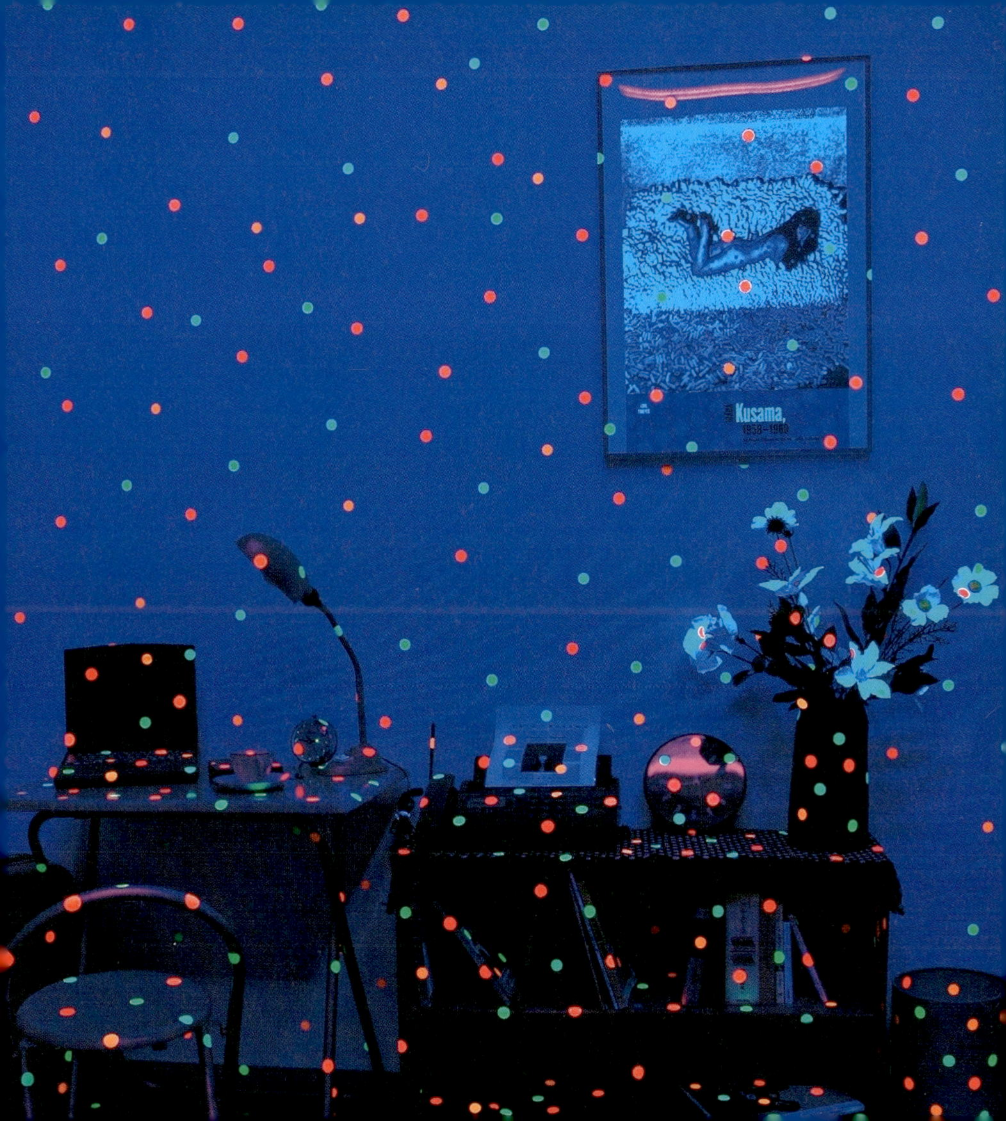
Kusama,

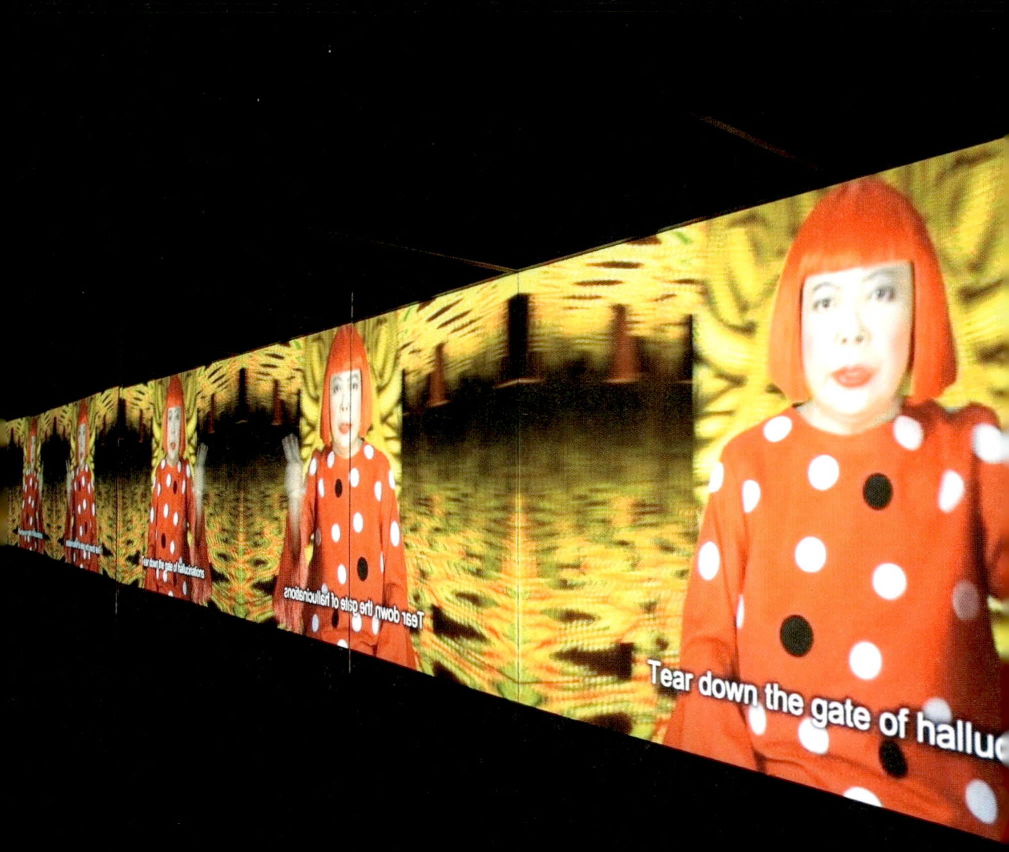
Tear down the gate of halluc

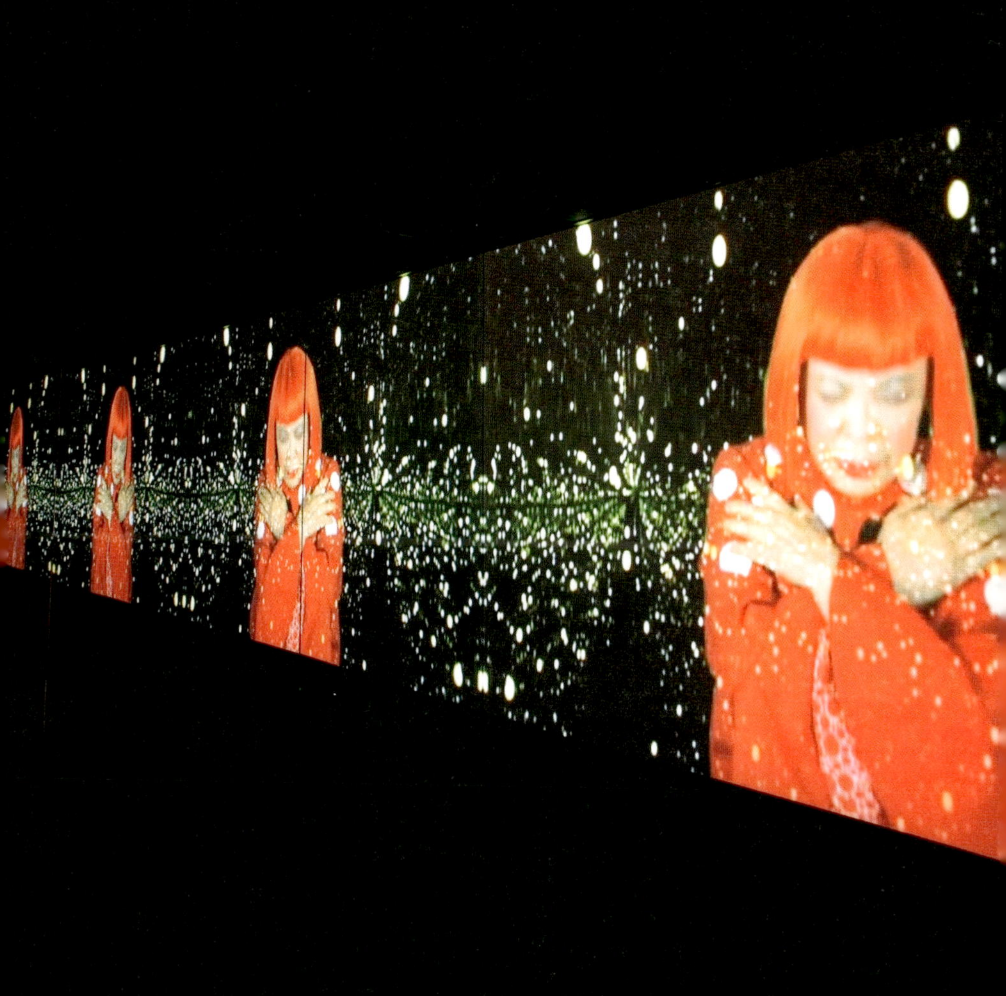

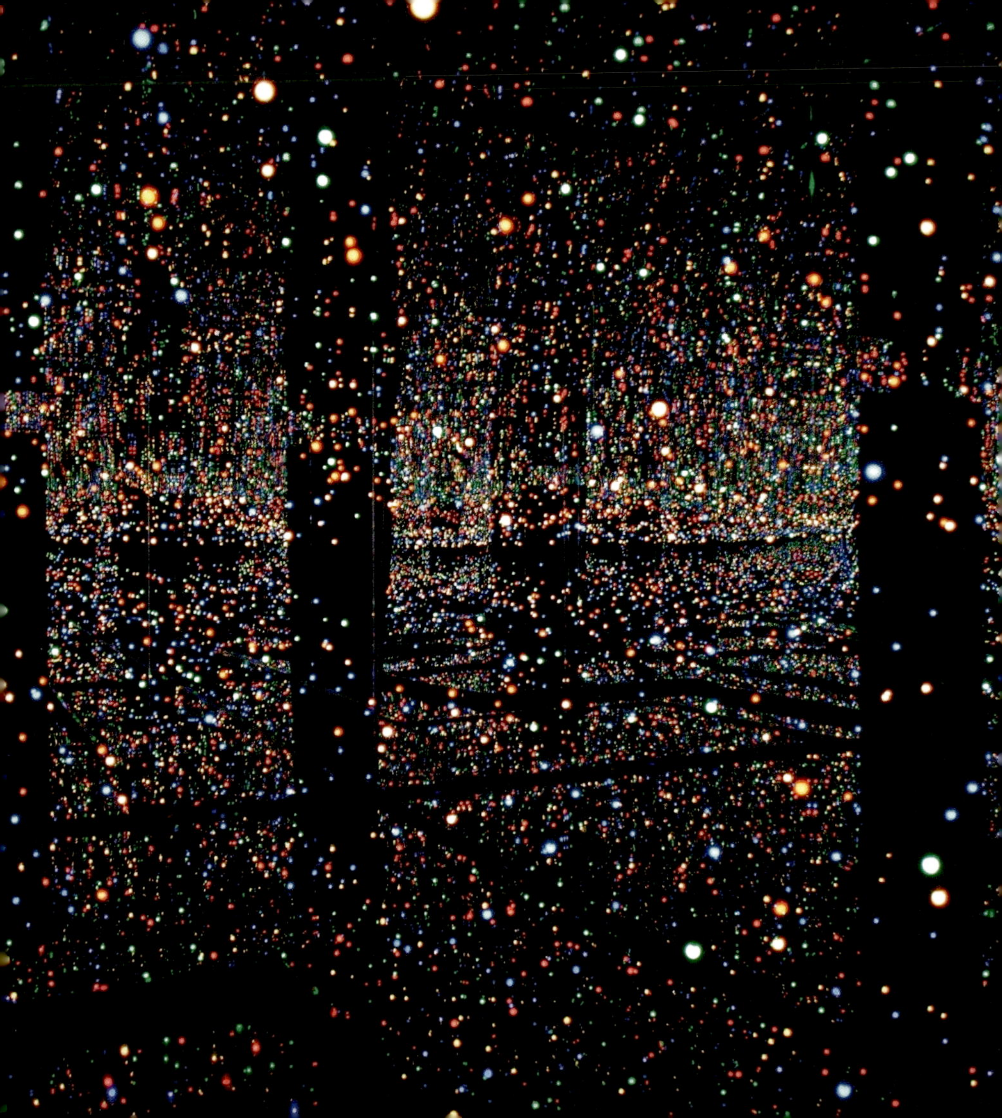

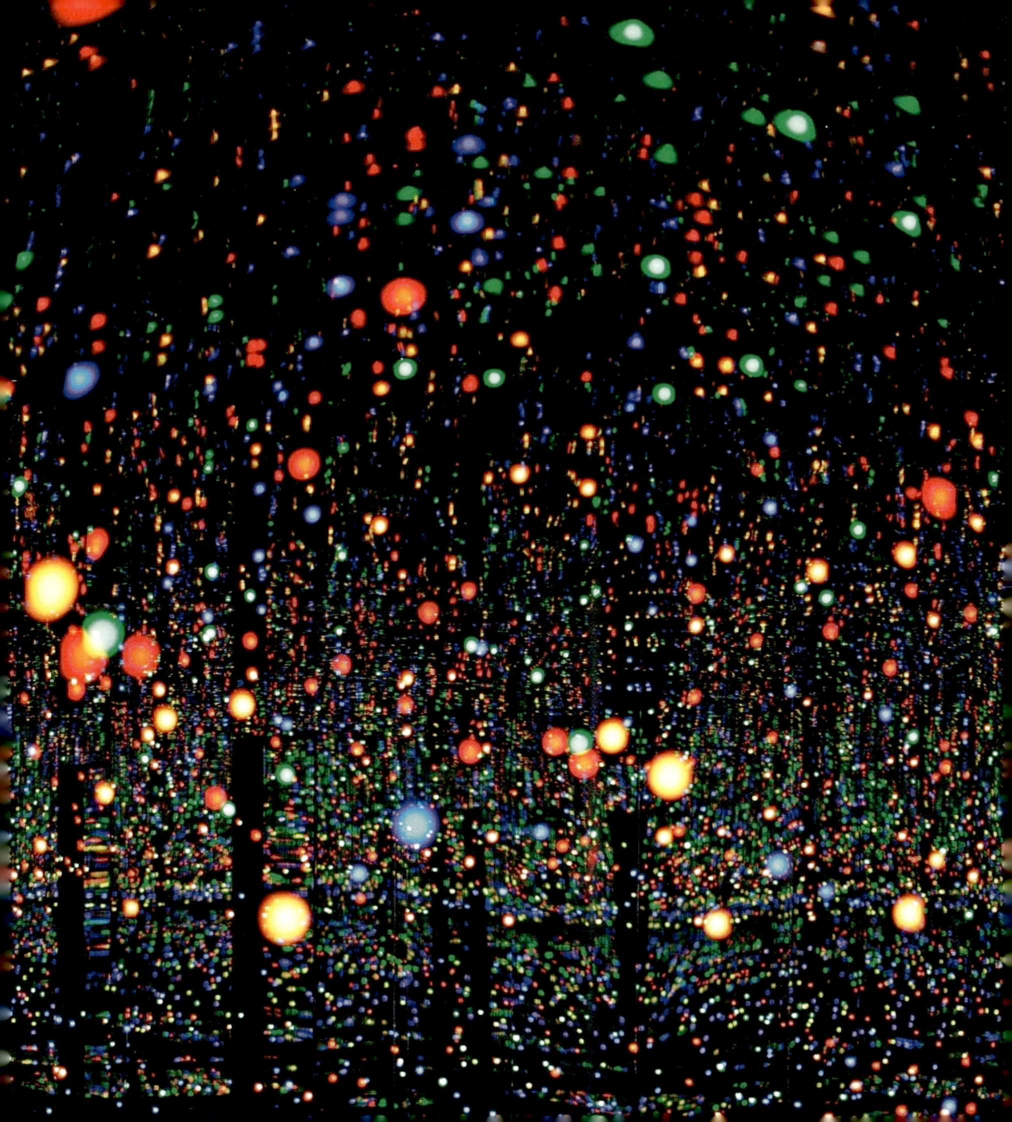

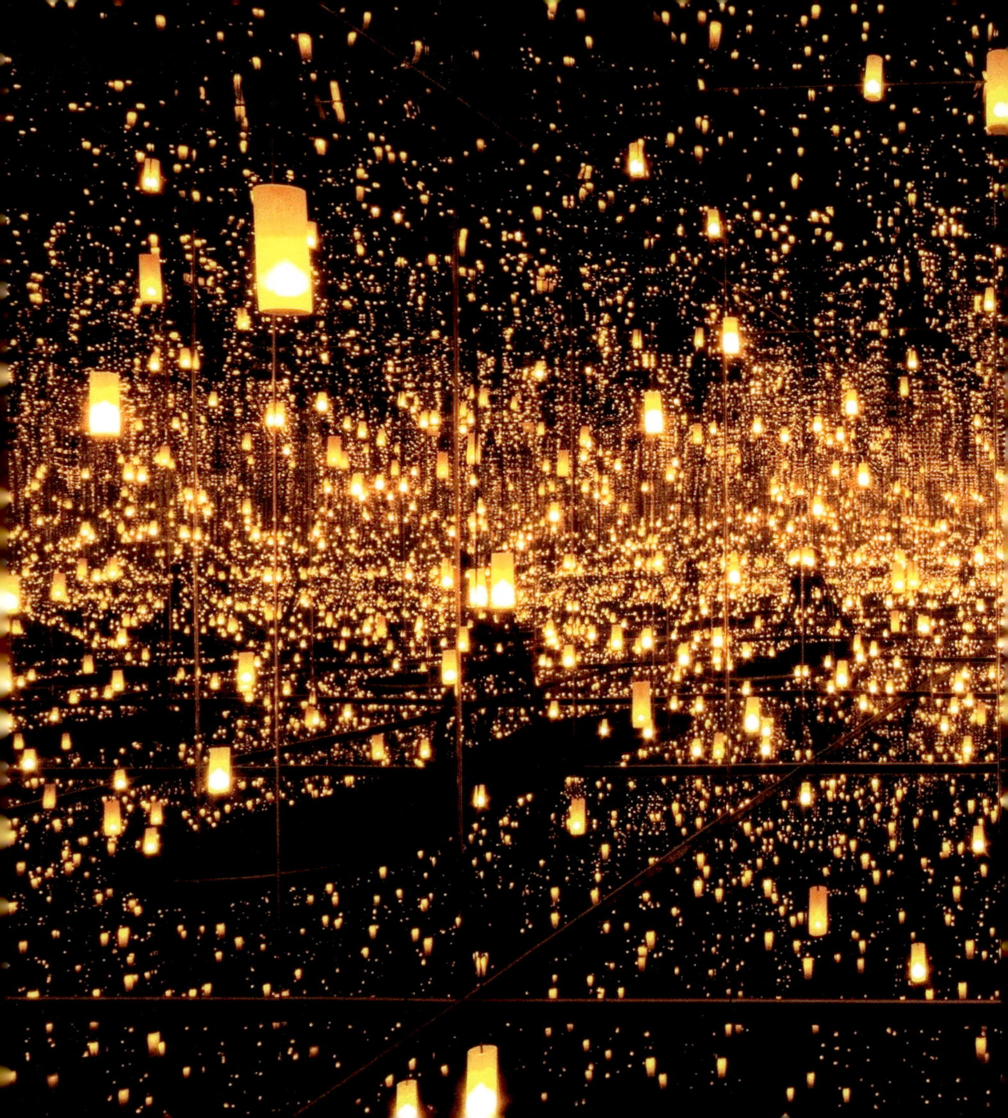

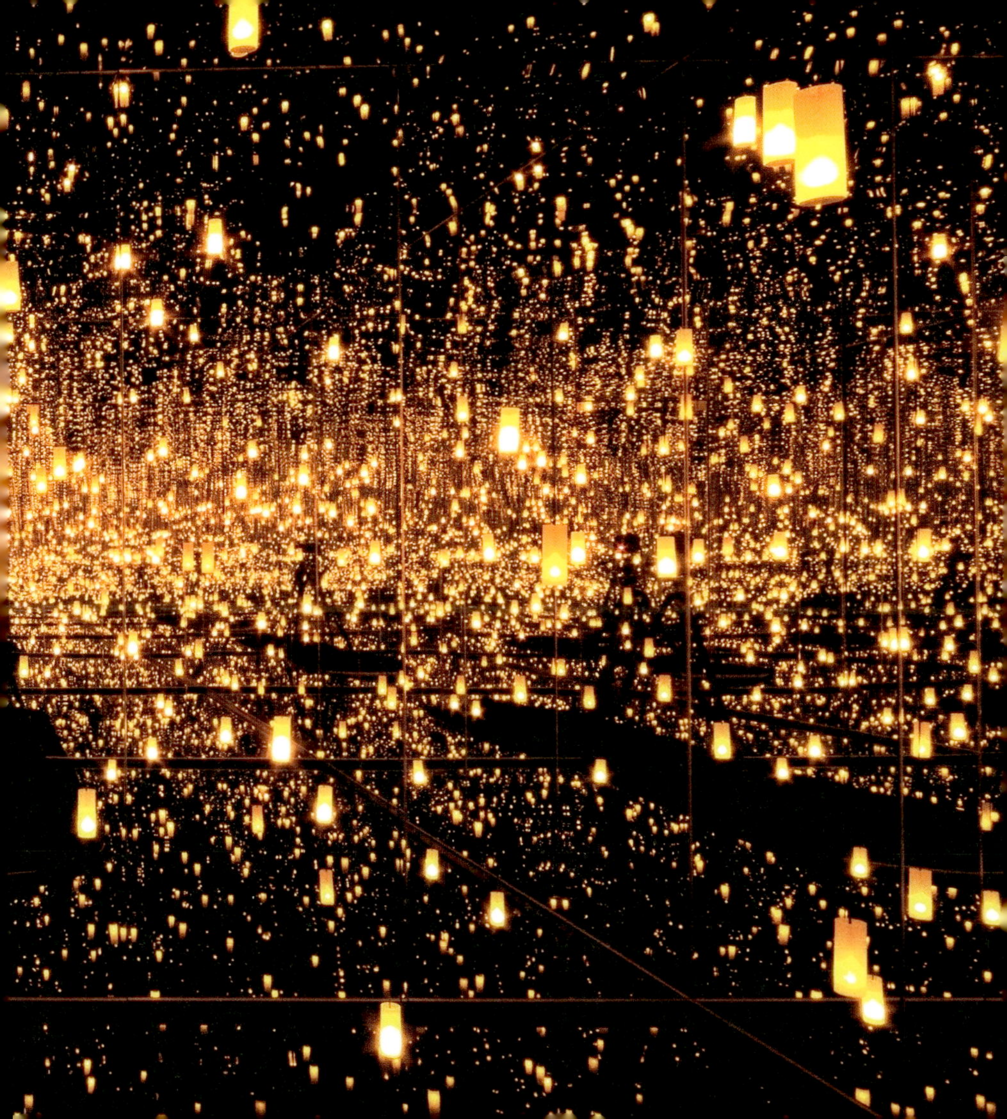

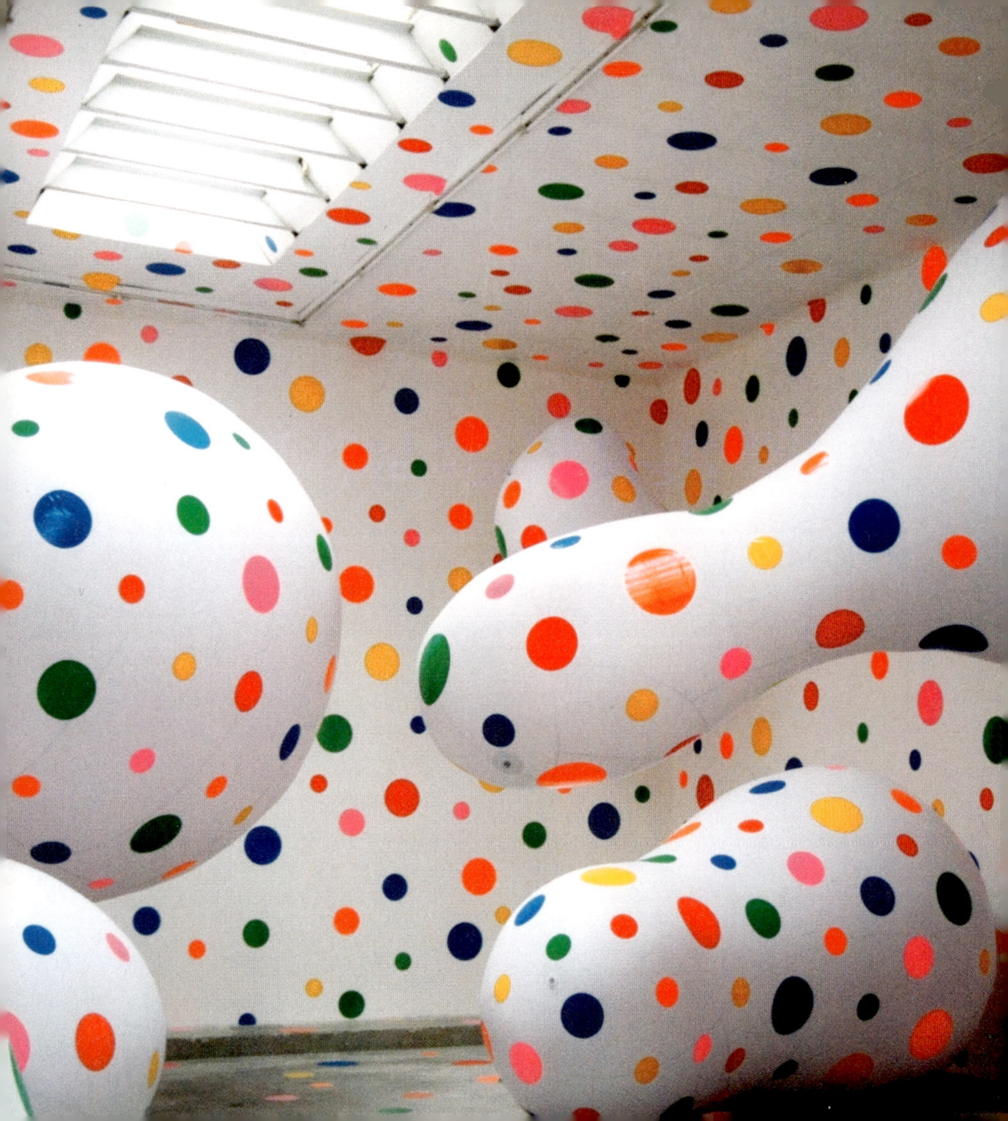

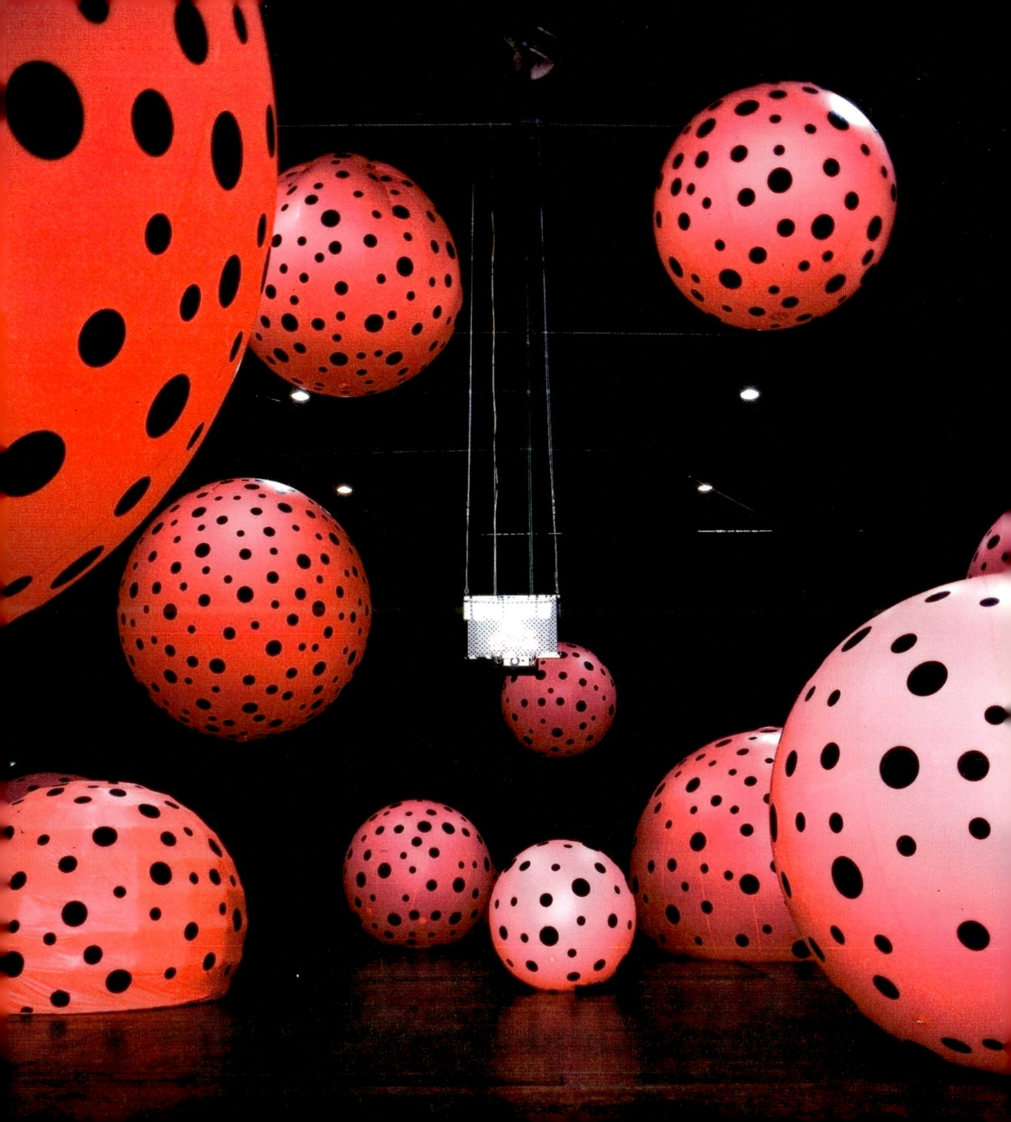

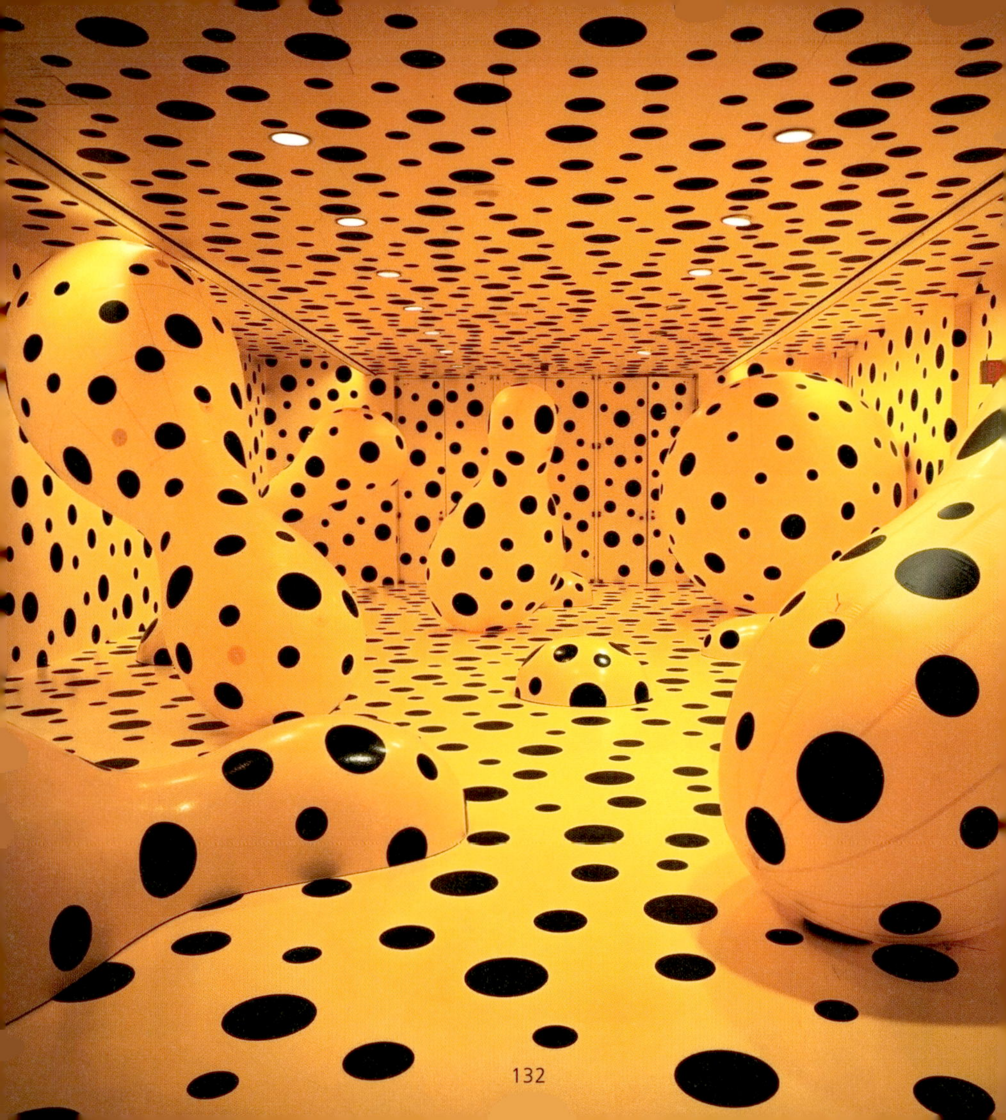

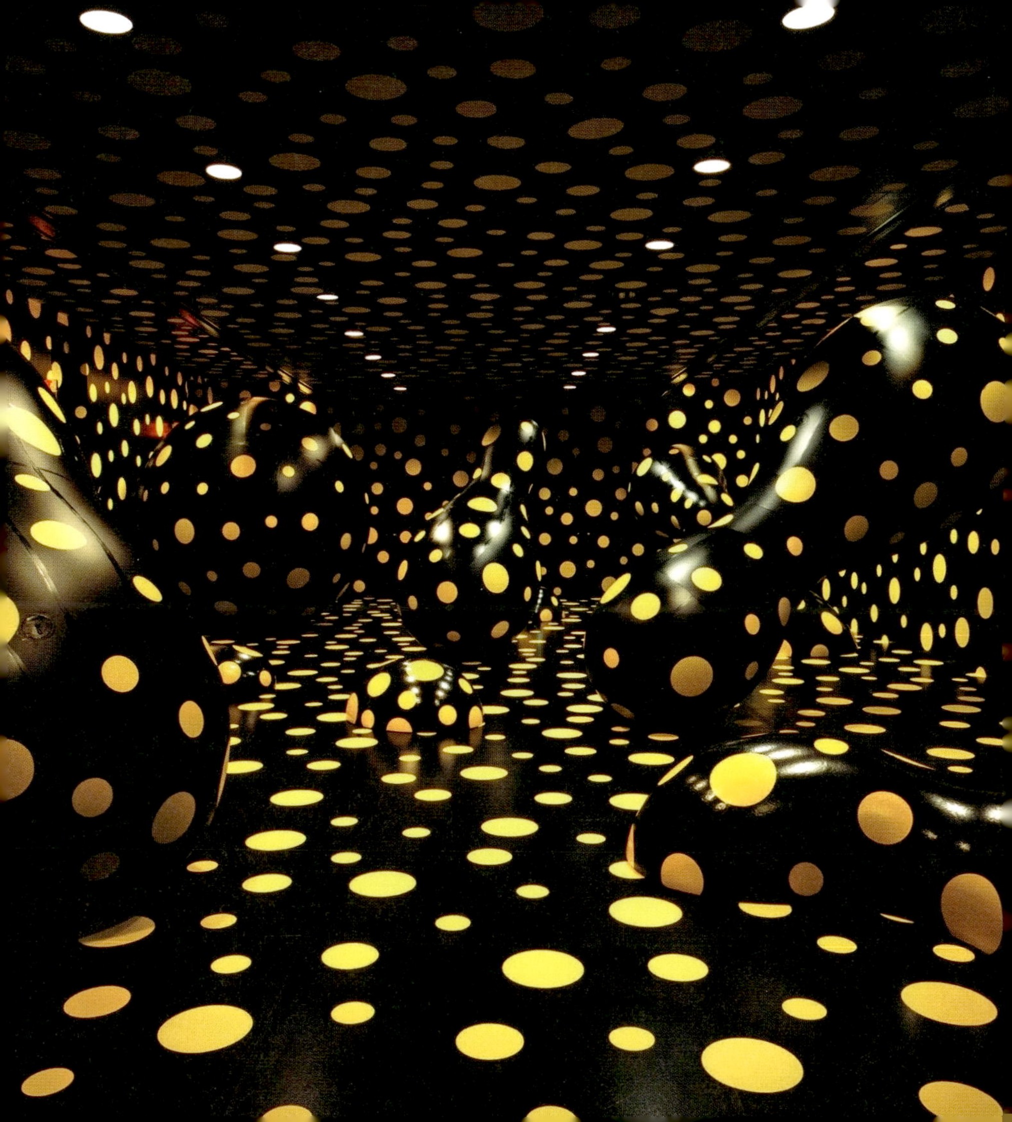

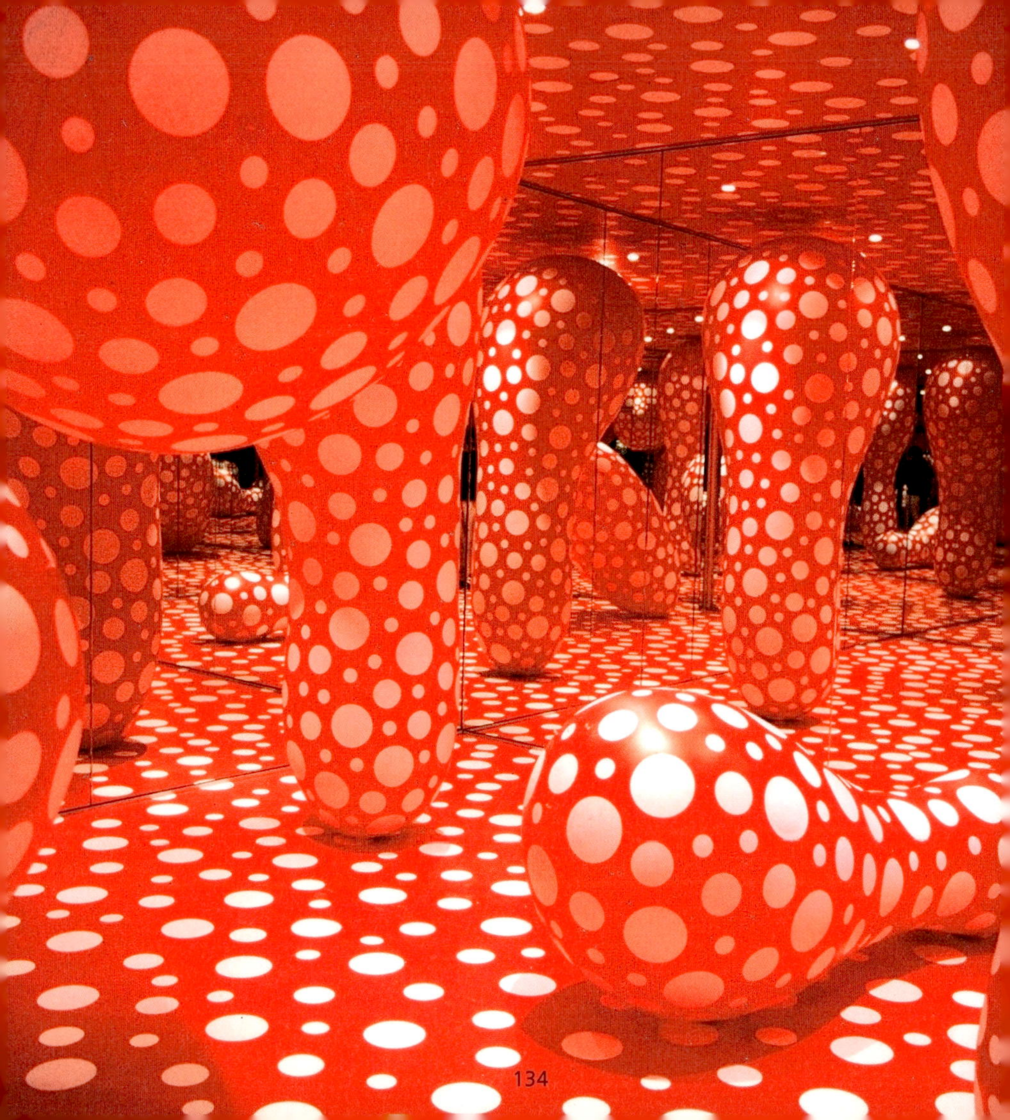

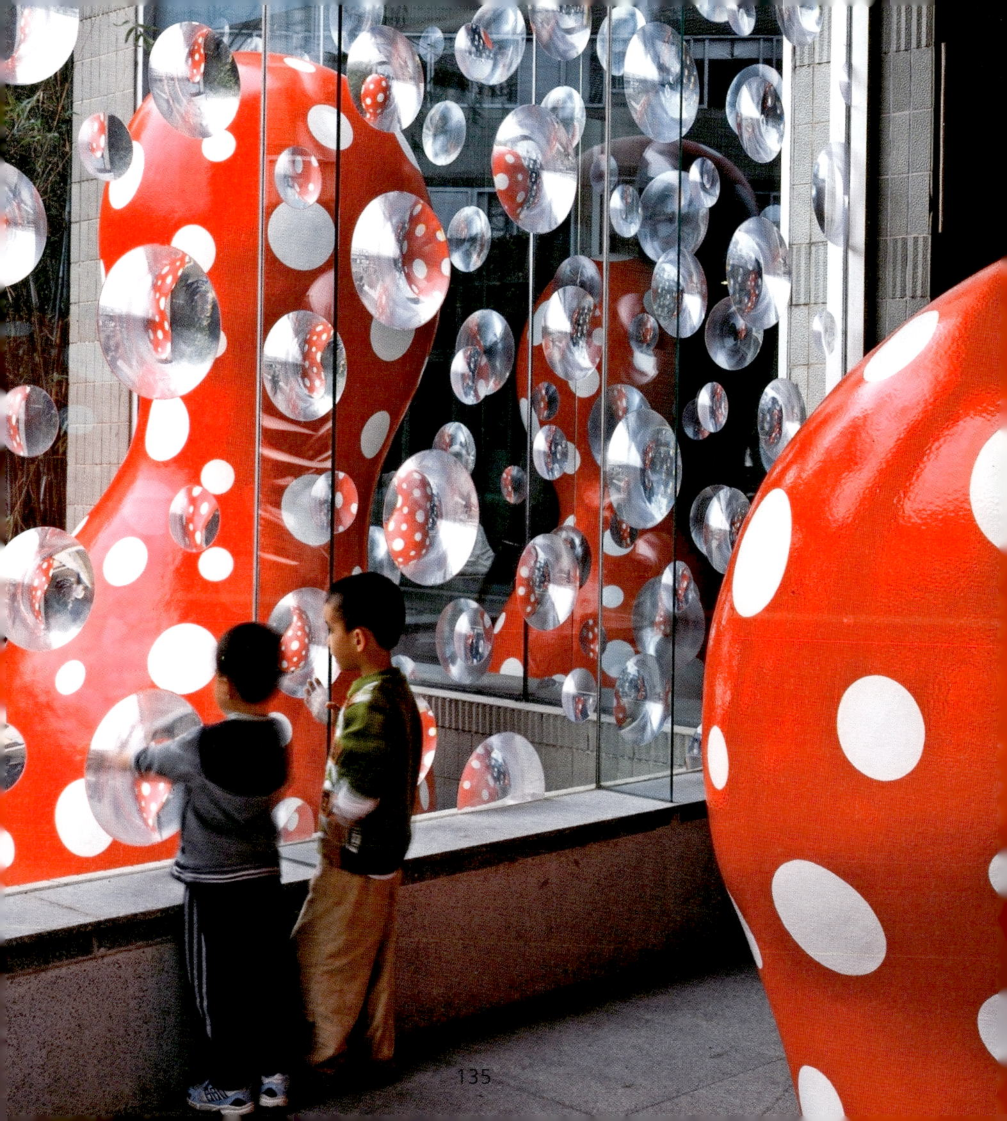

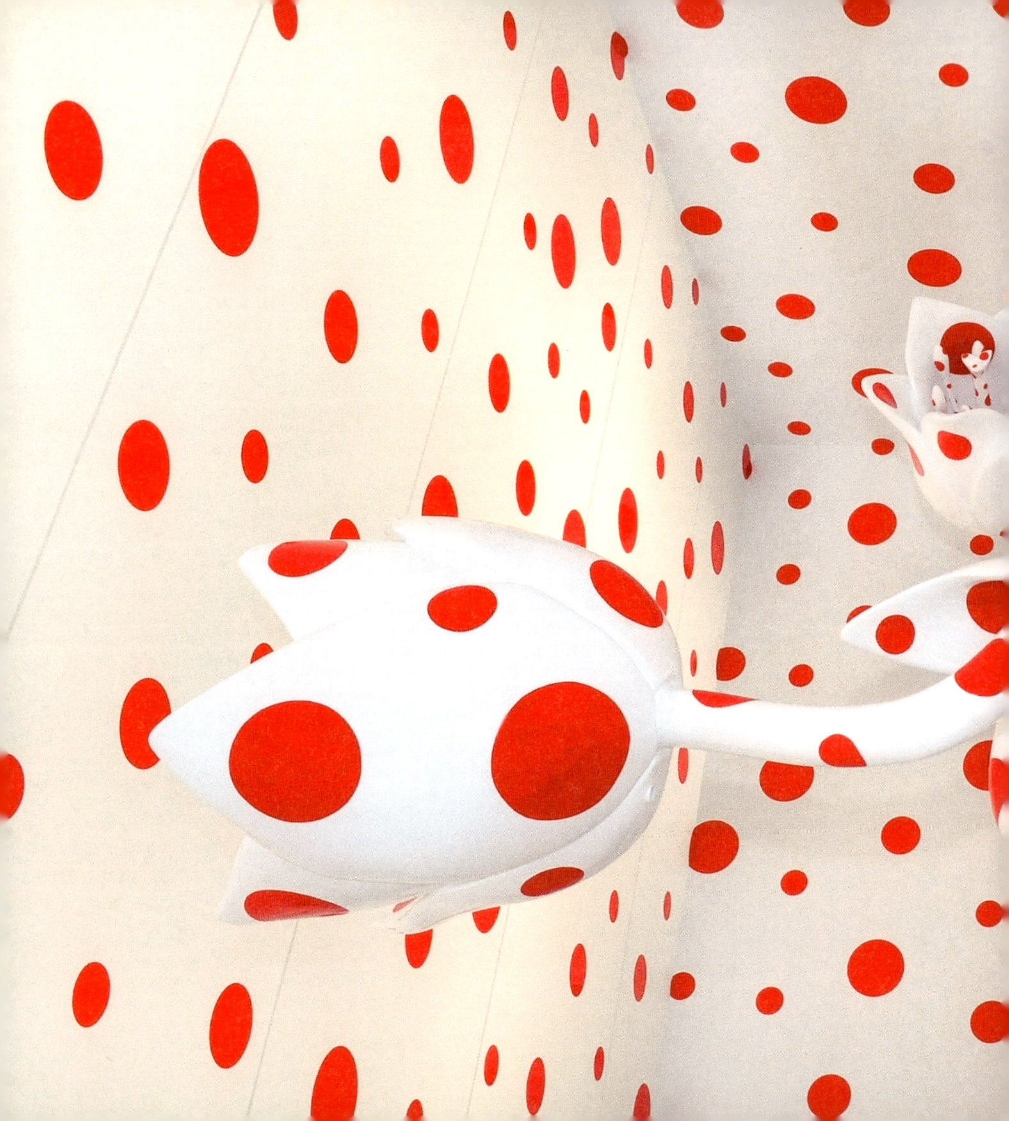

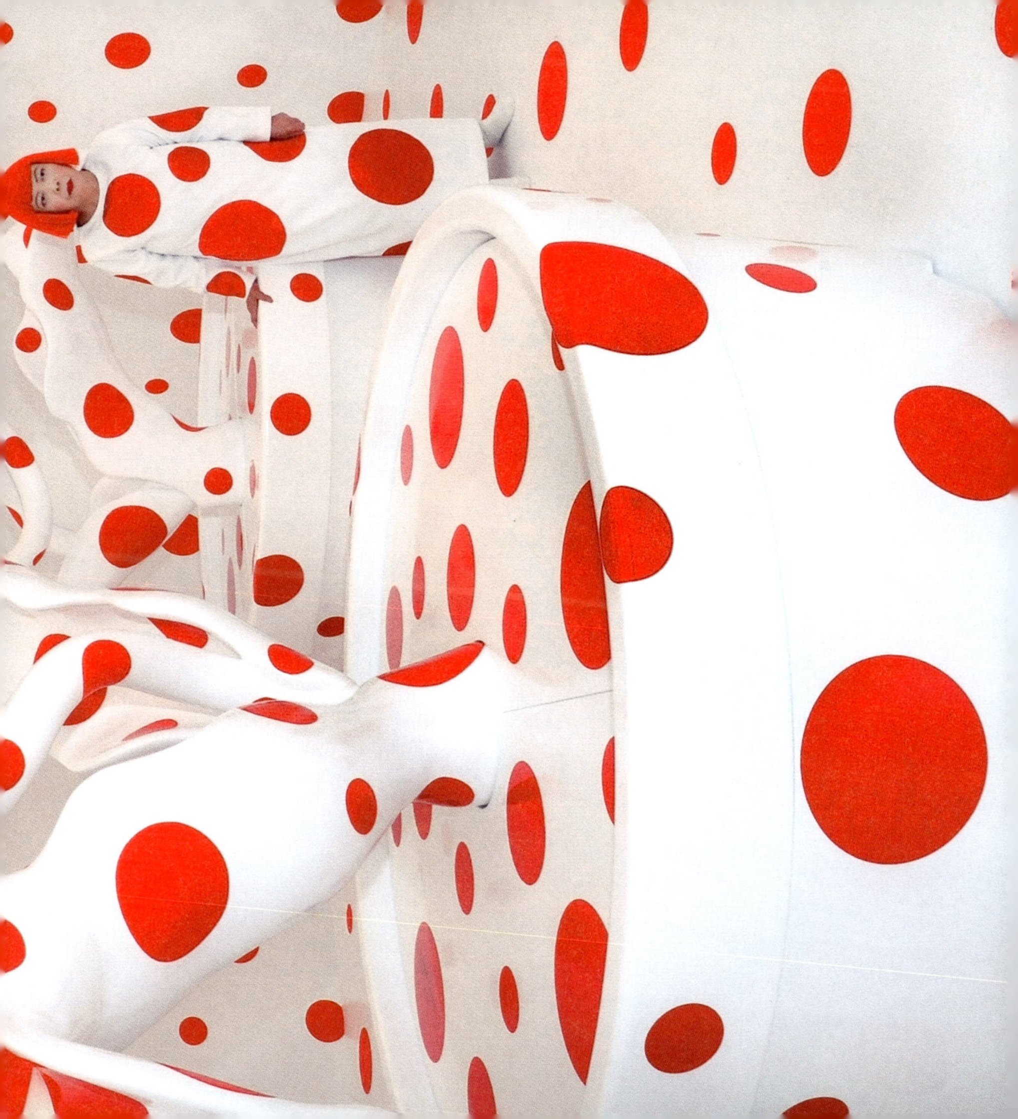

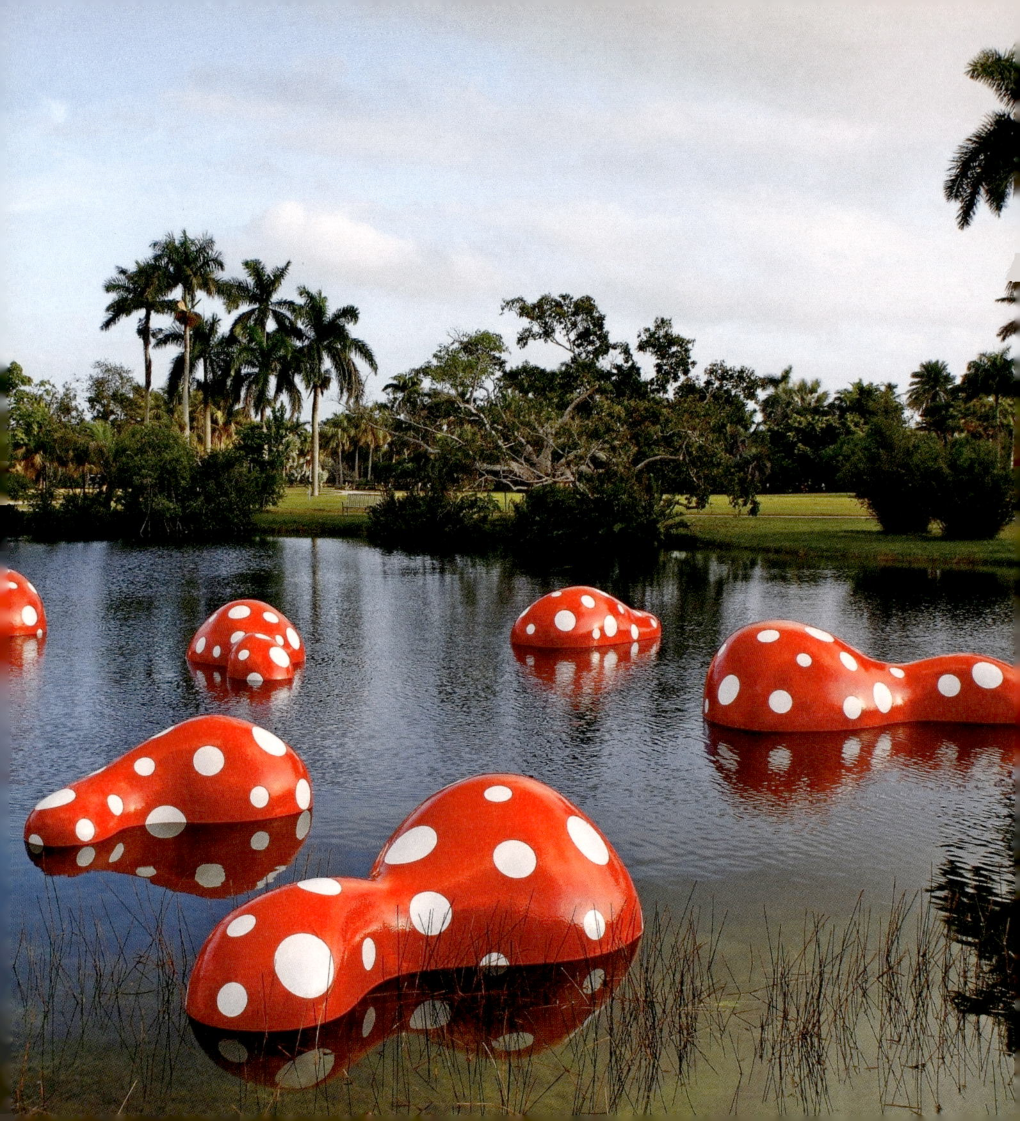

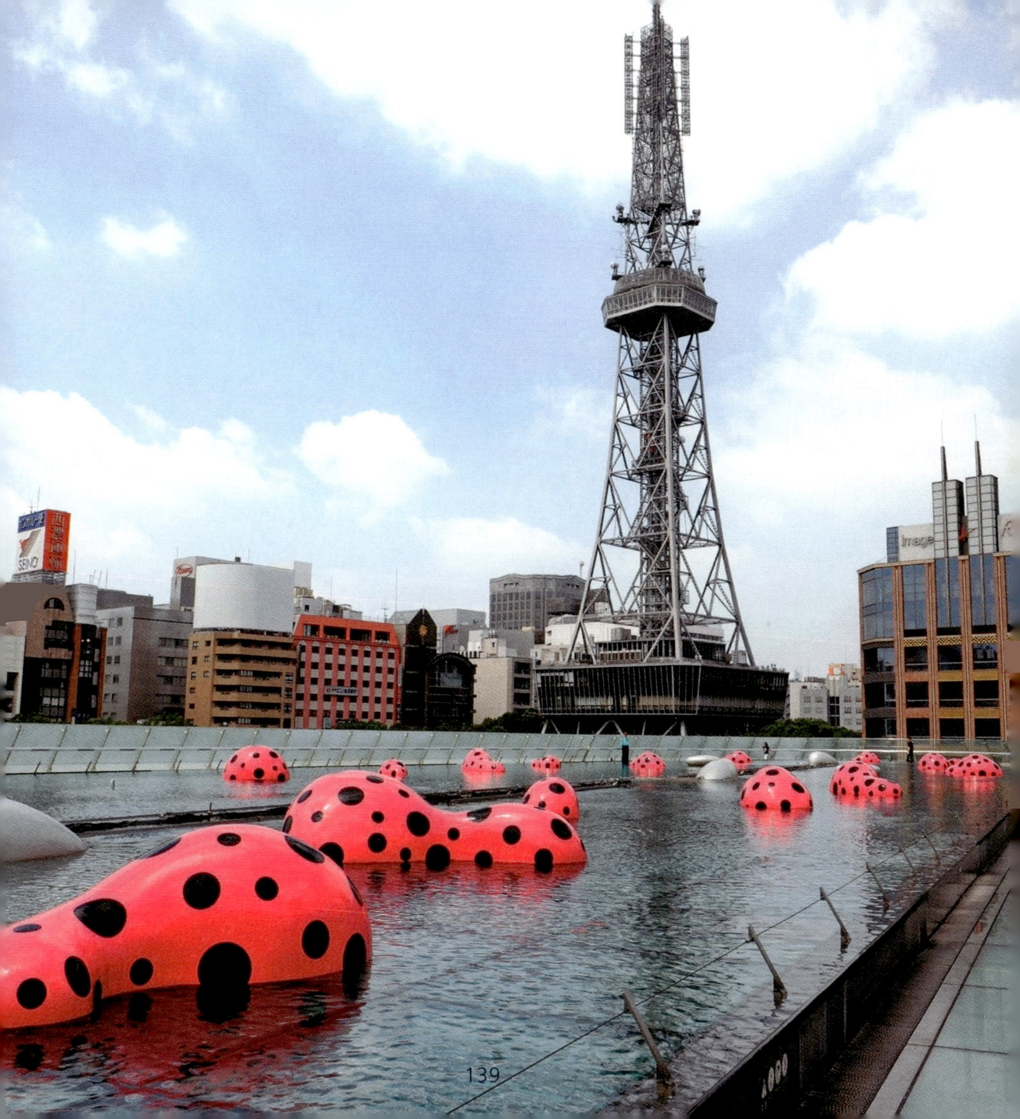
SEINO
Image

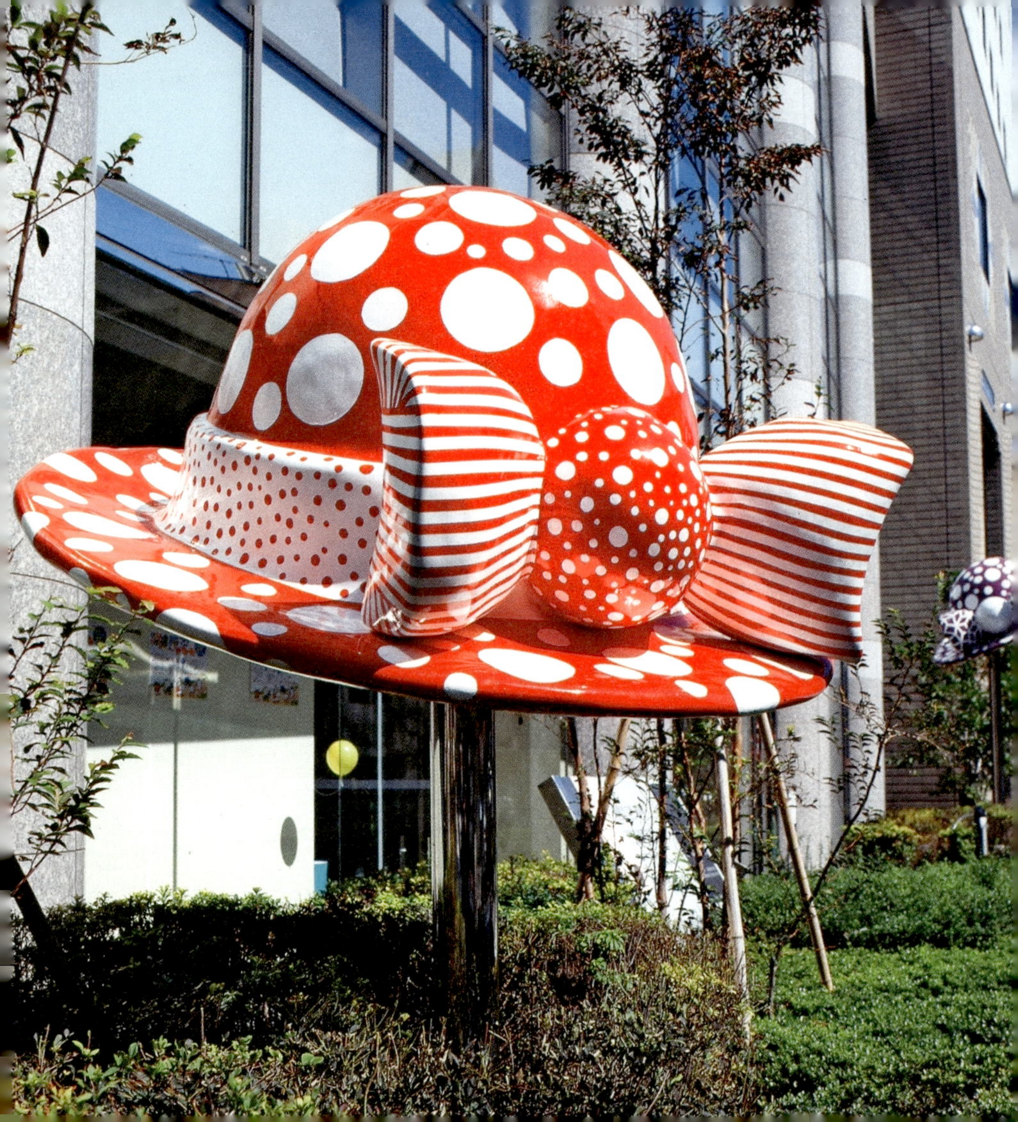

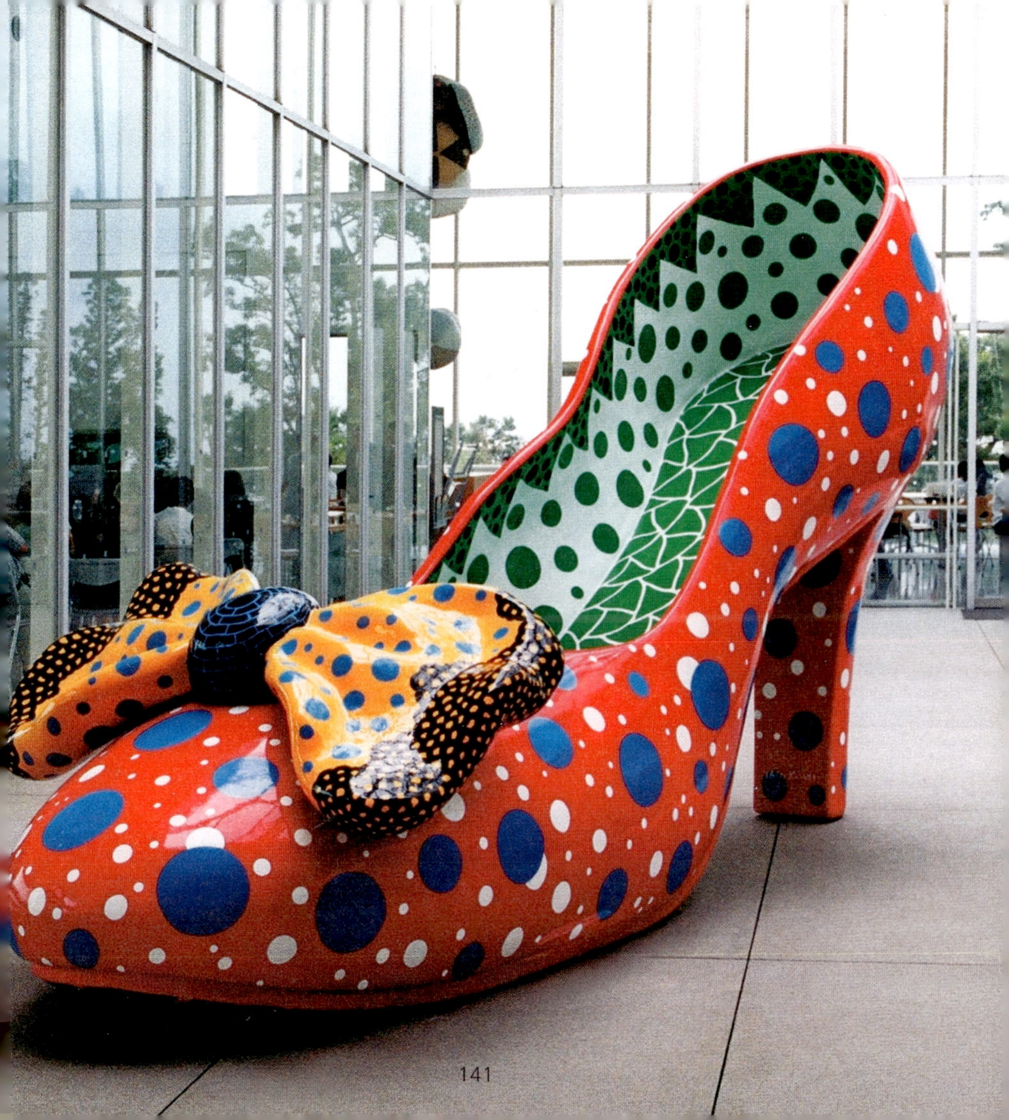

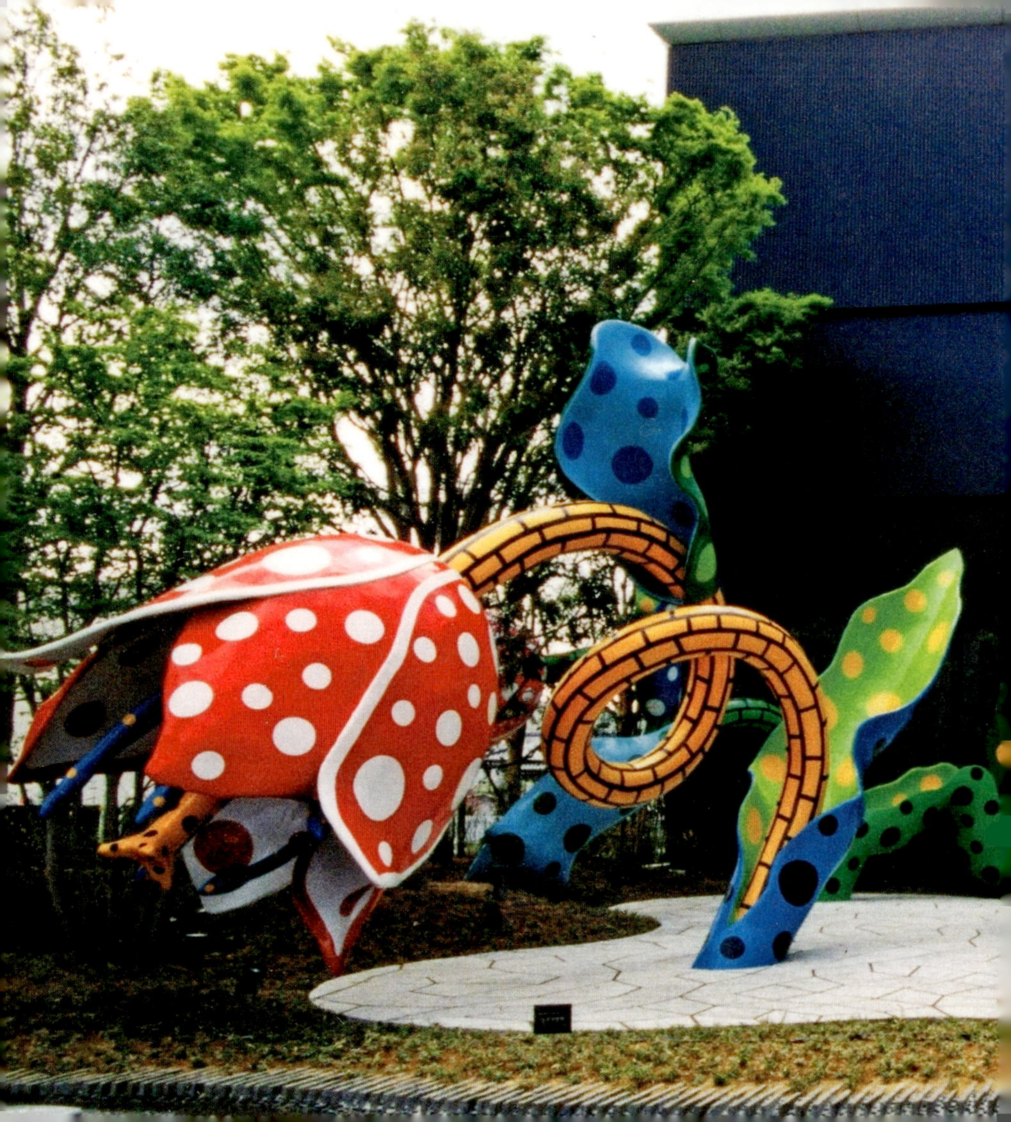

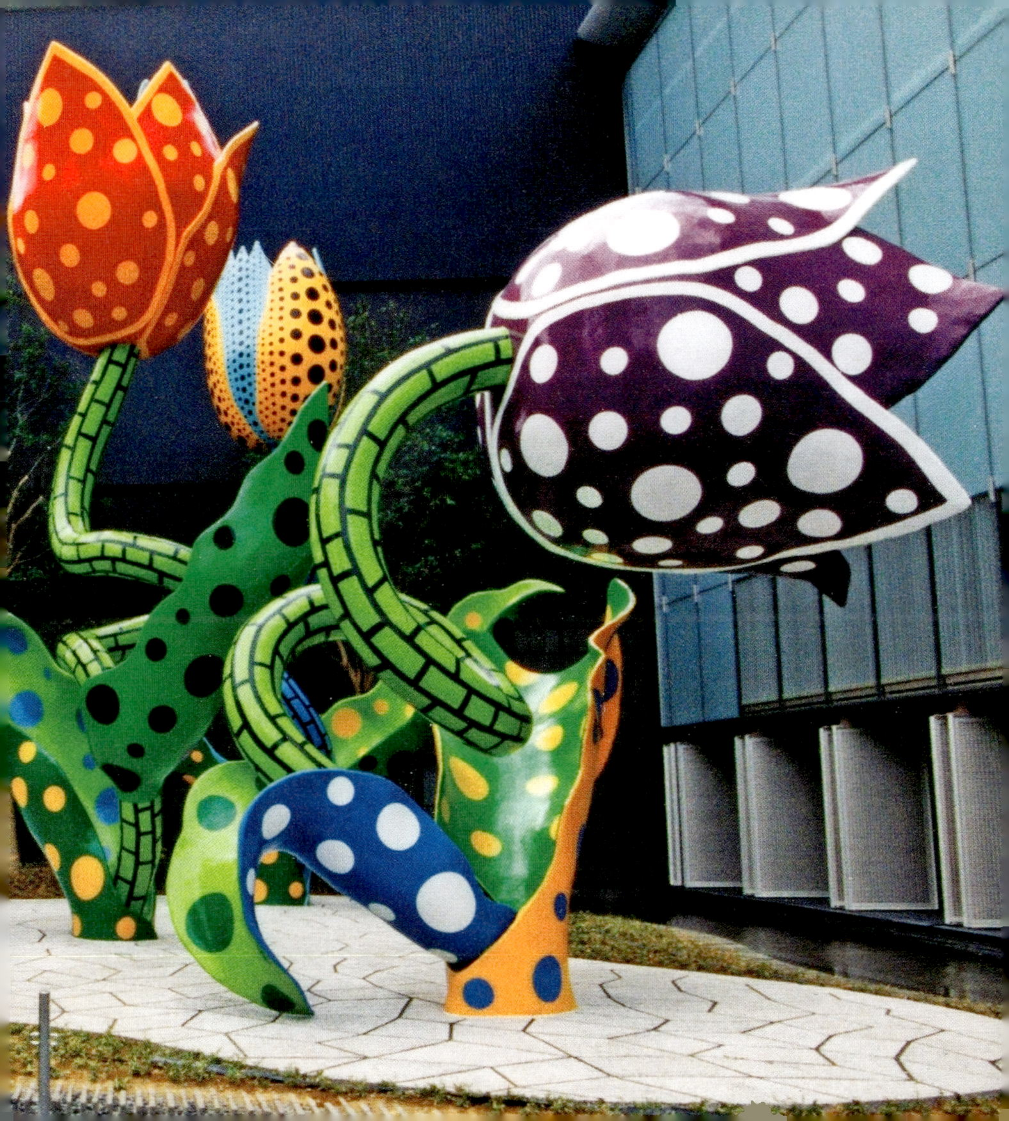

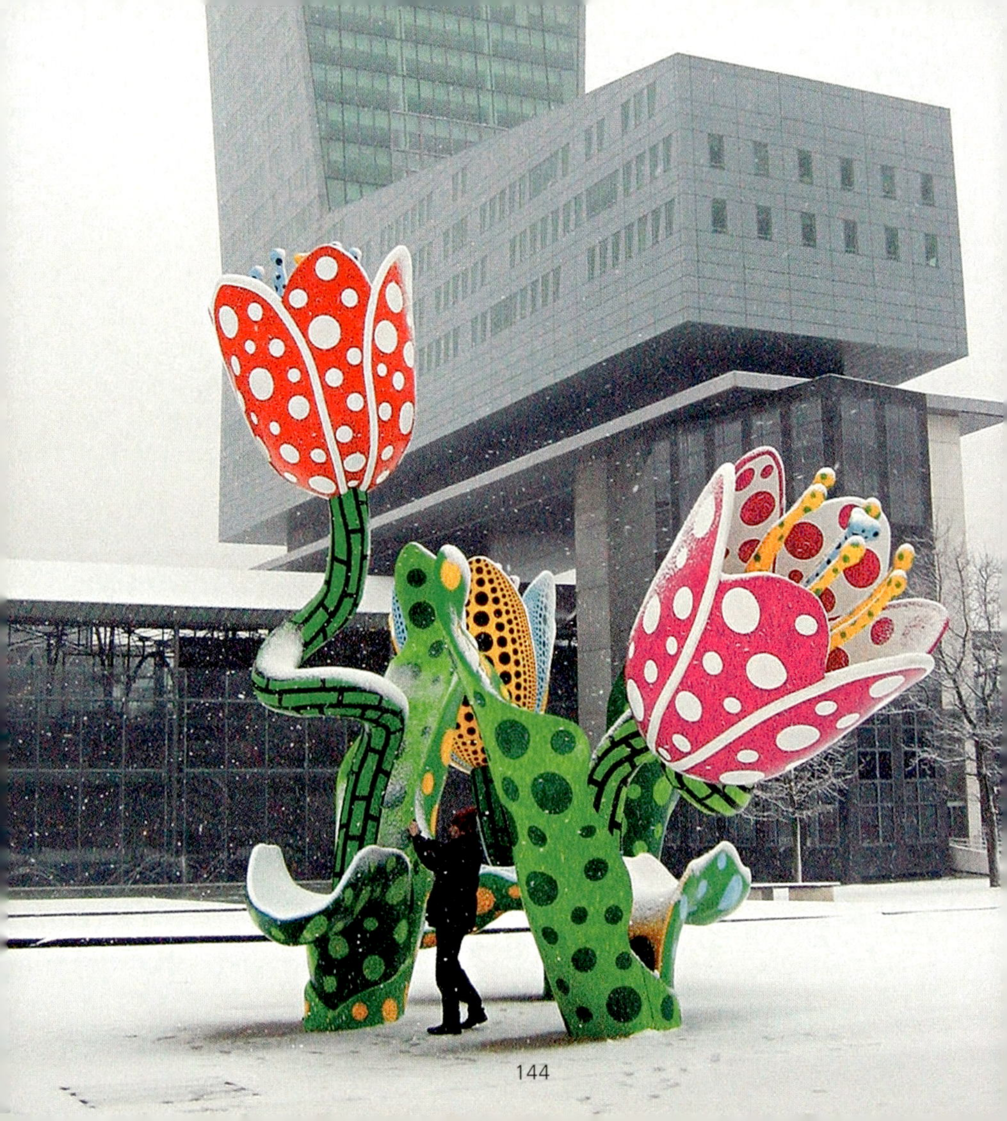

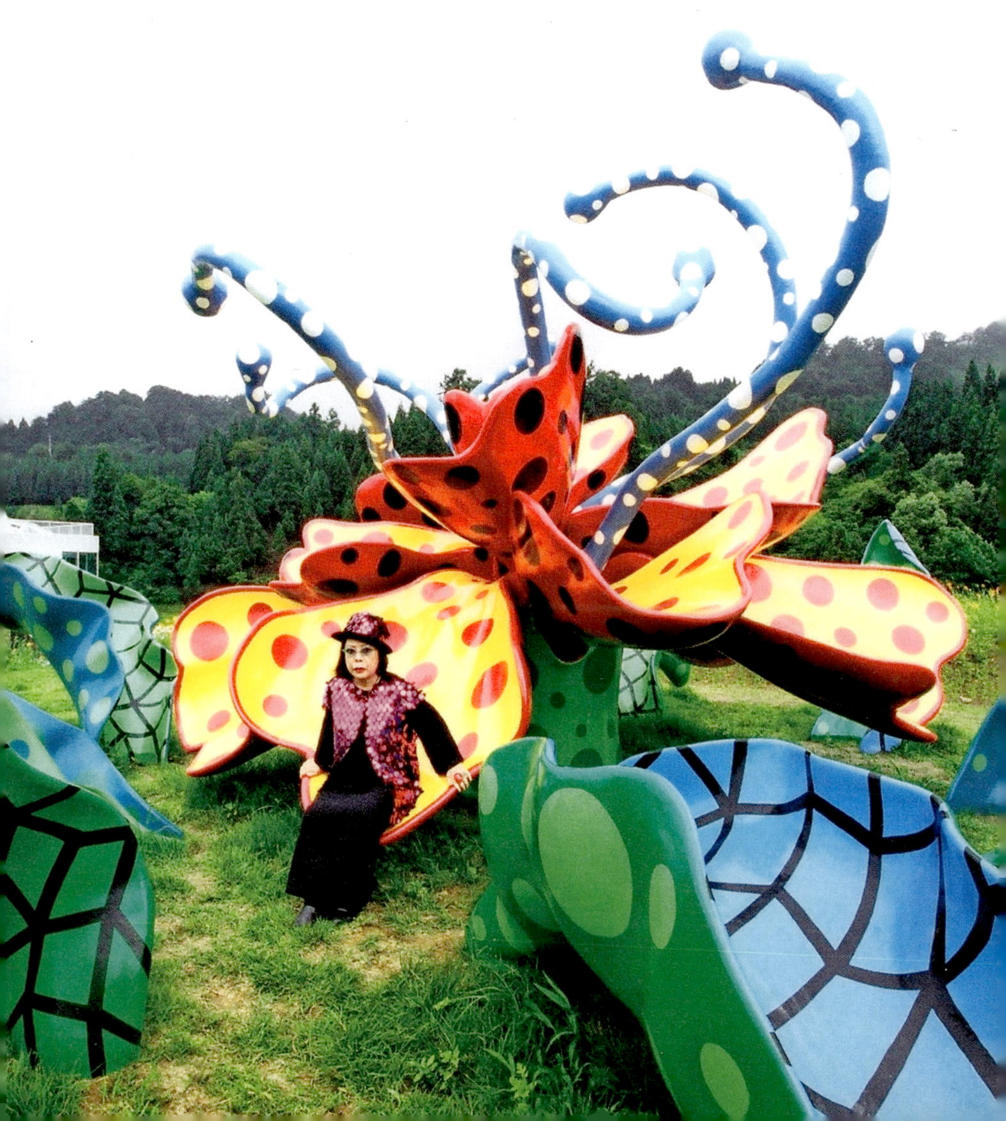

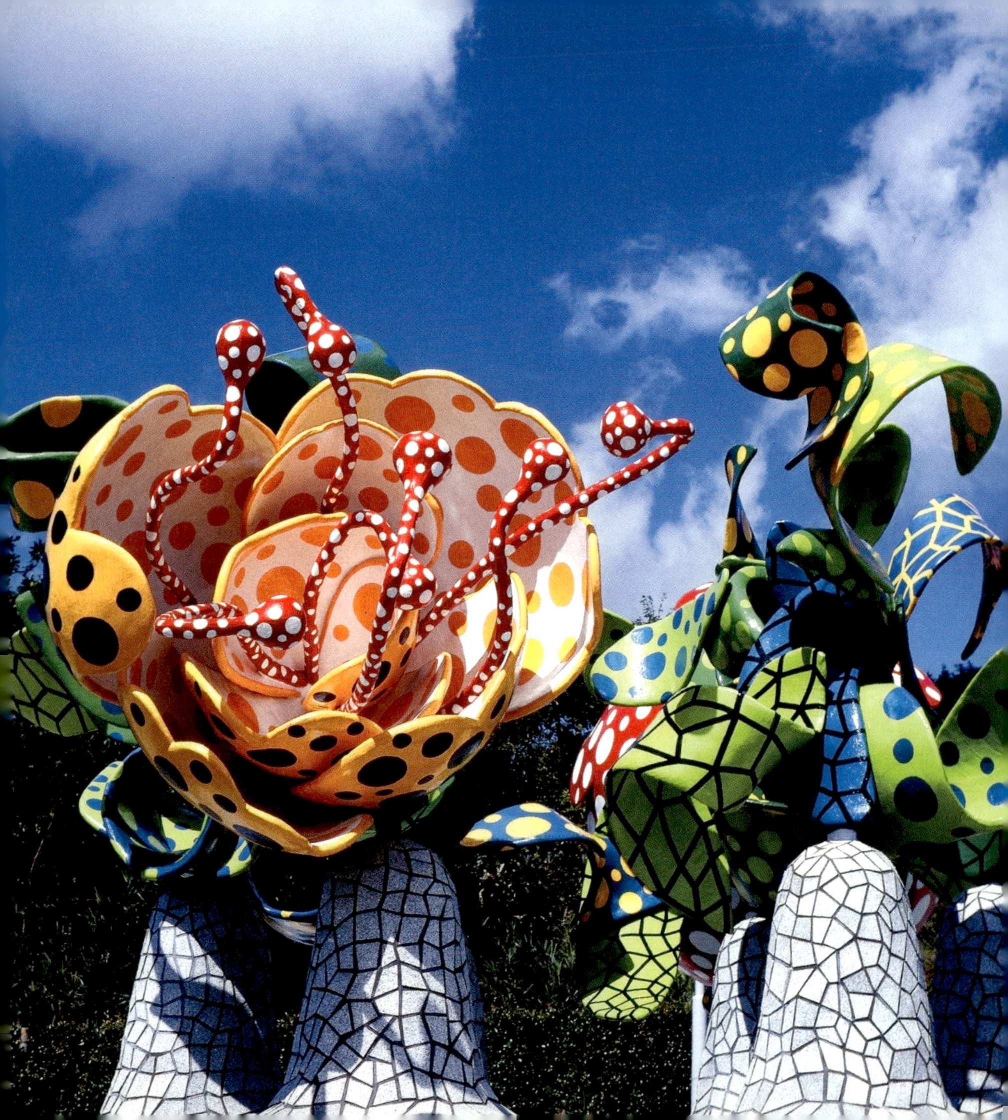

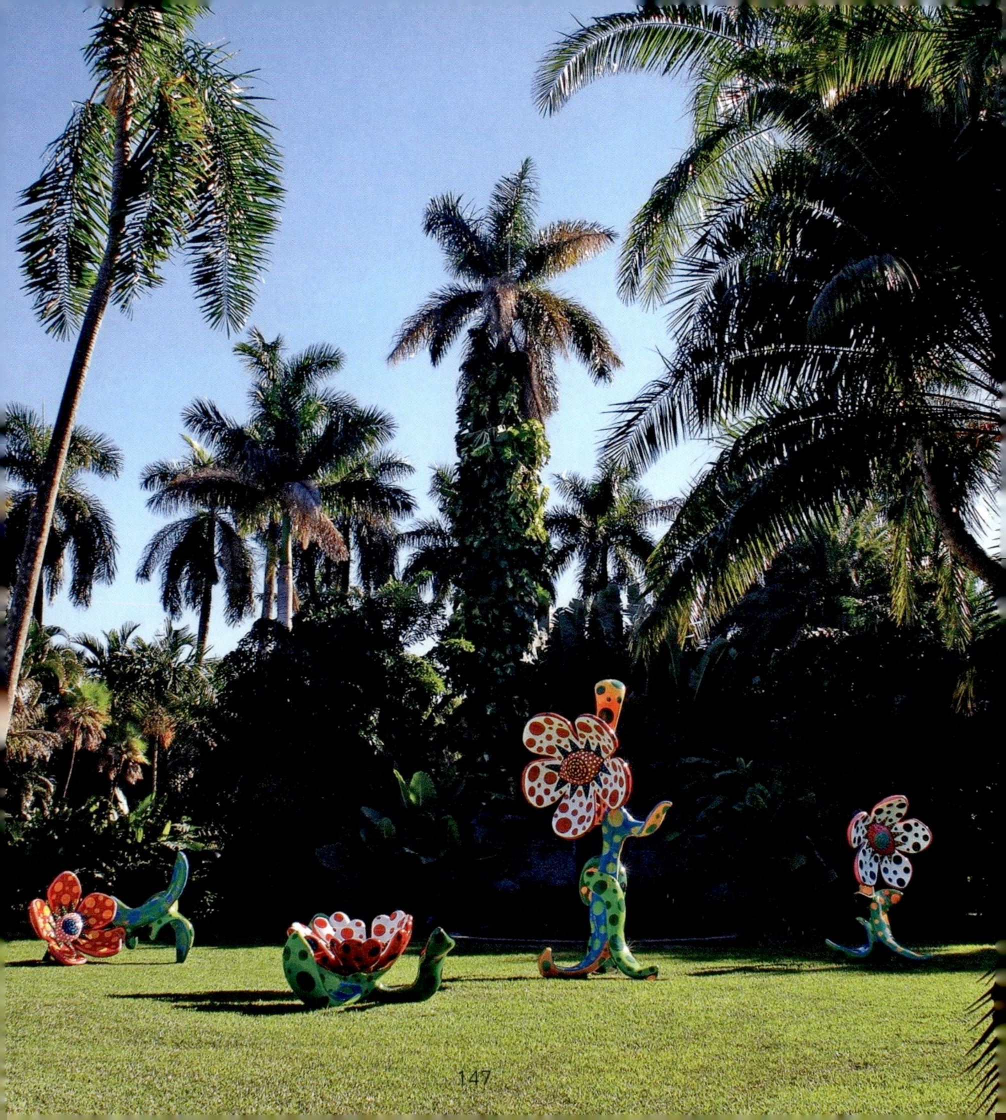

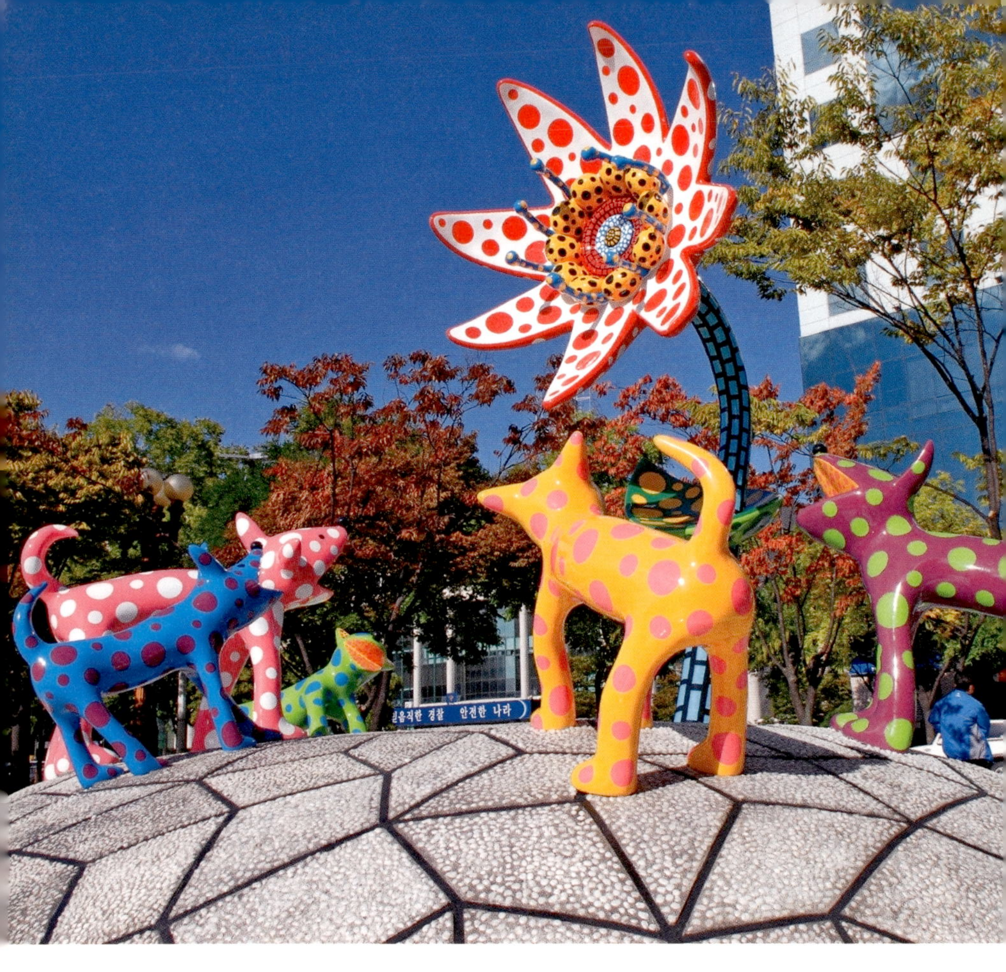

음직한 경찰 안전한 나라

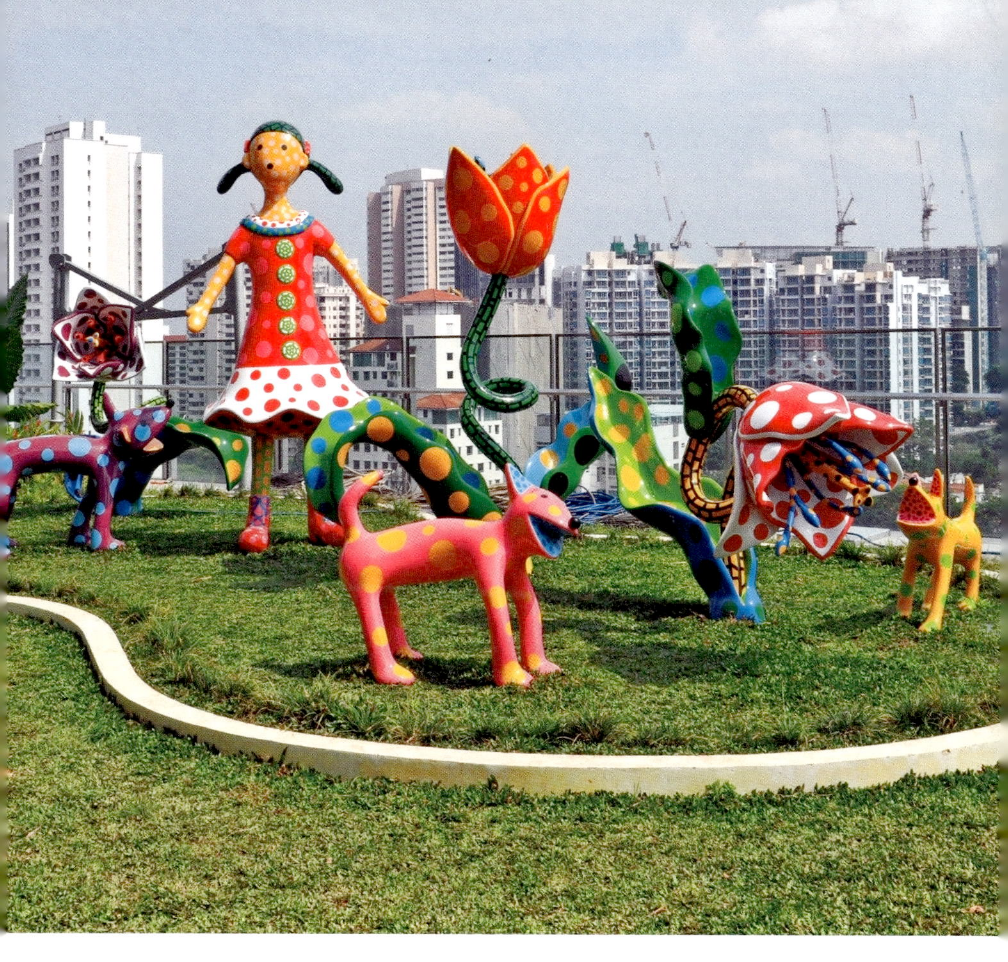

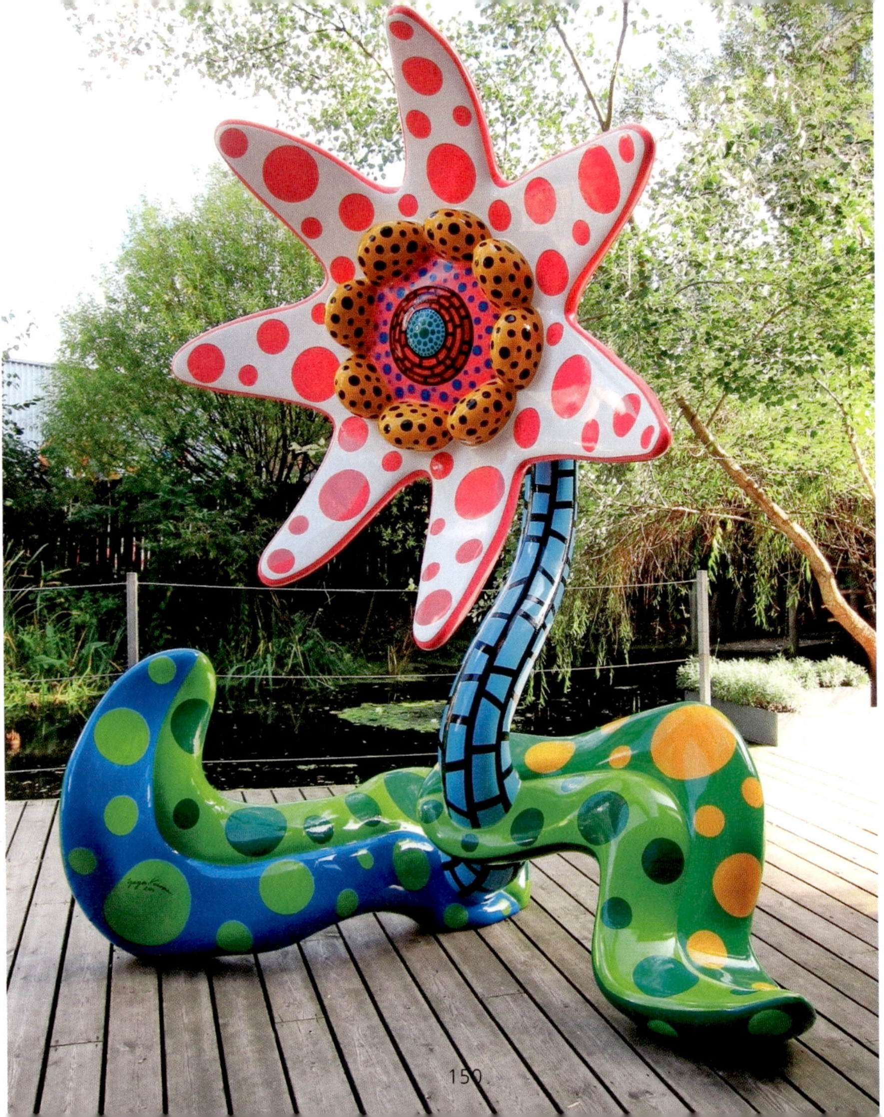

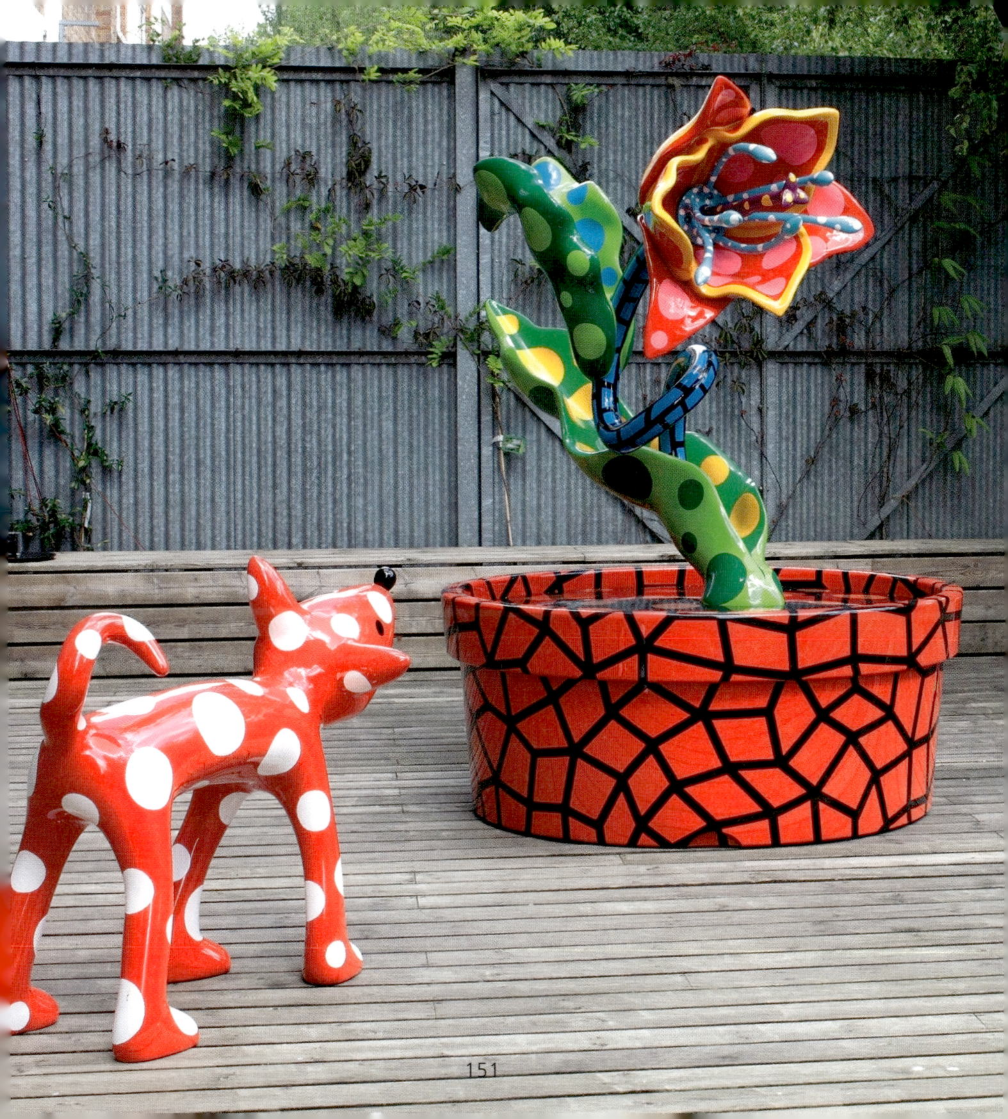

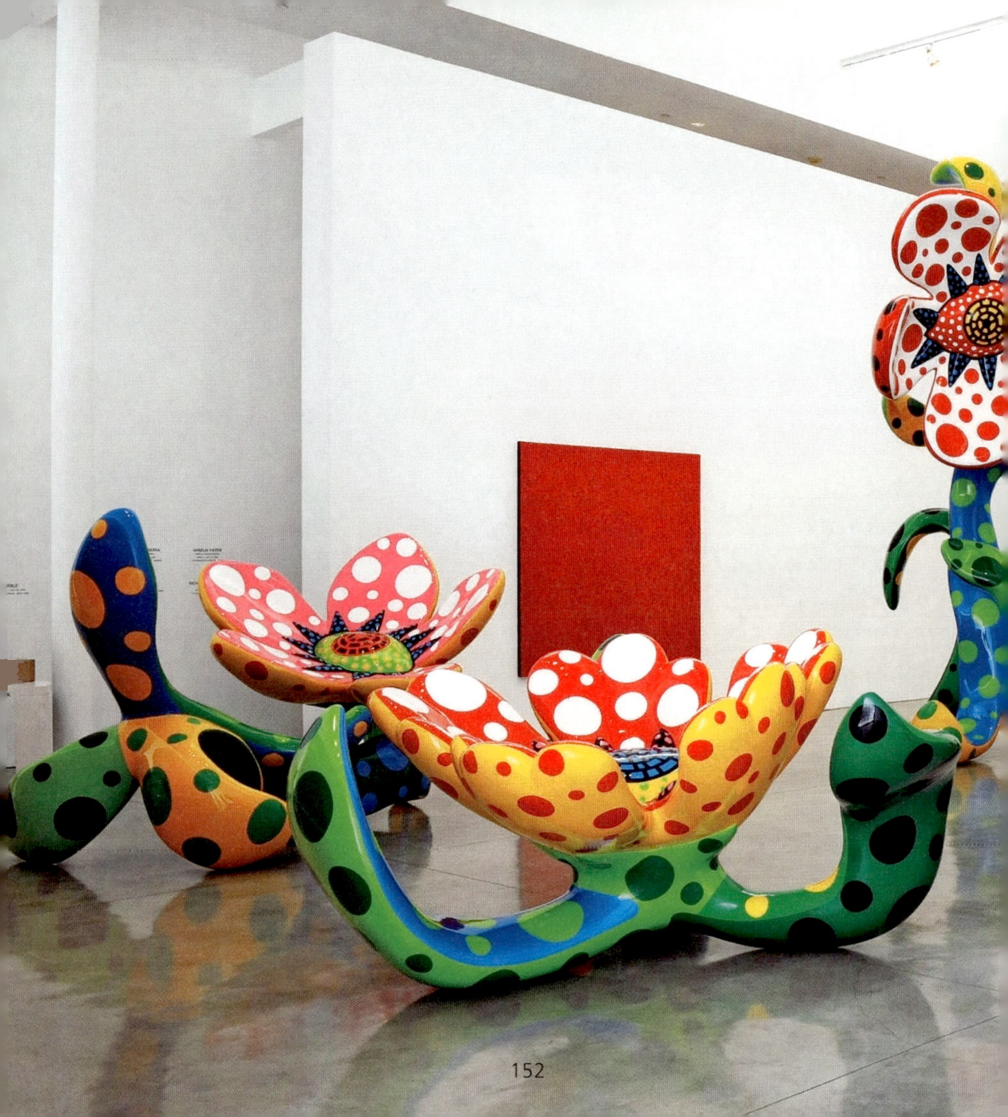

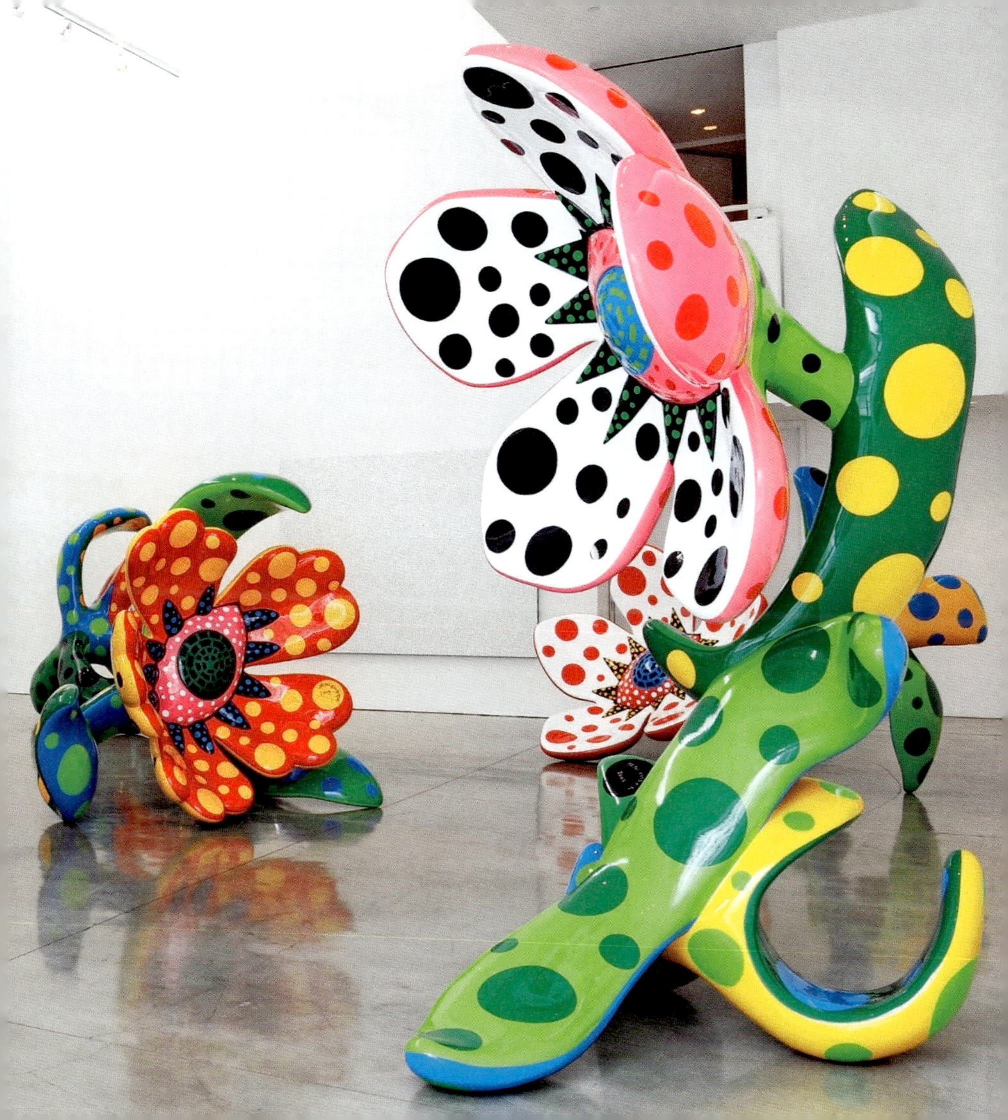

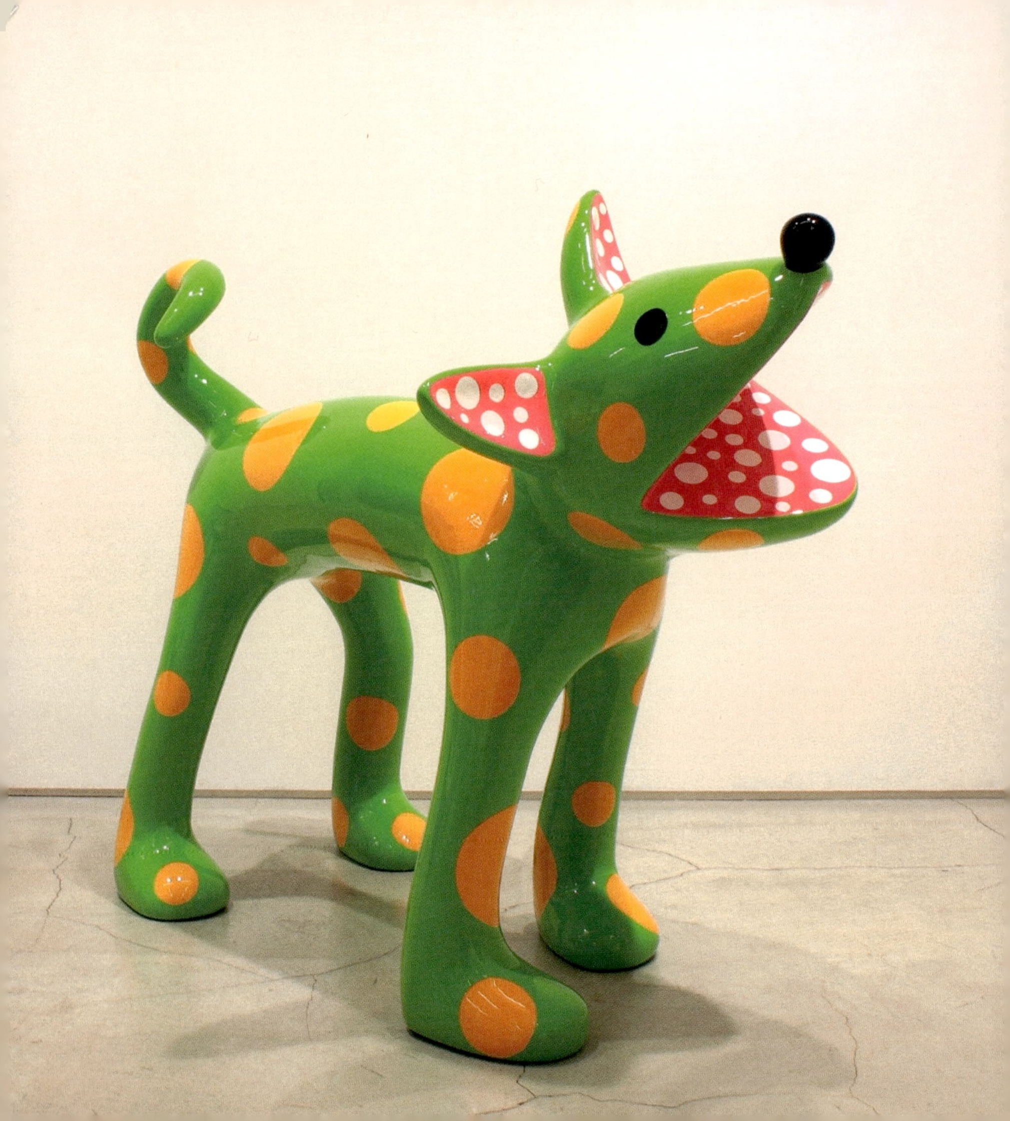

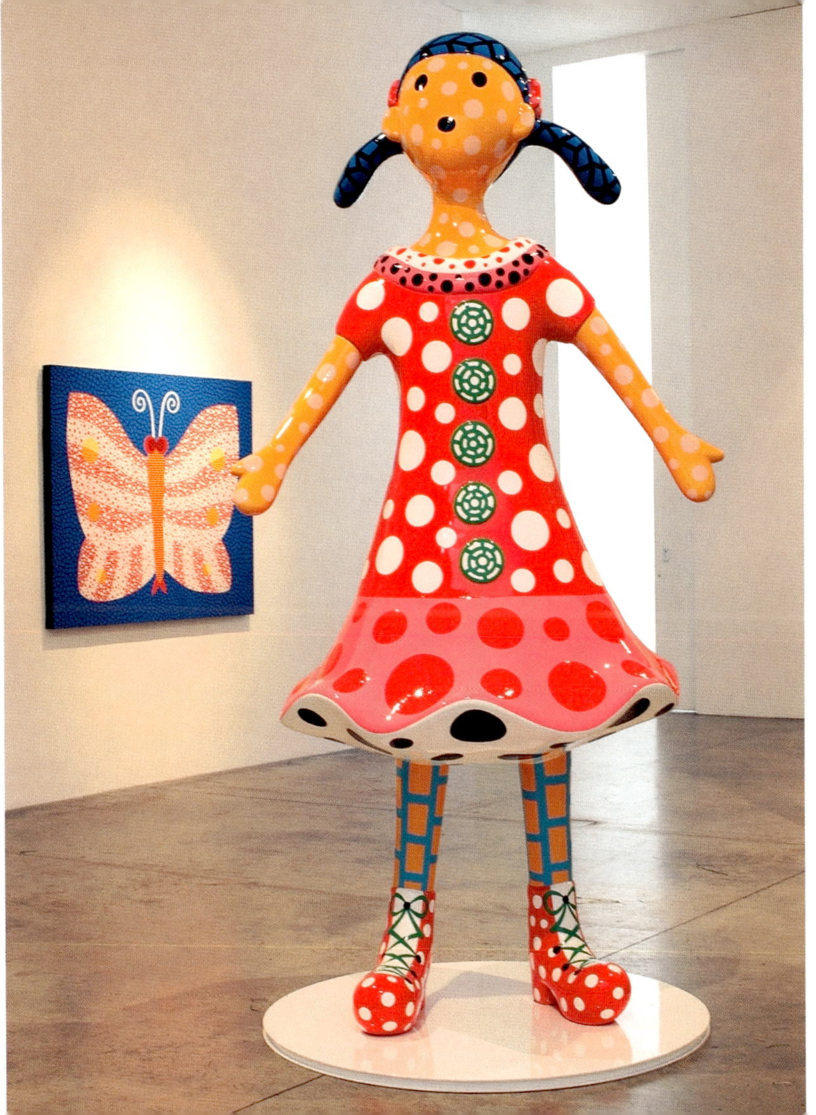

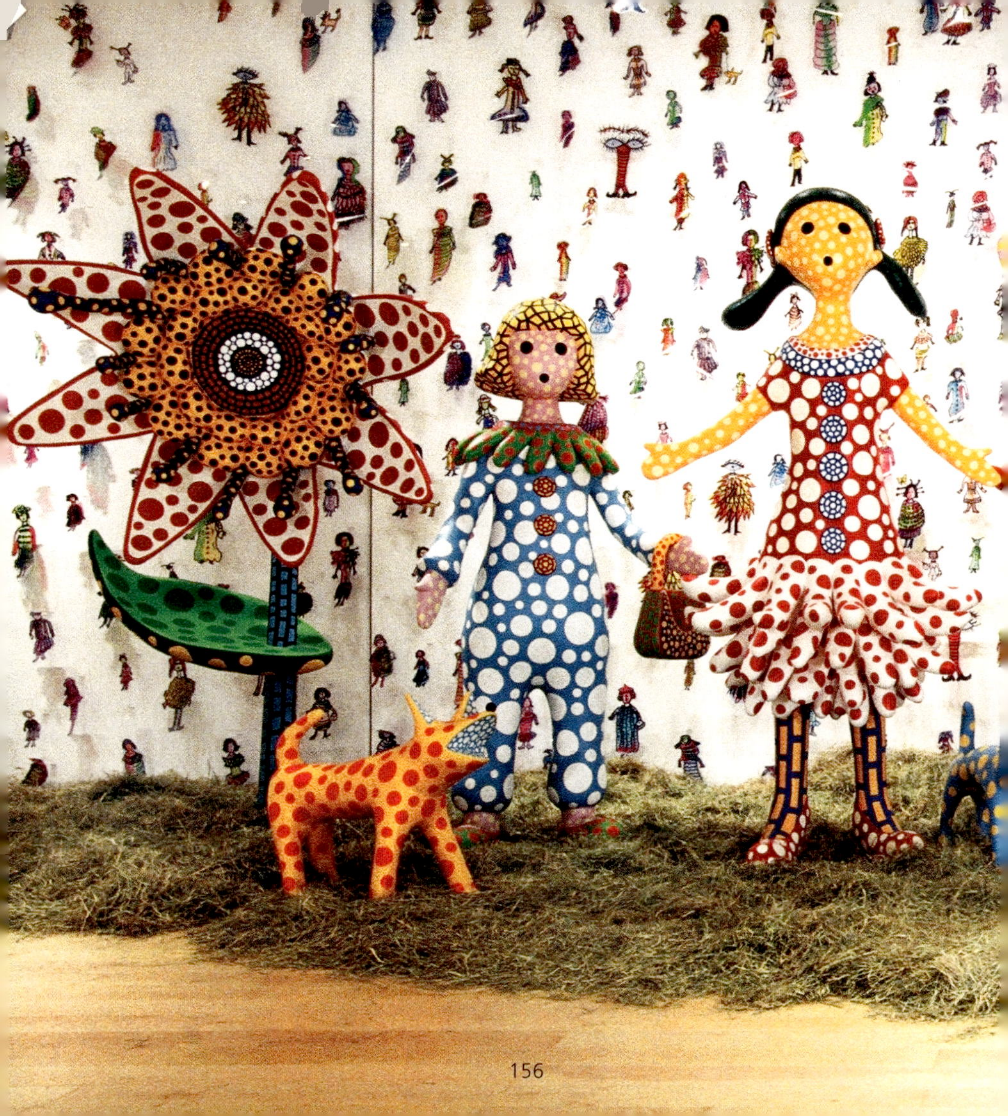

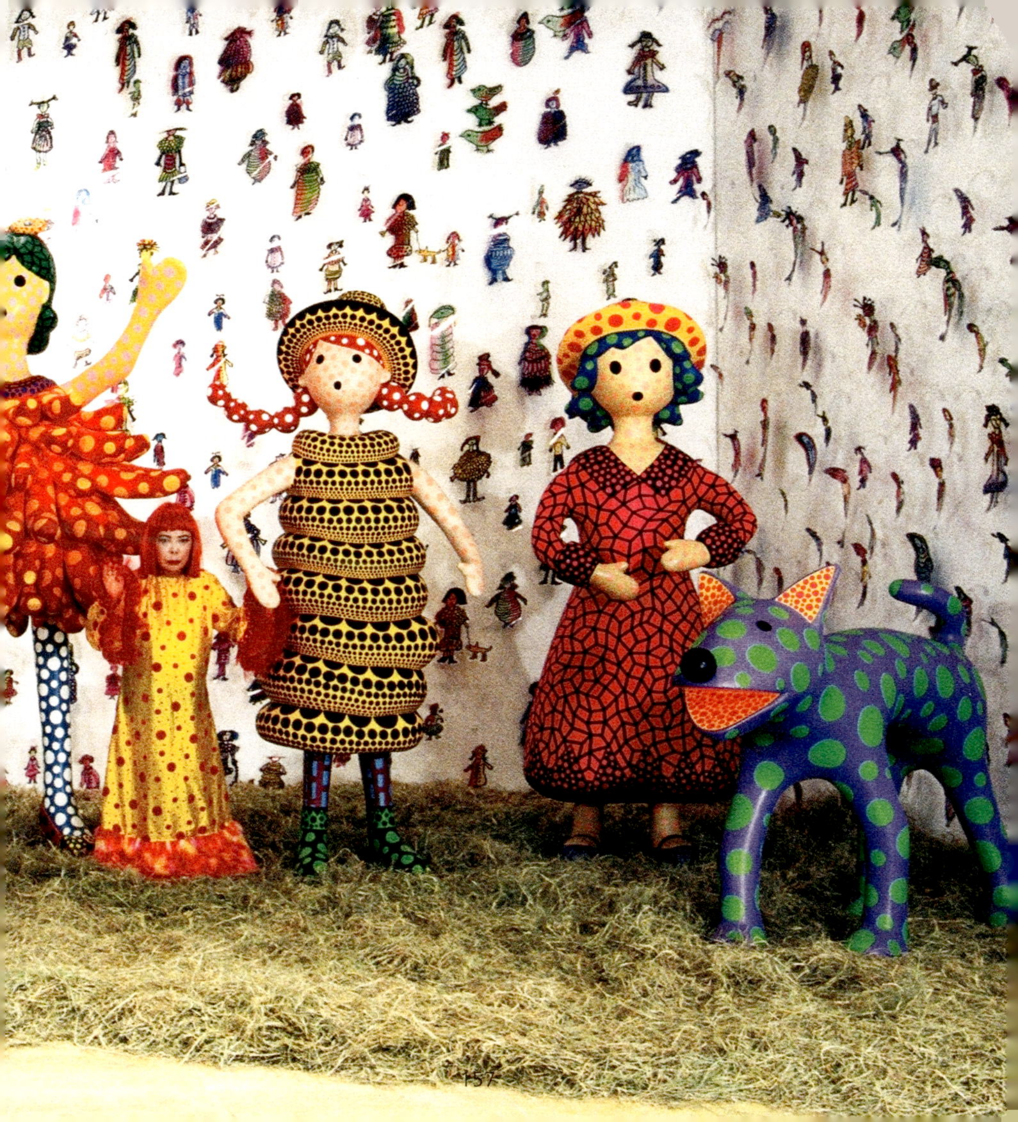

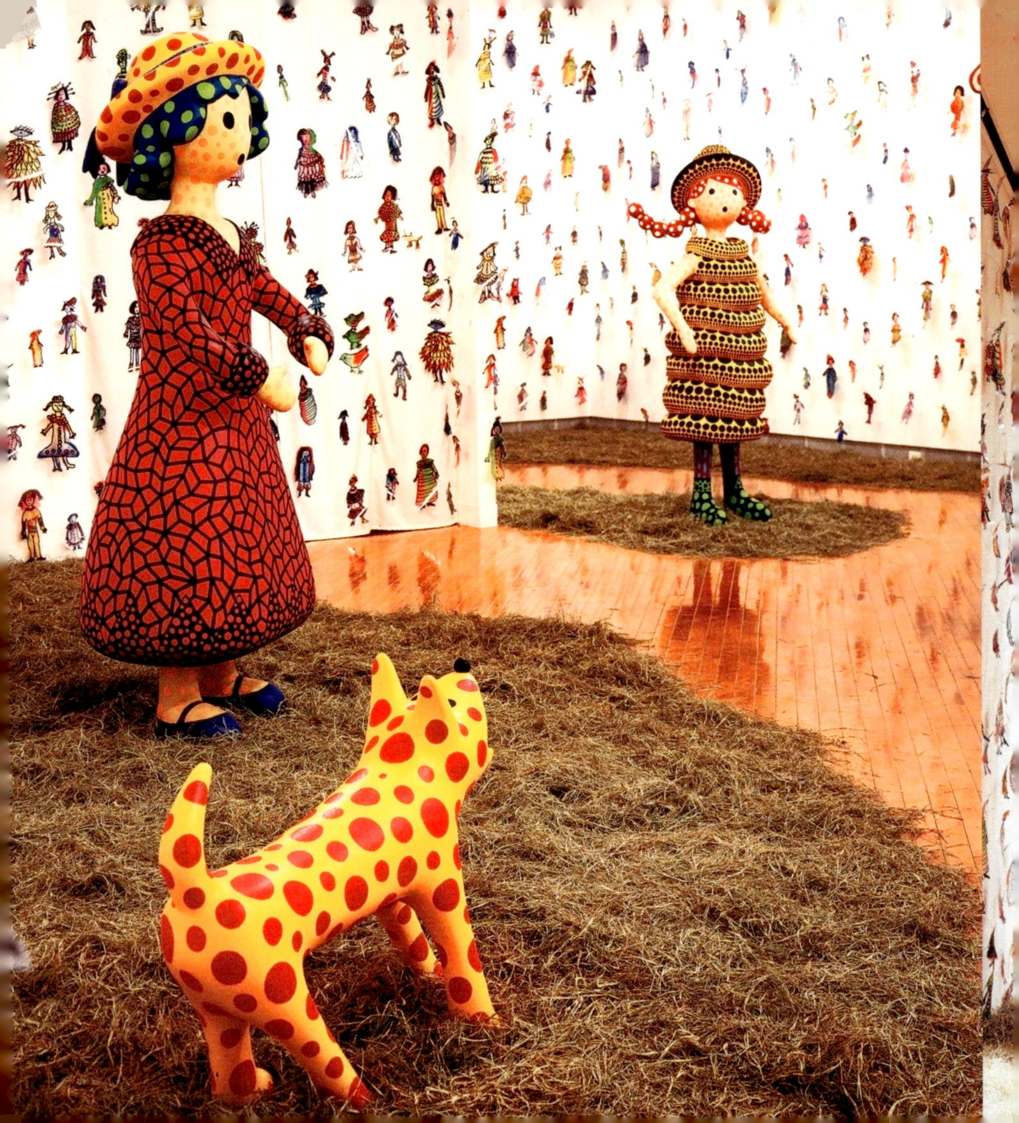

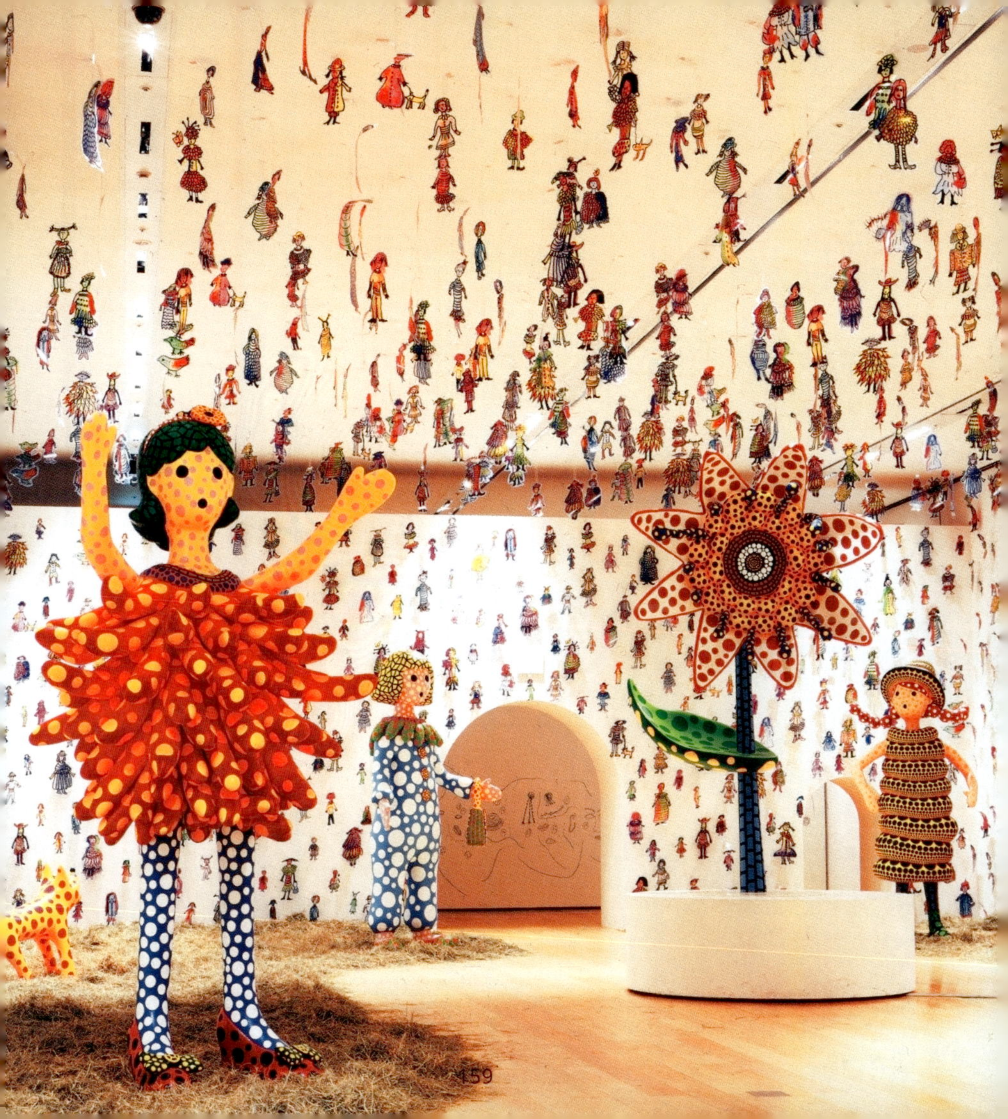

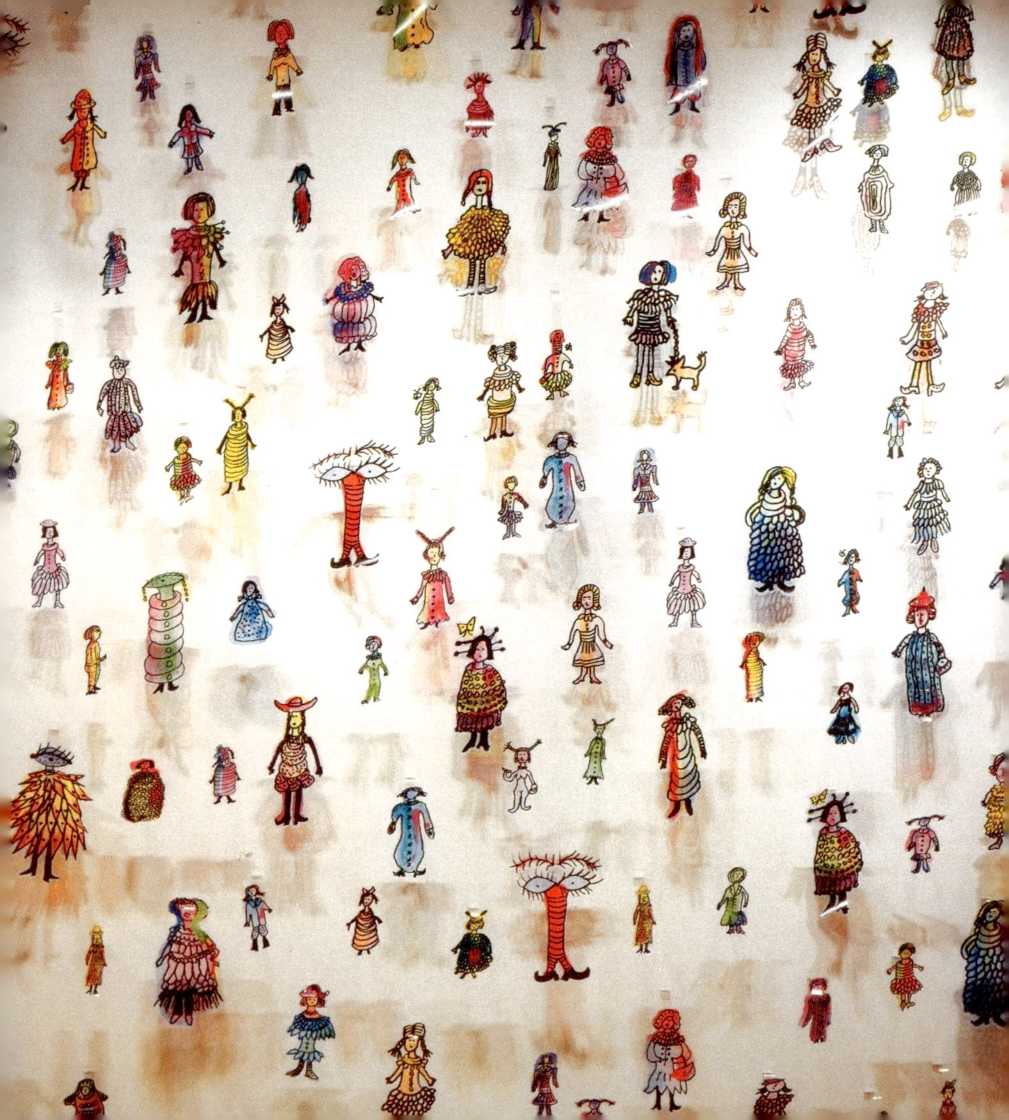

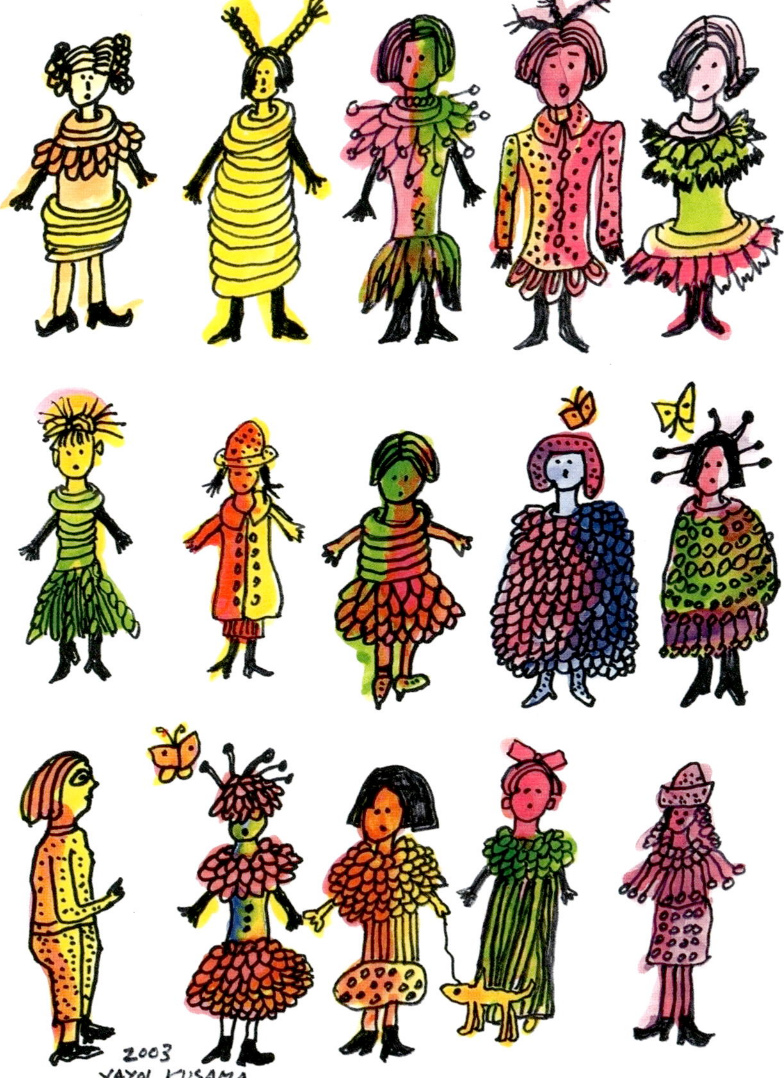
2003
YAYOI KUSAMA

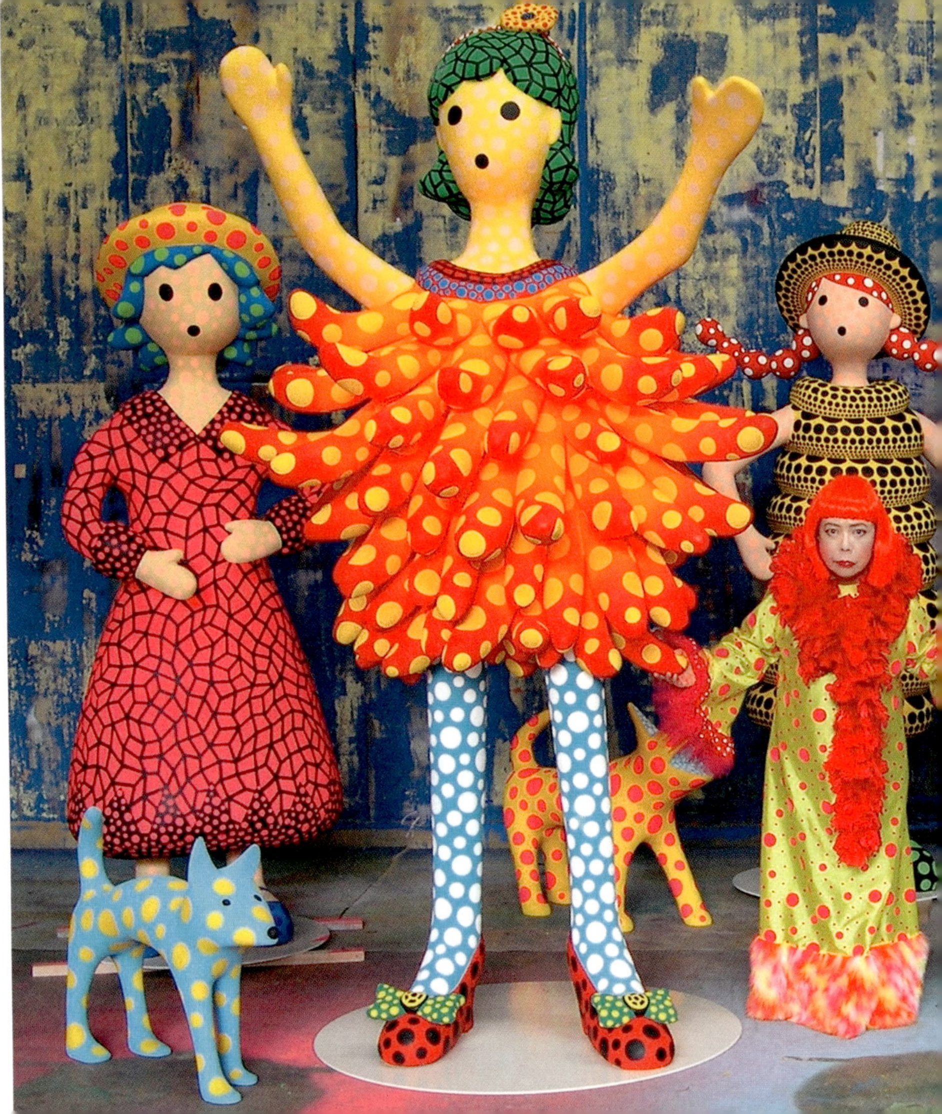

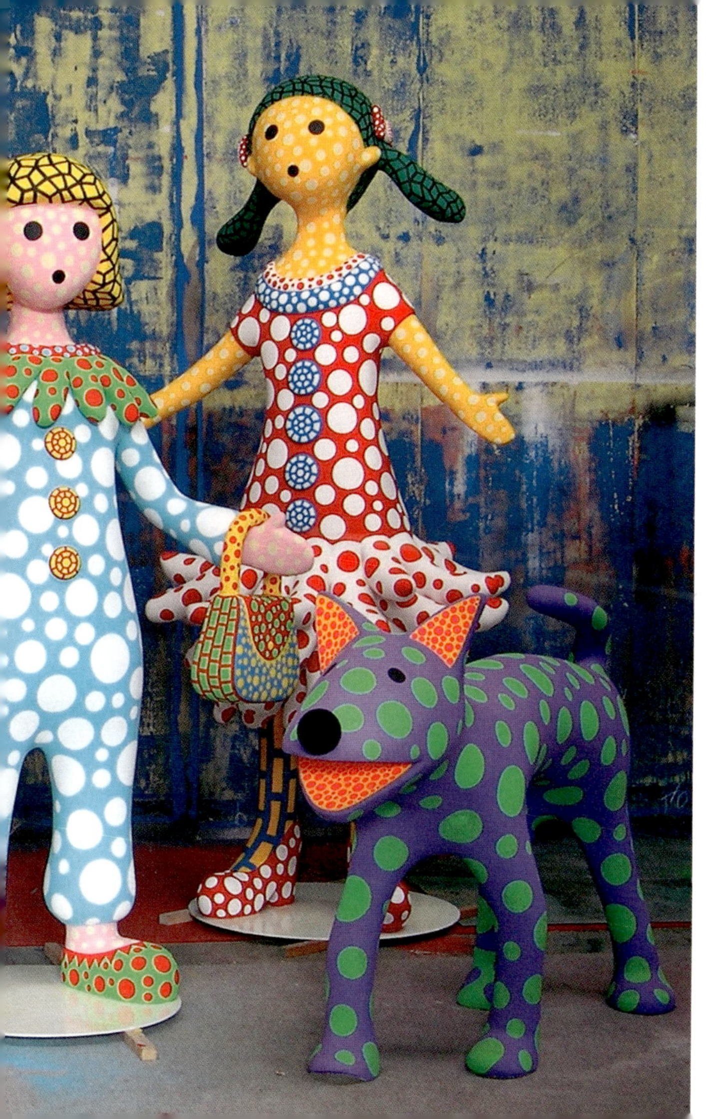

人生は真実素晴らしいとつくづく思い、

体が震えるほど、芸術の世界は尽きることなく興味があり、

私にはこの世界しか希望のわく、生きがいのある場所は他にないのだ。

そして、そのためには如何なる苦労をしても悔いはない。

私はそのようにこれまで生きてき、これからもそう生きてゆく。

I feel how truly wonderful life is,
and I tremble with an undying fascination for the world of art,
the only place that gives me hope and makes life worthwhile.
And no matter how I may suffer for my art, I will have no regrets.
This is the way I have always lived my life,
and it is the way I shall go on living it.

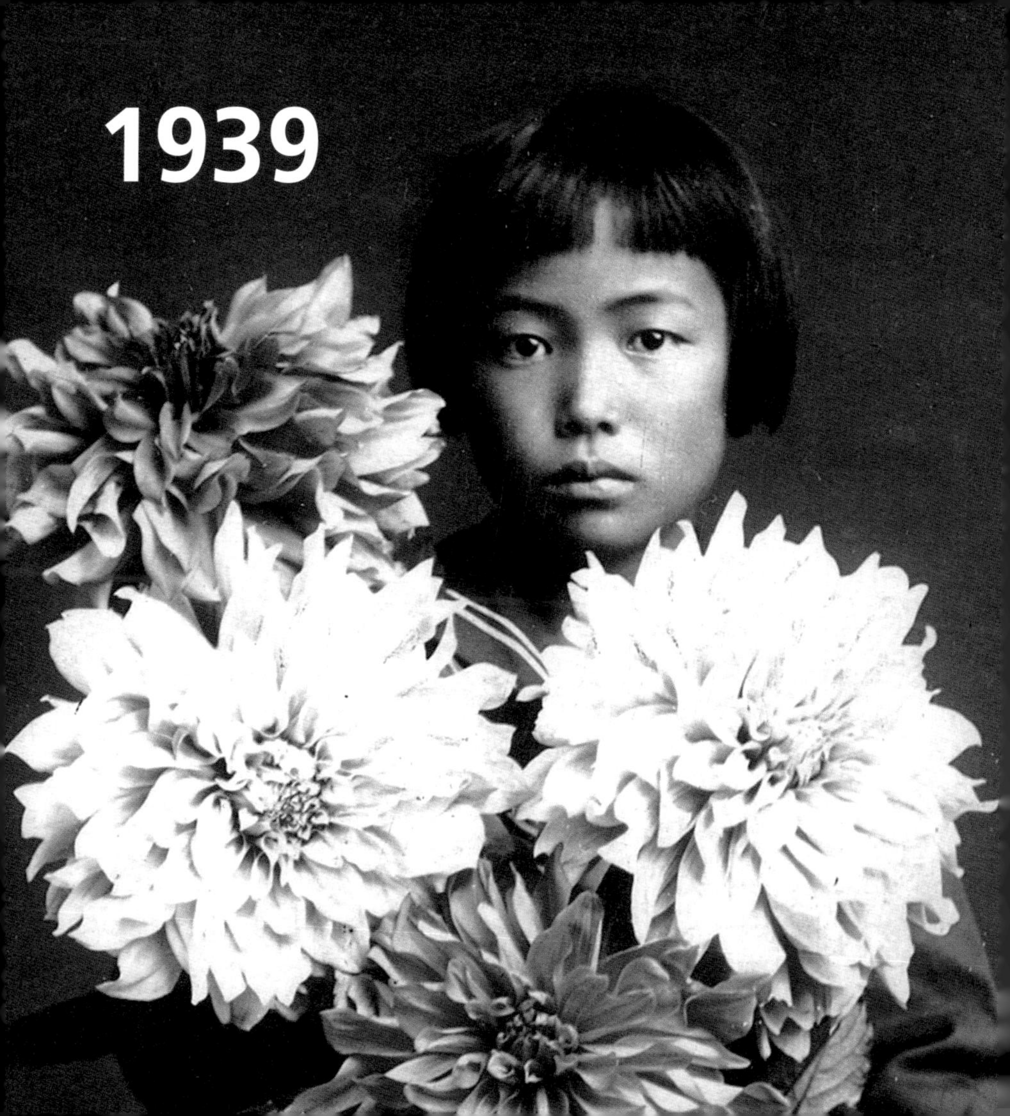
1939

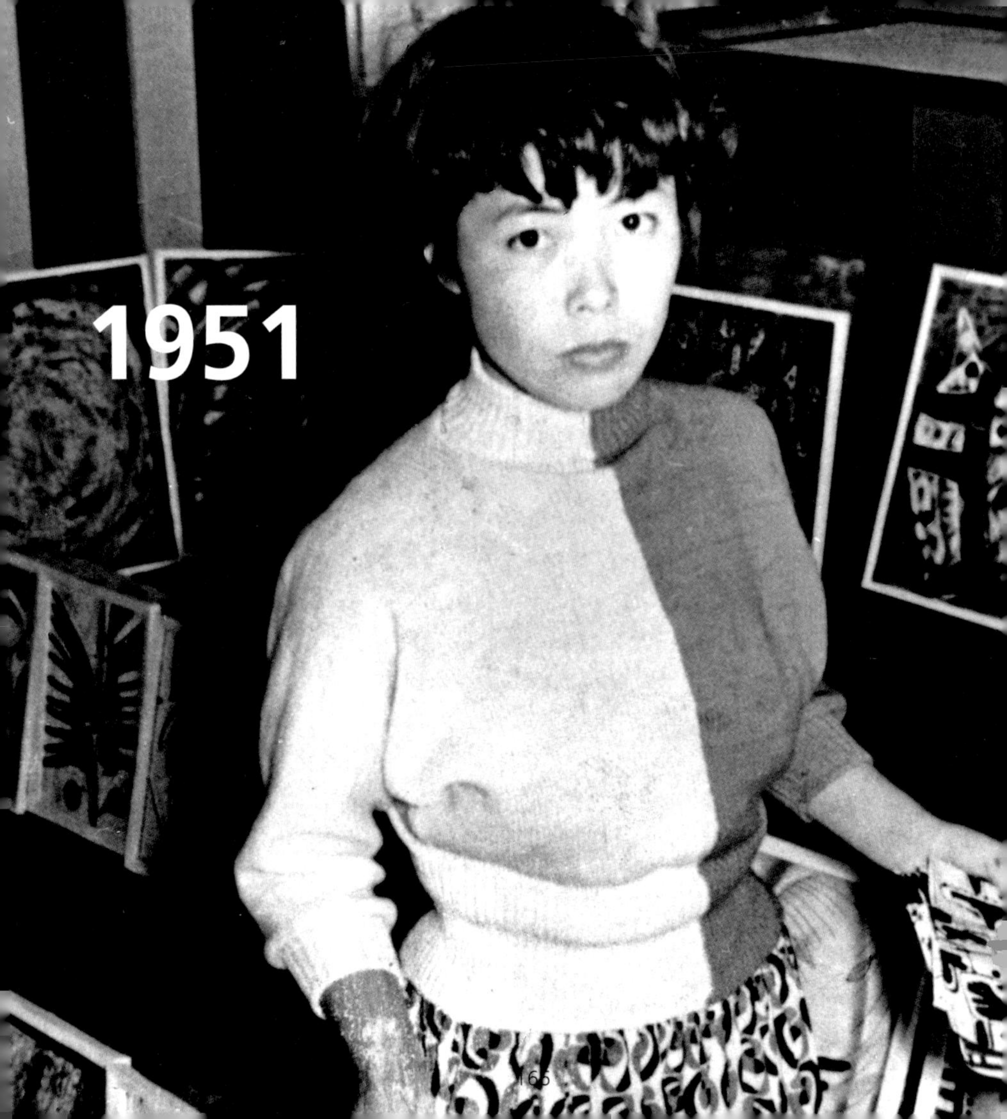

1951

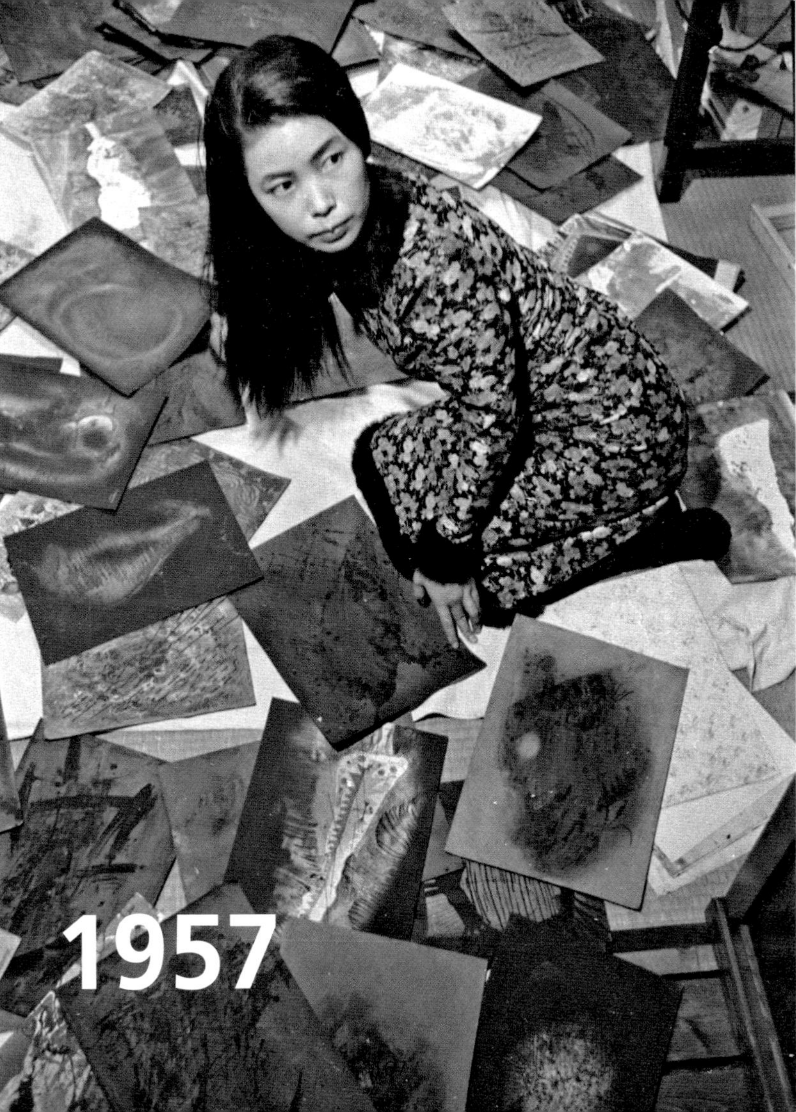
1957

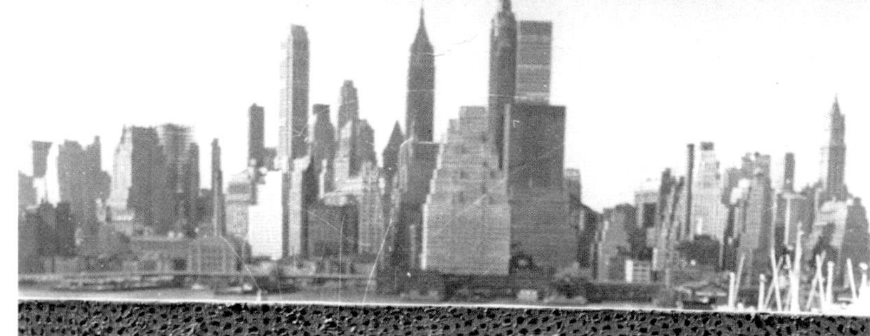

1958

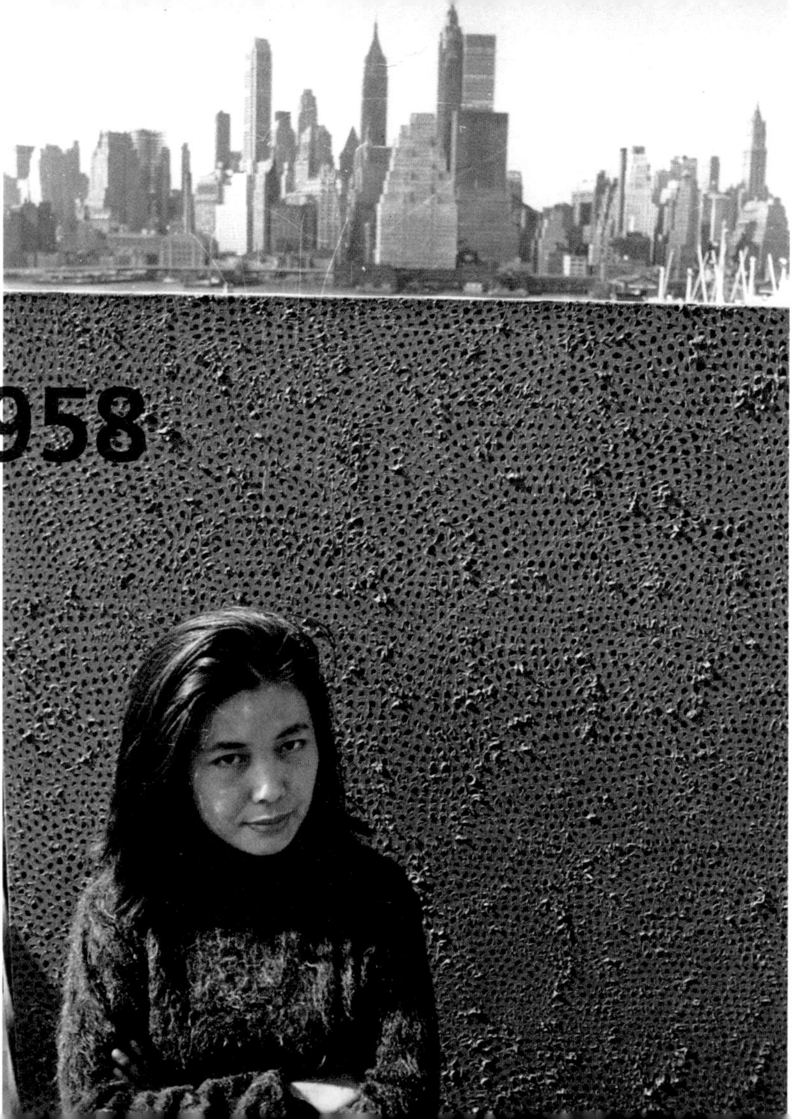

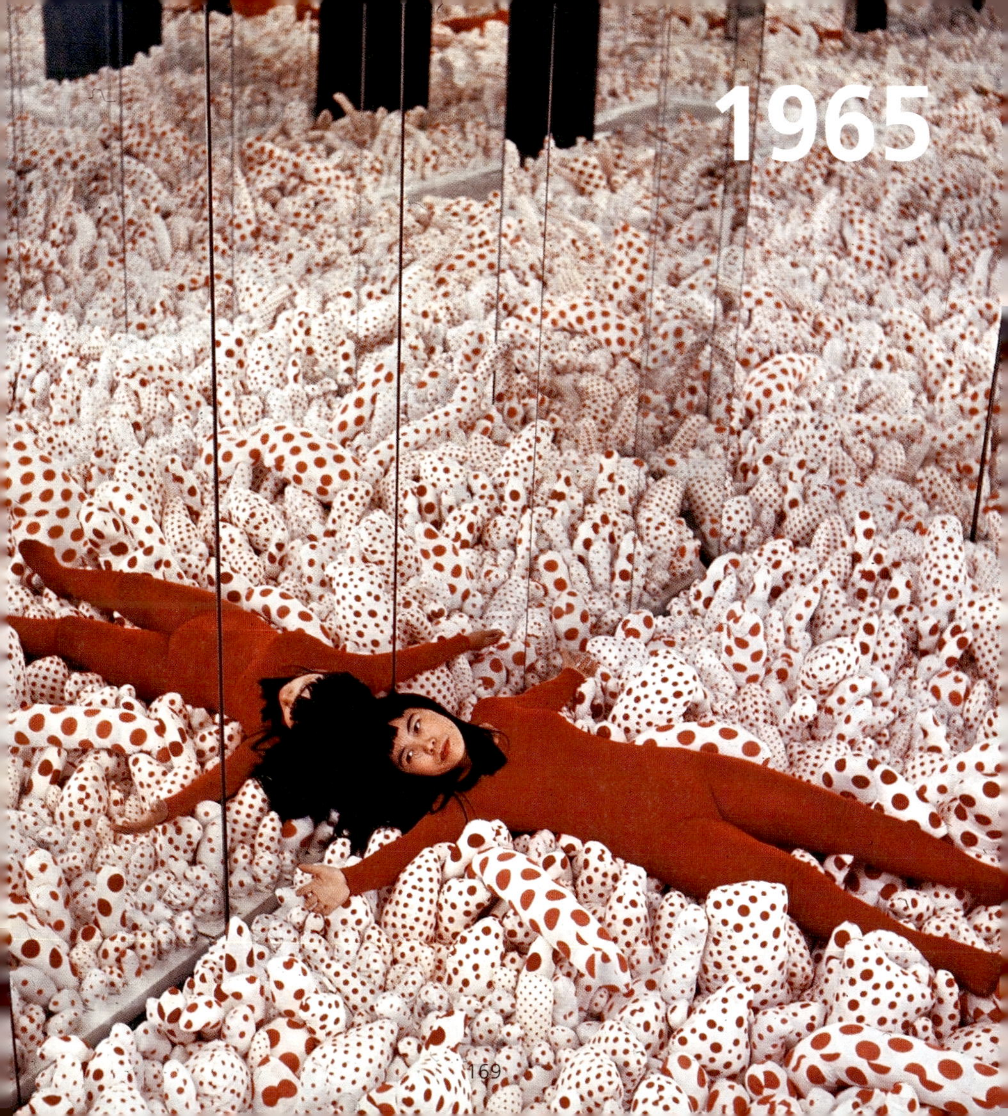
1965

1966

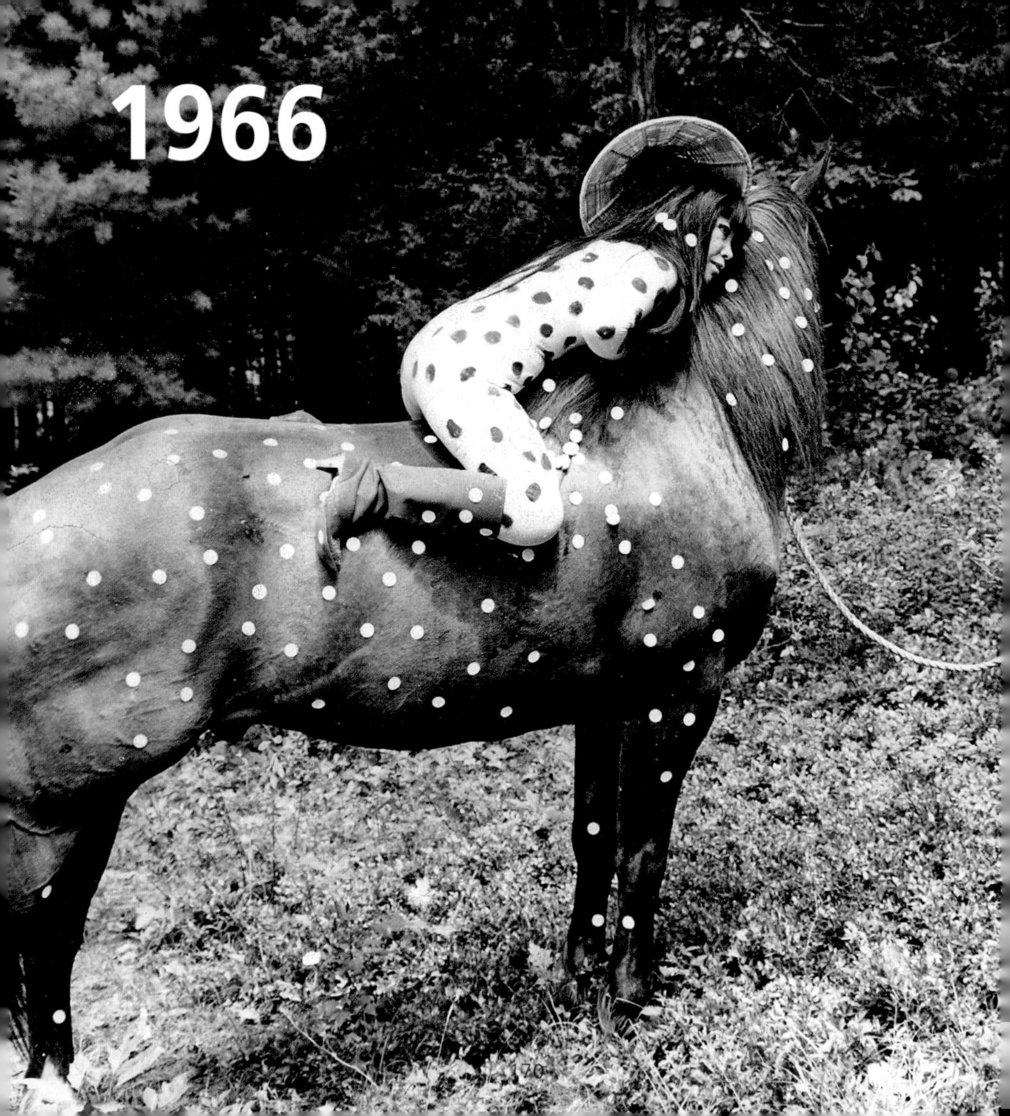

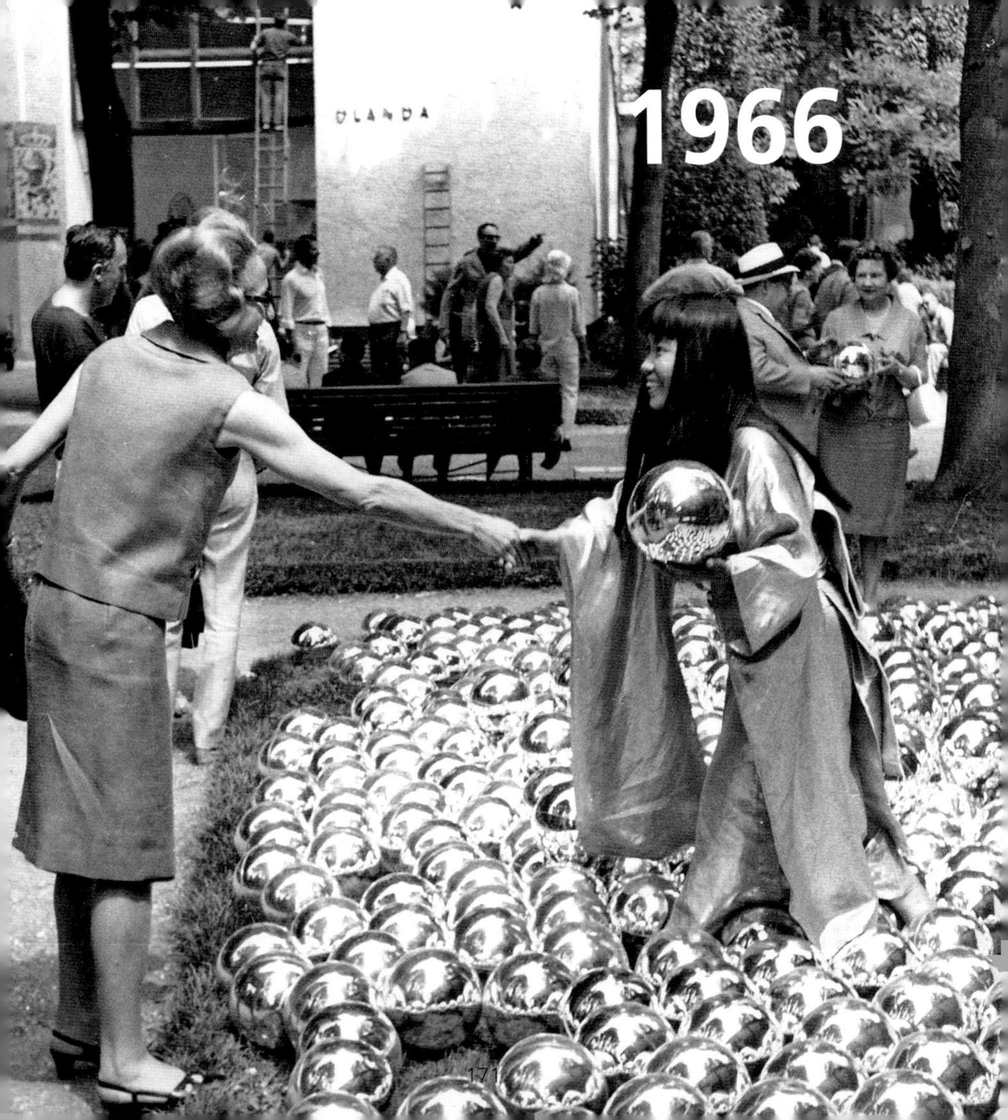
1966

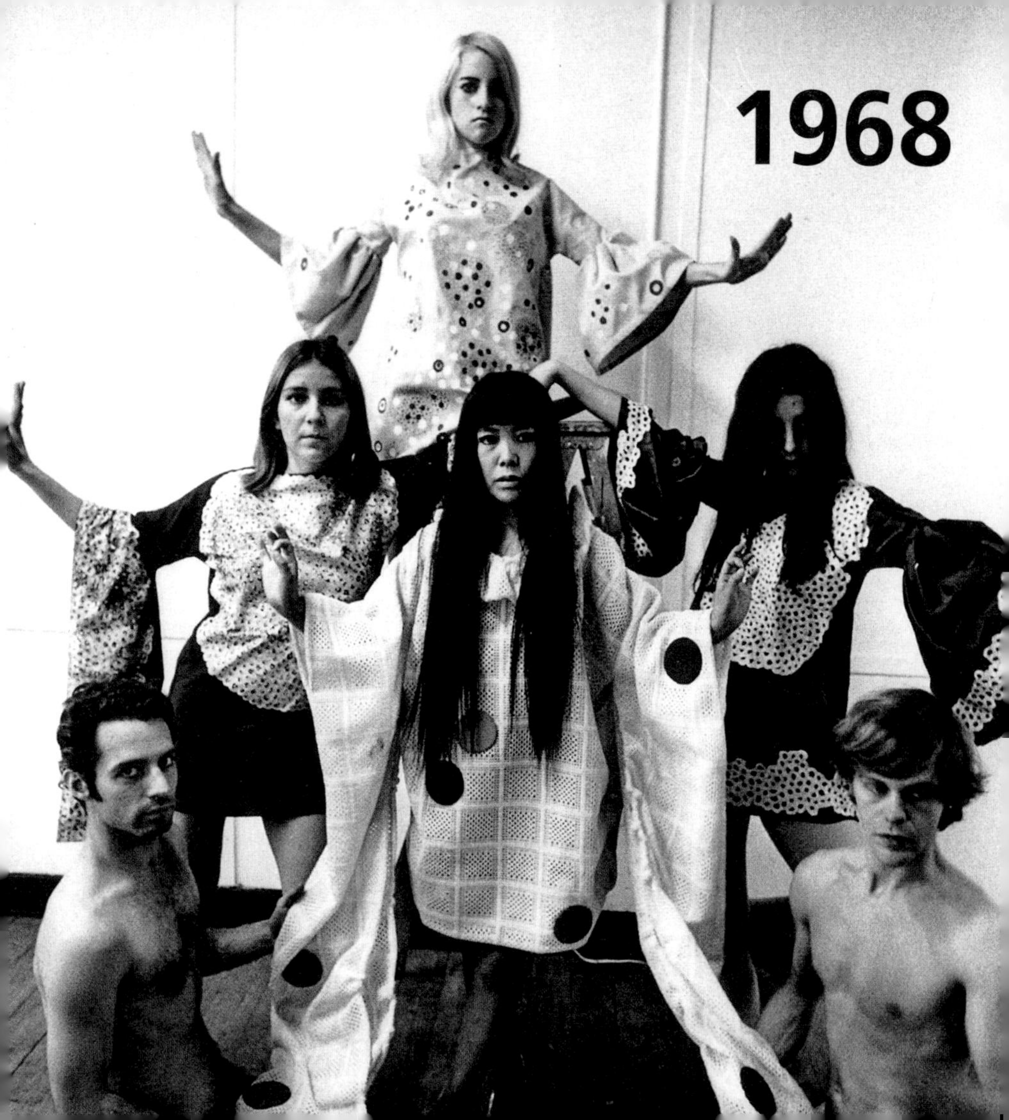
1968

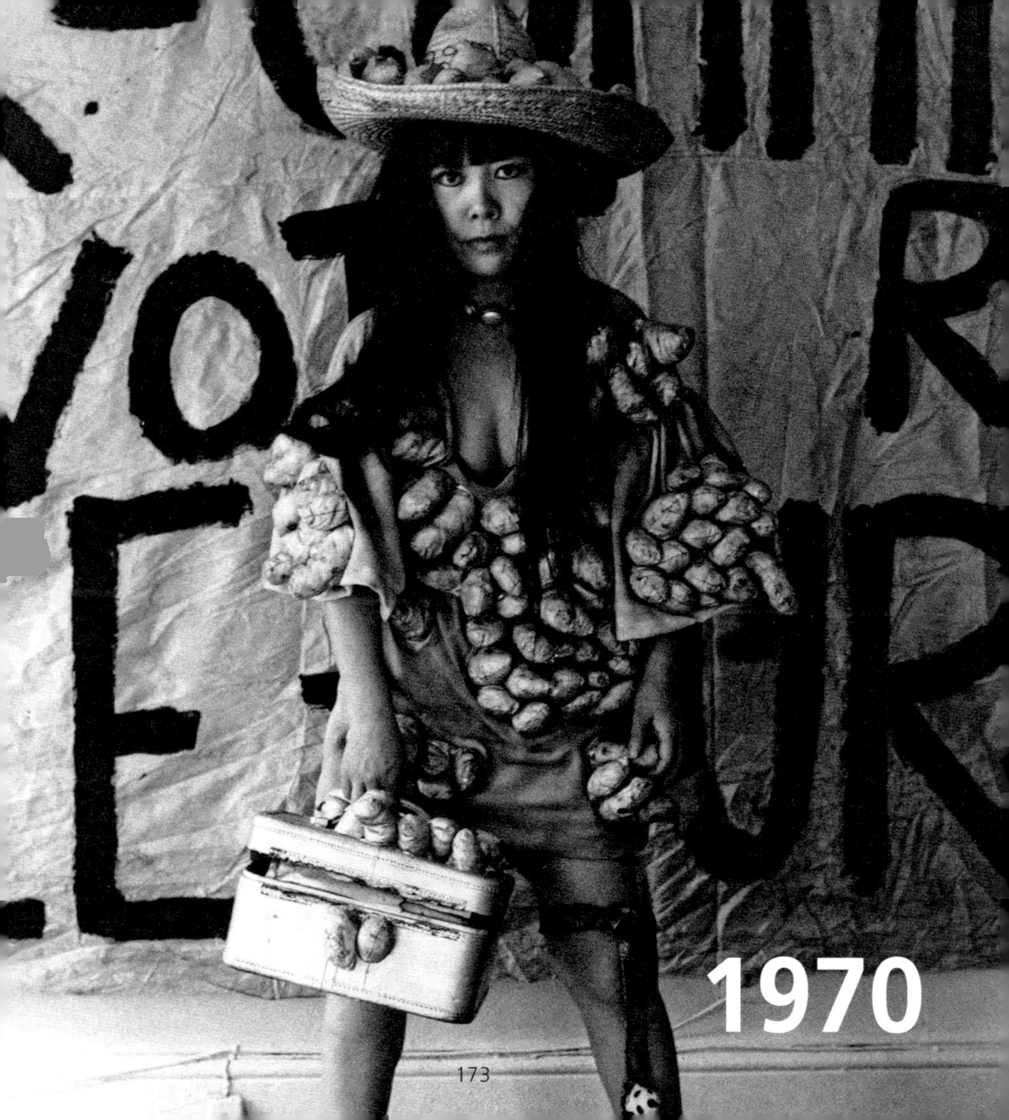

1970

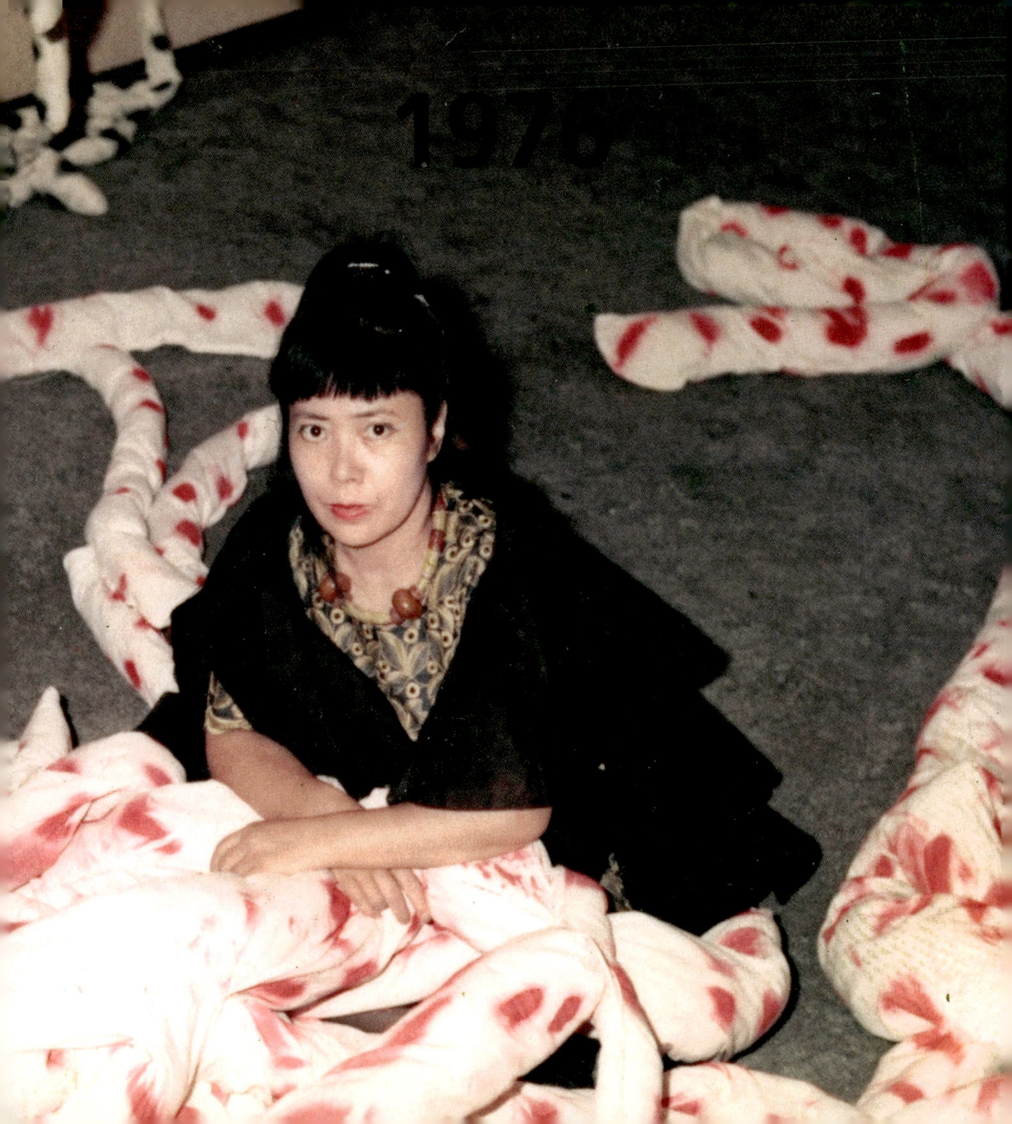
1970

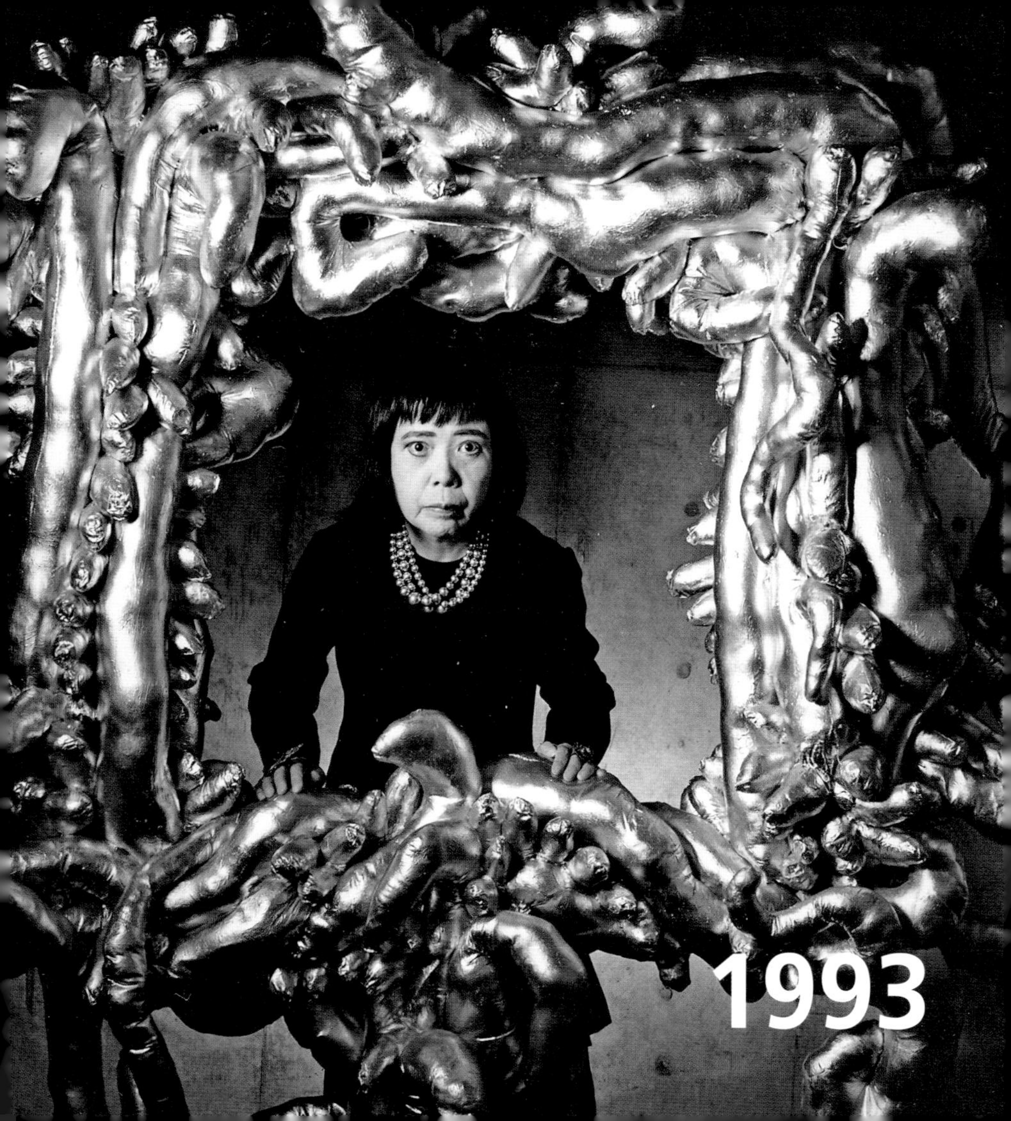
1993

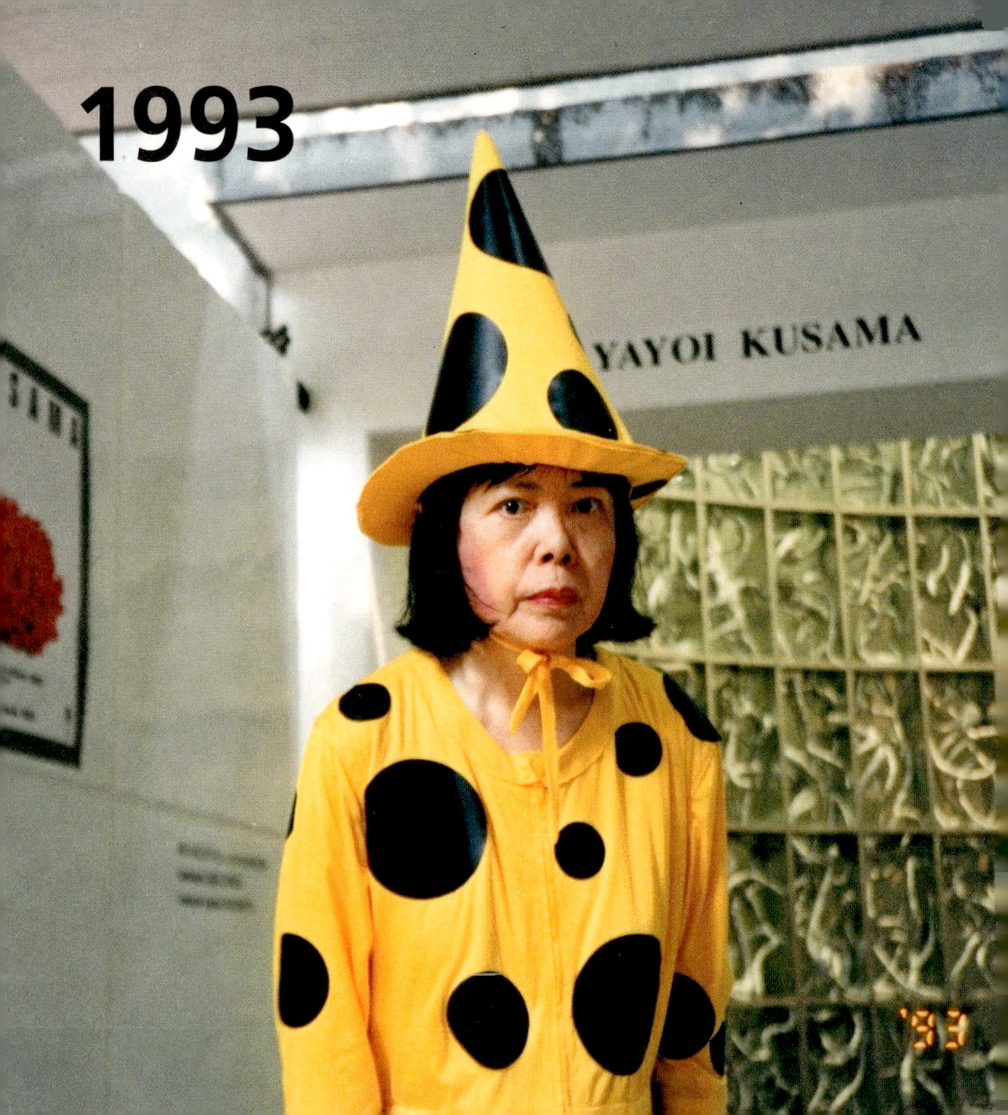
1993
YAYOI KUSAMA
'93

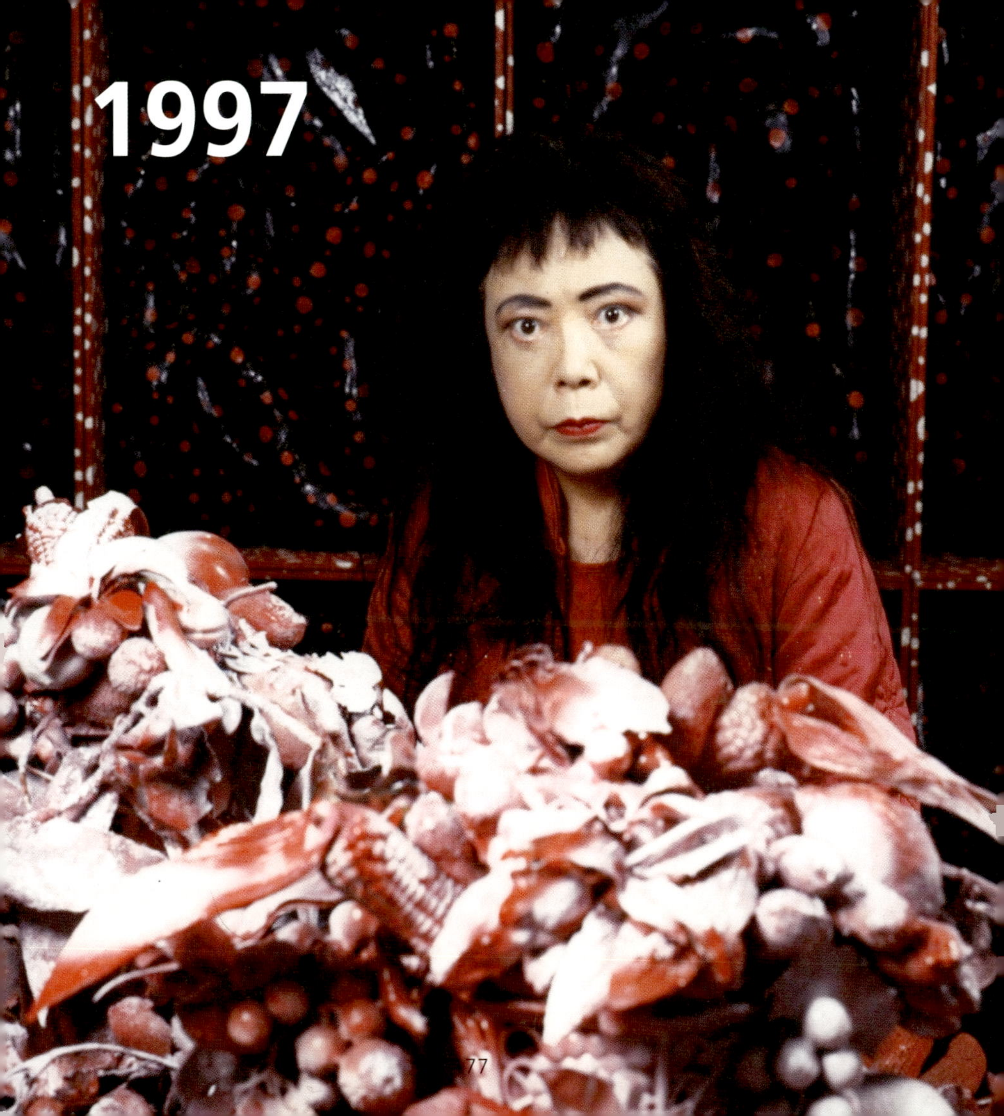

1997

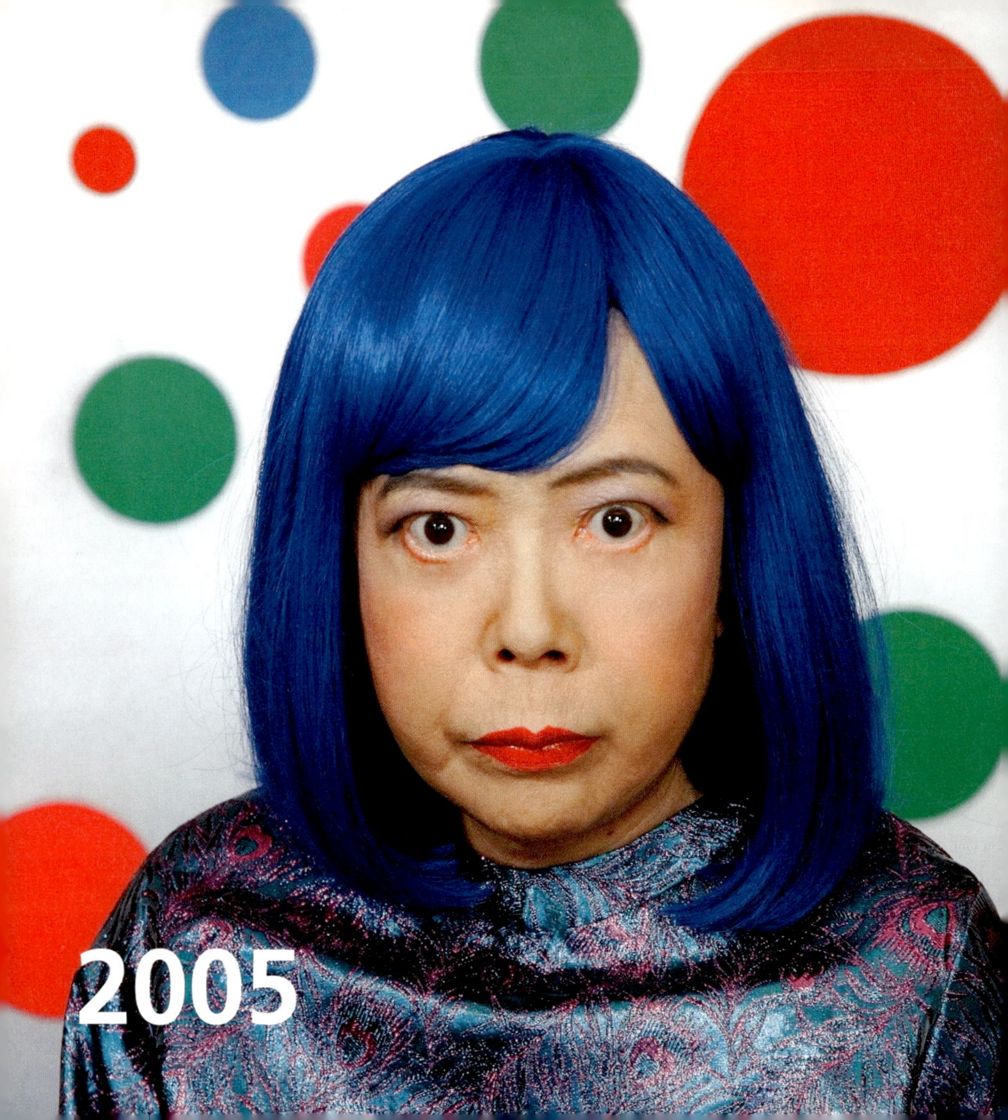
2005

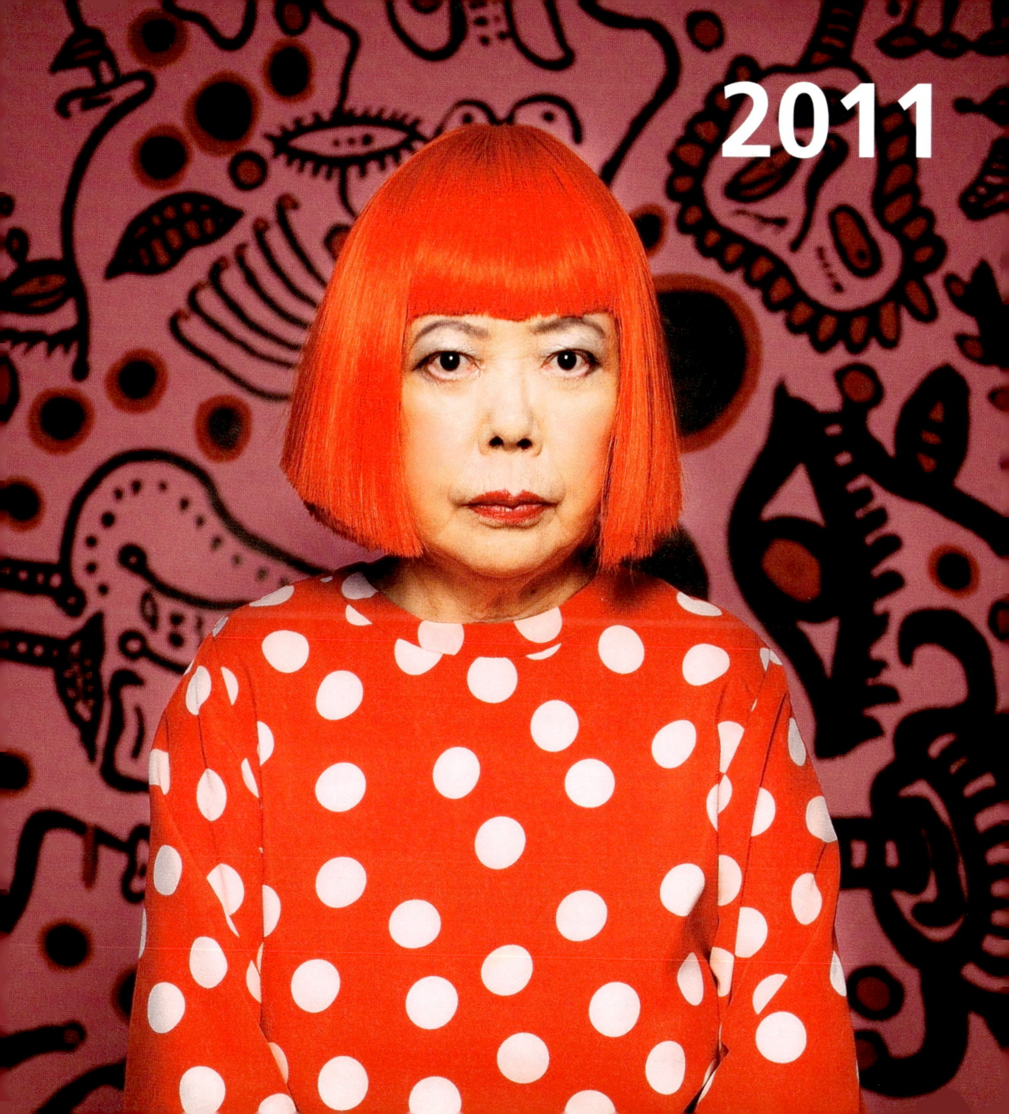
2011

Index of Works

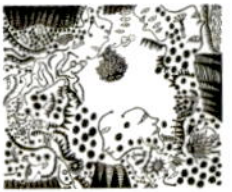

p.5
わが恋のすべて、そして
夜の夢をたべたい（部分）
ALL ABOUT MY LOVE,
AND I LONG TO EAT A
DREAM OF THE NIGHT
(detail)
2009
H130.3×162.0cm
Acrylic on canvas

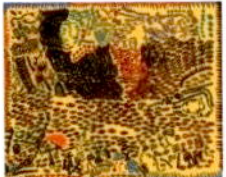

p.11
人の世のすべてを語る、
そして平和が来るのを
待っている
IT TELLS EVERYTHING
ABOUT THE WORLD OF
PEOPLE, AND AWAITS
THE ARRIVAL OF PEACE
2010, H130.3×162.0cm
Acrylic on canvas

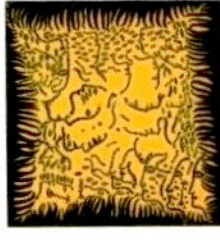

p.12
生老病死
Birth, Aging, Sickness and
Death
2008
H194.0×194.0cm
Acrylic on canvas

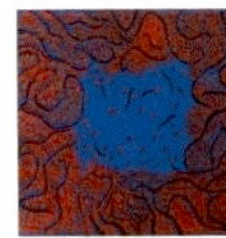

p.13
宇宙空間
COSMIC SPACE
2008
H194.0×194.0cm
Acrylic on canvas

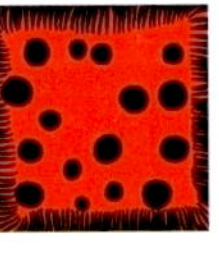

p.14
宇宙は何もないところから
発生する
THE UNIVERSE
EMERGES FROM
NOWHERE
2008
H194.0×194.0cm
Acrylic on canvas

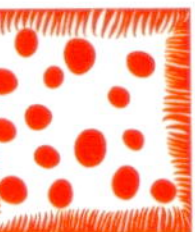

p.15
火の玉宇宙
UNIVERSE, FIREBALLS
2008
H194.0×194.0cm
Acrylic on canvas

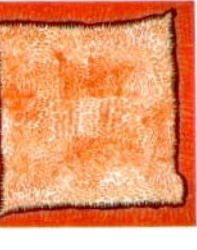

p.16
瞑想
MEDITATION
2008
H194.0×194.0cm
Acrylic on canvas

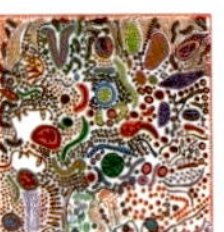

p.17
果てしない人間の一生
ENDLESS LIFE OF
PEOPLE
2010
H194.0×194.0cm
Acrylic on canvas

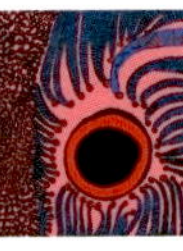

p.18
誰からも太陽は愛されてい
THE SUN IS LOVED BY
EVERYBODY
2009
H162.0×162.0cm
Acrylic on canvas

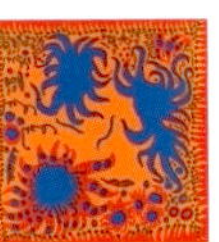

p.19
愛が花咲いたときの喜び
JOY I FEEL WHEN LOVE
HAS BLOSSOMED
2009
H194.0×194.0cm
Acrylic on canvas

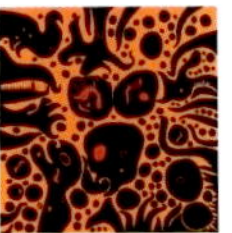

p.20
失恋の痛み、
そして自殺したい
PAIN OF LOVE LOST,
AND A WISH TO COMM
SUICIDE
2009
H194.0×194.0cm
Acrylic on canvas

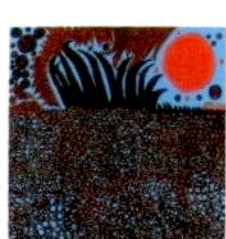

p.21
朝、太陽は地平線に
のぼってきた
MORNING, THE SUN HAS RISEN ABOVE THE HORIZON
2009
H162.0×162.0cm
Acrylic on canvas

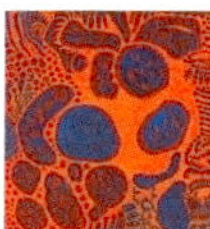

p.22
秘められた時
SECRET MOMENTS
2010
H162.0×162.0cm
Acrylic on canvas

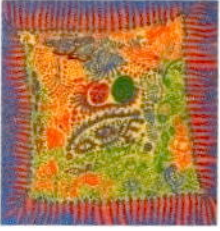

p.23
命の消滅
OBLITERATION OF LIFE
2011
H162.0×162.0cm
Acrylic on canvas

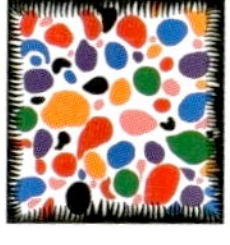

p.24
いまわしい戦争のあとでは
幸福で心が一杯になるばかり
ONCE THE ABOMINABLE WAR IS OVER, HAPPINESS FILLS OUR HEARTS
2010
H194.0×194.0cm
Acrylic on canvas

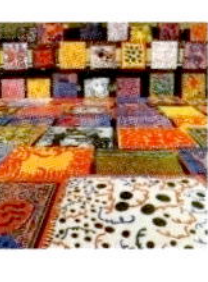

p.25
"我が永遠の魂"100枚の
絵　武蔵大学講堂にて
100 paintings of "My Eternal Soul" at Musashi University, Tokyo
2011

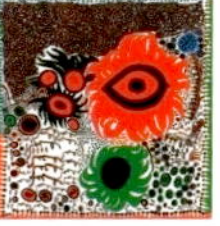

p.26
花園にうずもれた心
THE HEART BURIED IN A FLOWER GARDEN
2009
H194.0×194.0cm
Acrylic on canvas

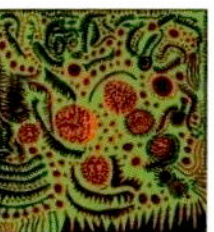

p.27
月の出を待っている
WAITING FOR THE MOON TO APPEAR
2011
H162.0×162.0cm
Acrylic on canvas

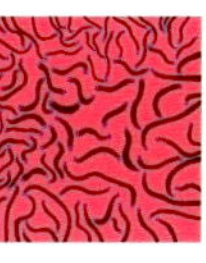

p.28
さざなみ
RIPPLES
2010
H162.0×162.0cm
Acrylic on canvas

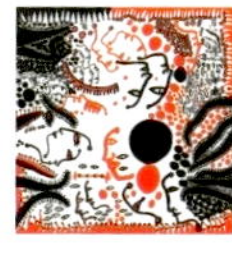

p.29
心から生命の賛美を
うたい上げたい
I WANT TO SING MY HEART OUT IN PRAISE OF LIFE
2009
H194.0×194.0cm
Acrylic on canvas

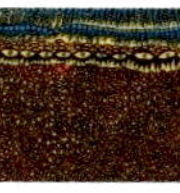

p.30
ふるさとの川岸に立ちて
涙をこぼす
STANDING ON THE RIVERBANK OF MY HOMETOWN I SHED TEARS
2009
H112.0×145.0cm
Acrylic on canvas

p.31
INFINITY-RED-DOTS [APB]
2011
H162.0×162.0cm
Acrylic on canvas

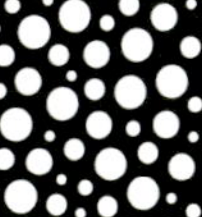

p.32
宇宙 [ABOM]
COSMOS [ABOM]
2008
H194.0×194.0cm
Urethane on canvas

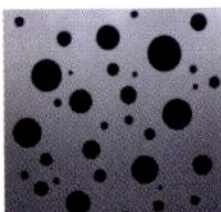

p.33
DOTS-OBSESSION
[TOBBQW]
2008
H194.0×194.0cm
Urethane on canvas

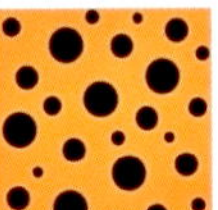

p.34
COSMOS [THOPS]
2008
H194.0×194.0cm
Urethane on canvas

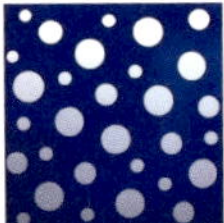

p.35
DOTS-OBSESSION
[TOSIA]
2008
H194.0×194.0cm
Urethane on canvas

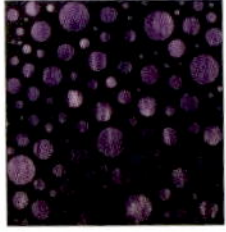

p.36
THE END OF THE
UNIVERSE [ATWON]
2008
H100.0×100.0cm
Acrylic on canvas

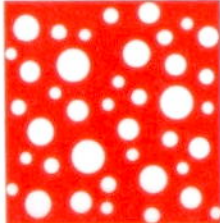

p.37
STARS OF INFINITY
[ZOAQ]
2008
H194.0×194.0cm
Urethane on canvas

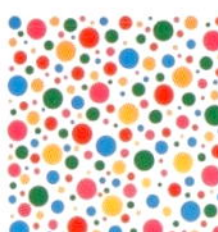

p.38
THE COSMOS [BKNS]
2010
H194.0×194.0cm
Acrylic on canvas

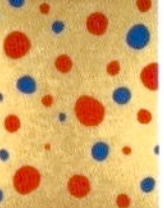

p.40
星たちの消滅(金)
OBLITERATION OF
STARS (GOLD)
2010
H259.0×194.0cm
Acrylic on canvas

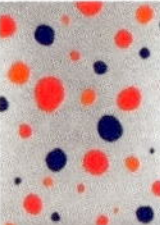

p.41
星たちの消滅(銀)
OBLITERATION OF
STARS (SILVER)
2010
H259.0×194.0cm
Acrylic on canvas

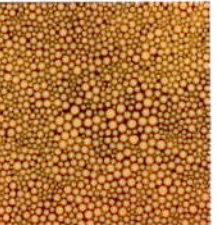

p.42
INFINITY-DOTS
[ASNIH]
2010
H194.0×194.0cm
Acrylic on canvas
back cover
(部分 detail)

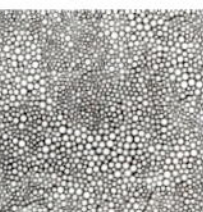

p.43
INFINITY-DOTS
[XHIA]
2010
H194.0×194.0cm
Acrylic on canvas

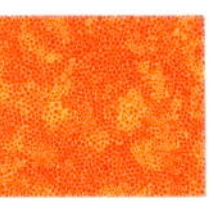

p.44
INFINITY-STARS
2011
H130.3×162.0cm
Acrylic on canvas

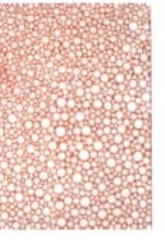

p.45
水玉 [ZXABOT]
DOT [ZXABOT]
2008
H130.3×97.0cm
Acrylic on canvas

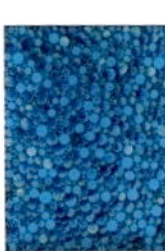

p.46
UNIVERSE [AJKN]
2010
H145.5×112.0cm
Acrylic on canvas

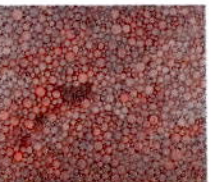

p.47
DOTS-OBSESSION
[BROQ]
2011
H130.3×162.0cm
Acrylic on canvas

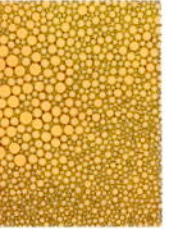

p.48
DOTS [XYZTT]
2008
H145.5×112.0cm
Acrylic on canvas

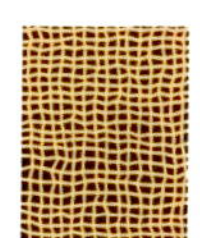

p.49
INFINITY-NETS
[TSWA]
2009
H145.5×112.0cm
Acrylic on canvas

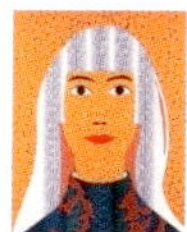

p.50
SELF-PORTRAIT
[AAWOY]
2010
H227.3×181.8cm
Acrylic on canvas

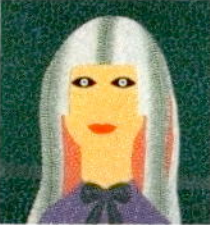

p.51
PORTRAIT [XOT]
2009
H194.0×194.0cm
Acrylic on canvas

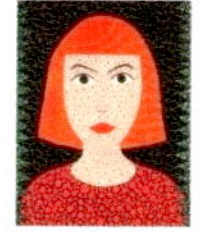

p.52
SELF-PORTRAIT
[OHBTY]
2011
H162.0×130.3cm
Acrylic on canvas

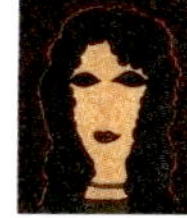

p.53
永遠の永遠の愛 [QPOWEY]
ETERNAL NEVER-ENDING LOVE
[QPOWEY]
2008
H227.3×181.8cm
Acrylic on canvas

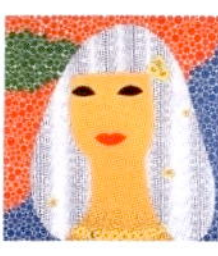

p.54
PORTRAIT [SSA]
2009
H194.0×194.0cm
Acrylic on canvas

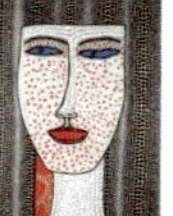

p.55
遠い目の異国で
IN A FOREIGN COUNTRY
OF BLUE-EYED PEOPLE
2011
H227.3×181.8cm
Acrylic on canvas

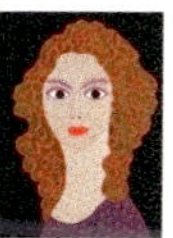

p.56
SELF-PORTRAIT
[OPXTO]
2010
H145.5×112.0cm
Acrylic on canvas

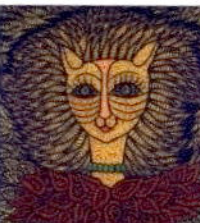

p.57
自画像
SELF-PORTRAIT
2009
H194.0×194.0cm
Acrylic on canvas

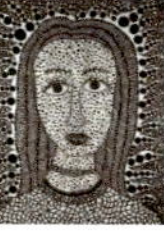

p.58
青春を前にした我が自画像
MY SELF-PORTRAIT
IN THE PRESENCE OF
ADOLESCENCE
2011
H227.3×181.8cm
Acrylic on canvas

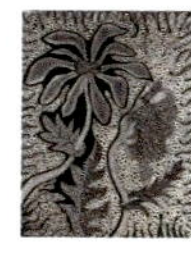

p.59
HEART FLOWERS
2011
H162.0×130.3cm
Acrylic on canvas

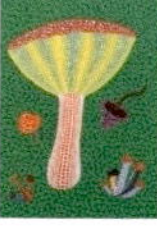

p.60
きのこ [AOWN]
MUSHROOMS [AOWN]
2010
H130.3×97.0cm
Acrylic on canvas

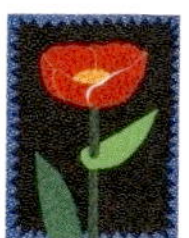

p.61
A FLOWER
2008
H227.3×181.8cm
Acrylic on canvas

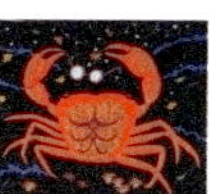

p.62
A-CRAB
2008
H181.8×227.3cm
Acrylic on canvas

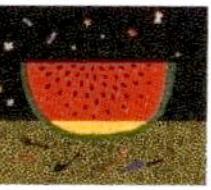

p.63
WATERMELON
2008
H181.8×227.3cm
Acrylic on canvas

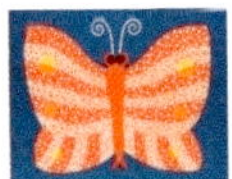

p.64
A BUTTERFLY
[ACHNO]
2011
H112.0×145.0cm
Acrylic on canvas

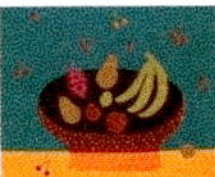

p.65
FRUITS [EPSOB]
2011
H112.0×145.0cm
Acrylic on canvas

p.66
INFINITY-NETS [UAXP]
2010
H145.5×145.5cm
Acrylic on canvas

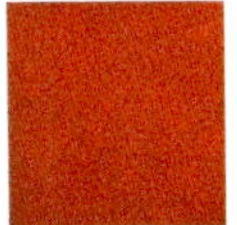

p.67
INFINITY-NETS [GKSG]
2010
H162.0×162.0cm
Acrylic on canvas

p.68
無限の網 [JOAATT]
INFINITY-NETS
[JOAATT]
2009
H100.0×100.0cm
Acrylic on canvas

p.69
INFINITY-NETS
[WAASSO]
2008
H100.0×100.0cm
Acrylic on canvas

p.70
UNIVERSE [RYPK]
2010
H194.0×194.0cm
Acrylic on canvas

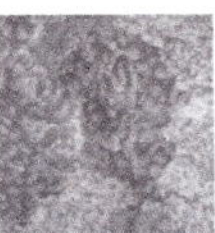

p.71
無限の網 [ZSSOQAA]
INFINITY-NETS
[ZSSOQAA]
2008
H100.0×100.0cm
Acrylic on canvas

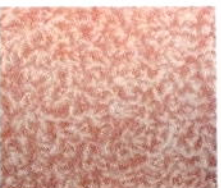

p.72
INFINITY-NETS [DSR]
2011
H181.8×227.3cm
Acrylic on canvas

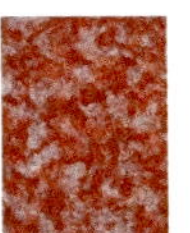

p.73
INFINITY-NETS
[XZABB]
2008
H145.5×112.0cm
Acrylic on canvas

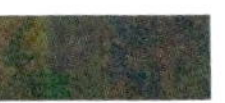

p.74-75
輪廻転生
TRANSMIGRATION
2011
H194.0×521.2cm
Acrylic on canvas

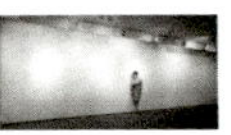

p.78-79
約10mの無限の網の作品
ステファン・ラディチ画廊
にて
Kusama with her Infinity
Nets painting (33 feet) at
Stephen Radich Gallery
in New York
1961

p.80-81
No.AB
1959
H210.3×414.4cm
Oil on canvas
Collection : Toyota
Municipal Museum of Ar

p.82
Yellow Net
1960
H240.0 × 294.6cm
Oil on canvas

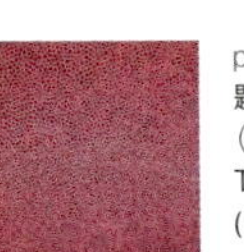

p.83
題不明
（無限の網の絵）
Title Unknown
(Infinity-Nets painting)
c.1959
Oil on canvas

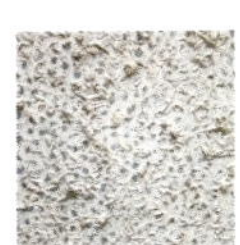

p.84
No.F（部分）
No.F（detail）
1959
H105.4×132.1cm
Oil on canvas

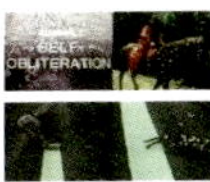

p.86-87
草間の自己消滅
Kusama's Self-Obliteration
1968
Film

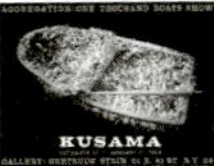

p.88
集合：1000艘のボートショー（ポスター）
AGGREGATION : ONE THOUSAND BOATS SHOW (Poster)
1964

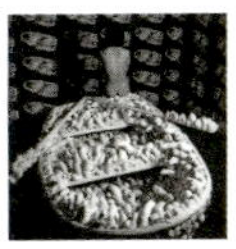

p.89
集合：1000艘のボートショー
"AGGREGATION : ONE THOUSAND BOATS SHOW" at Gertrude Stein Gallery, New York
1964

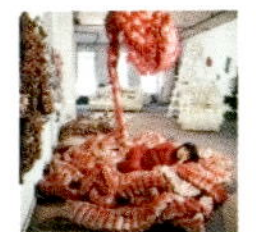

p.90-91
"My Flower Bed"（1962）と草間、ニューヨークのスタジオにて
Kusama Lying on the base of "My Flower Bed" (1962) at her studio in New York
c.1965
Photo by Peter Moore

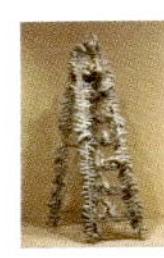

p.92
Traveling Life
1964
H248.0×82.0×151.0cm
Collection: The National Museum of Modern Art, Kyoto

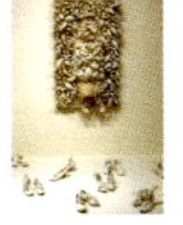

p.93
"The Man" 1963
The Man (1963)
Collection: Hiroshima City Museum of Contemporary Art
集積の靴 1963
Accumulation shoes (1963)
Courtesy : Mudima Foundation, Milan

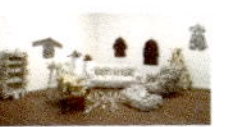

p.94-95
集積作品（1962-64）
展示風景（テートモダン）
Accumulation pieces (1962-64), installation view at Tate Modern, London, 2012

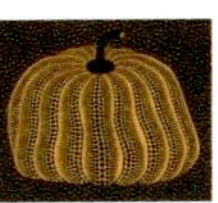

p.96
PUMPKIN [SOMEM]
2010
H130.3×162.0cm
Acrylic on canvas

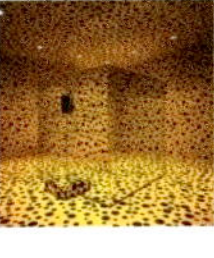

p.98
ミラールーム（かぼちゃ）
Mirror Room (Pumpkin)
1991
H200×200×200cm
Mixedmedia
Collection: Hara Museum of Contemporary Art, Tokyo

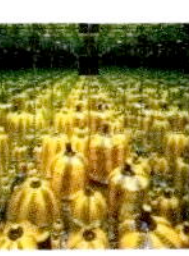

p.99
ミラールーム（かぼちゃ）（内側）
Mirror Room (Pumpkin) (Inside)
1991
H200×200×200cm
Mixedmedia
Collection: Hara Museum of Contemporary Art, Tokyo

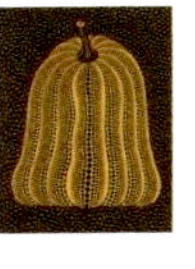

p.100
A-PUMPKIN [BAGN8]
2011
H162.0 ×130.3cm
Acrylic on canvas

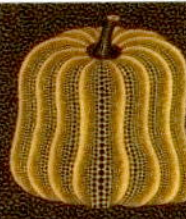

p.101
PUMPKIN [BEPNO]
2011
H145.0×145.0cm
Acrylic on canvas

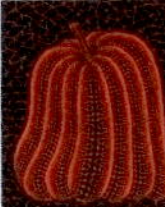

p.102 左
A Pumpkin（3枚組）
2003
H53.0×45.5cm
Acrylic on canvas

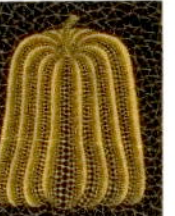

p.102 右
A Pumpkin（3枚組）
2003
H53.0×45.5cm
Acrylic on canvas

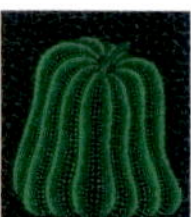

p.103
A Pumpkin（3枚組）
2003
H53.0×45.5cm
Acrylic on canvas

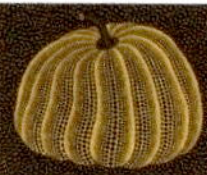

p.104
PUMPKIN [TWPOT]
2010
H130.3×162.0cm
Acrylic on canvas

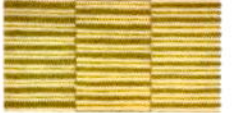

p.105
イエロー・ドッツ
Yellow Dots
1982
H194.0×390.0cm
Acrylic on canvas
Collection: Kitakyushu Municipal Museum of Art

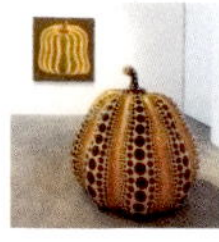

p.106
かぼちゃの彫刻と絵
Pumpkin sculpture and painting
2011
Installation view:
Victoria Miro, London

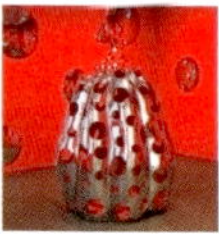

p.107
宇宙にとどけ、水玉かぼちゃ
Reach Up to Universe, Dotted Pumpkin
2010
H200×150×150cm
Paint on Aluminum
Installation view:
Gagosian Gallery Rome

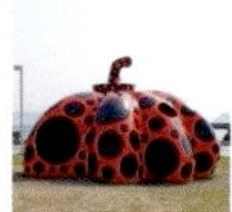

p.108
赤かぼちゃ
Red Pumpkin
2006
H395×φ696cm
Urethane on G.R.C.
Miyanoura Port Square, Naoshima

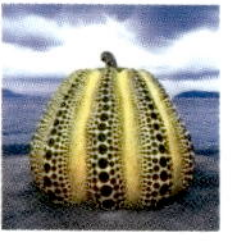

p.109
南瓜
Pumpkin
1994
H200×φ250cm
Urethane on F.R.P.
Collection: Benesse Holdings, Inc.

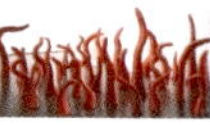

p.110-111
再生の瞬間
The Moment of Regeneration
2004
Mixedmedia

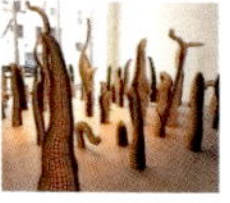

p.112
生命-反復するヴィジョン
Life-Repetitive Vision
1998
Mixedmedia

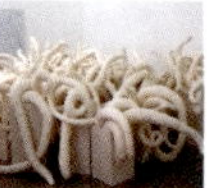

p.113
天と地
Heaven and Earth
1991
Mixedmedia

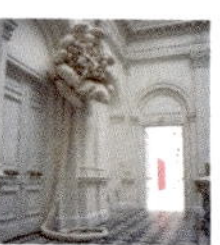

p.114-115
Death of an Illusion
2001
Mixedmedia
Courtesy: Galerie Piece Unique

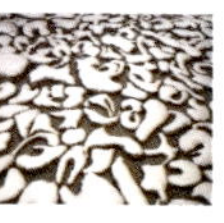

p.116
雲
The Clouds
1984
100点組、サイズ可変
100 pieces, variable dimensions
Mixedmedia

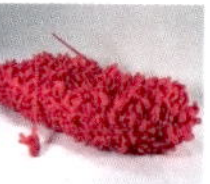

p.117
ピンク・ボート
Pink Boat
1992
90×350×180cm
Mixedmedia
Collection: Nagoya City Art Museum

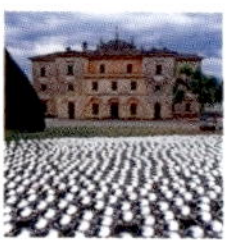

p.119
ナルシス・ガーデン
Narcissus Garden
2003
Installation view:
Fattoria di celle, Florence

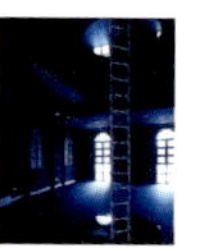

p.120
天国への階段
Ladder to Heaven at Sri Krishnan Temple
2006
Mixedmedia
Installation view:
Singapore Biennale

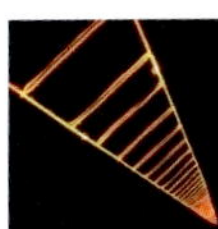

p.121
天国へのぼる階段は
やさしく
Tender Are the Stairs to Heaven
2004
360×φ120cm
Mixedmedia

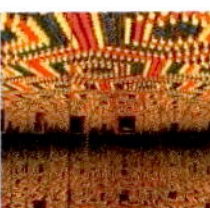

p.122
Infinity Mirrored Room-
信濃の灯
Infinity Mirrored Room-
Glowing Lights in Shinano
2001
240×144.4×144.4cm
Mixedmedia
Collection: Matsumoto City Museum of Art

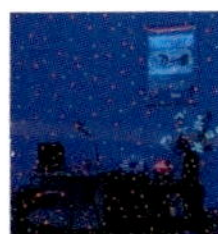

p.123
I'm Here, but Nothing
2004
Mixedmedia
Installation view:
The National Museum of Modern Art, Tokyo

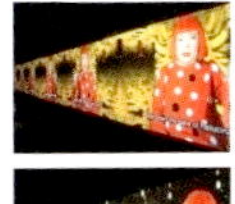

p.124-125
マンハッタン自殺未遂常習犯の歌
Manhattan Suicide Addict performance
2010
DVD, miirror
Installation view:
Queensland Art Gallery, Brisbane

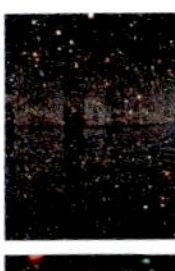

p.126-127
Infinity Mirrored Room -
Filled with the Brilliance of Life
2011
300×617.5×645.5cm
Mixedmedia

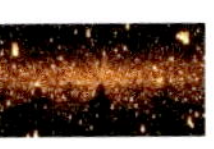

p.128-129
Infinity Mirrored Room -
Aftermath of Obliteration of Eternity
2009
415×415×287.4cm
Mixedmedia
Photo by Takao Miyakaku

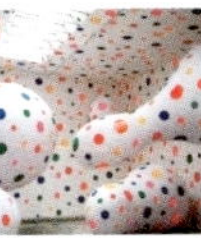

p.130
水玉強迫
ニューセンチュリー
Dots Obsession
New Century
2000
Mixedmedia
Installation view :
Le Consortium, Dijon

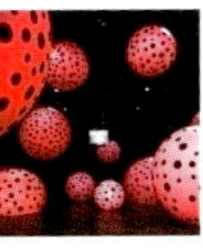

p.131
水玉強迫
水玉になった愛
Dots Obsession - Dots Transformed into Love
2008
Mixedmedia
Installation view:
La Villette, Paris

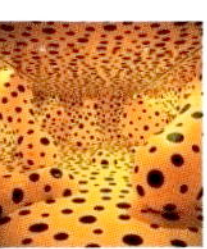

p.132
水玉強迫　昼
Dots Obsession - Day
2008
Mixedmedia
Installation view:
The Kennedy Center, Washington,D.C.

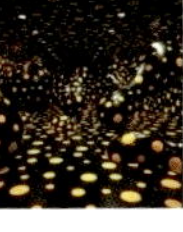

p.133
水玉強迫　夜
Dots Obsession - Night
2008
Mixedmedia
Installation view:
The Kennedy Center, Washington,D.C.

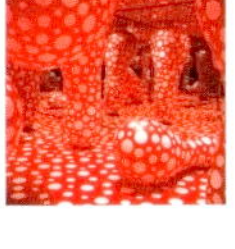

p.134
水玉強迫
Dots Obsession
1999
Mixedmedia
Installation view:
Les Abattoirs, Toulouse

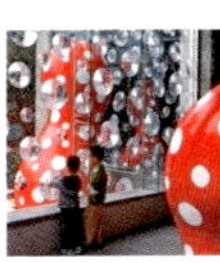

p.135
新たなる空間への道標
Guidepost to the New Space
2007
Mixedmedia
Installation view:
Guangzhou, China

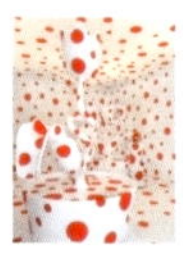

p.136-137
チューリップに愛を込めて、永遠に祈る
With All My Love for the Tulips, I Pray Forever
2012, Mixedmedia
Installation view:
The National Museum of Art, Osaka

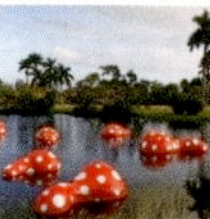

p.138
新たなる空間への道標
Guidepost to the New Space
2009
Fairchild Tropical Botanic Garden, Miami
Photo by Benjamin Thacker

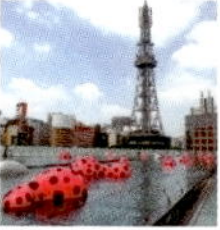

p.139
命の足跡
Footprints of Life
2010
Mixedmedia
Oasis 21, Nagoya
Aichi Triennale 2010

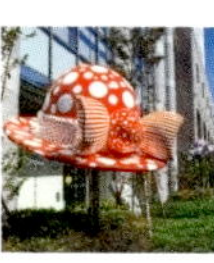

p.140
三つの帽子(部分)
Three Hats (detail)
1996
H95×180×180cm (各)
Paint on G.R.C.
Fukuoka Health Promotion Foundation

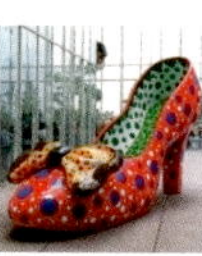

p.141
赤い靴
High Heel
2002
H255×430×173cm
Urethane on F.R.P.
Kirishima Open-Air Museum, Kagoshima

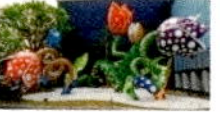

p.142-143
幻の華
The Visionary Flowers
2002
H1057×1830×1625cm
Urethane on G.R.C.
Matsumoto City Museum, Nagano

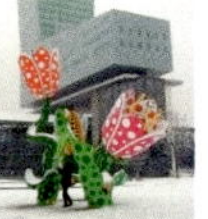

p.144
シャングリラのチューリップ
Tulips of Shangri-La
2003
H700×400×500cm
Paint on G.R.C.
Lille, France

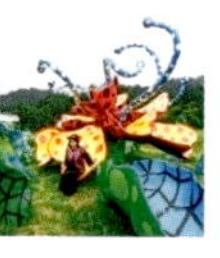

p.145
花咲ける妻有
Tsumari in Bloom
2003
H410×507×521cm
Paint on G.R.C.
Agraian Culture Center
Matsudai, Niigata

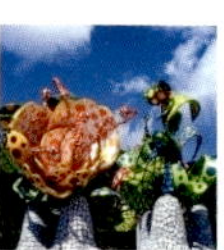

p.146
シャングリラの華
Flowers of Shangri-La
2000
H370×840×640cm
Paint on G.R.C.
Kirishima Open-Air Museum, Kagoshima

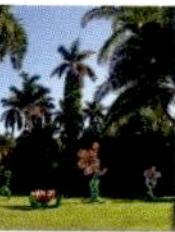

p.147
真夜中に咲く花
Flowers That Bloom at Midnight
2009
Urethane on F.R.P.
Fairchild Tropical Botanic Garden, Miami
Photo by Benjamin Thack

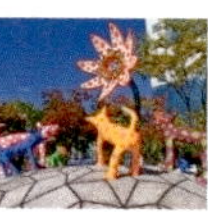

p.148
ハロー・アニャン、愛を込めて
Hello, Anyang with Love
2007
H390×590×400cm
Urethane on G.R.C., F.R.F
Pyeonghwa Park, Korea

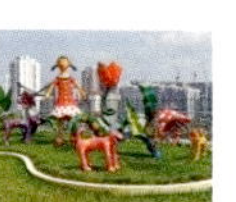

p.149
華さけるチューリップたちの楽園へゆこう
Let's Go to a Paradise of Glorious Tulips
2009
H265×907×558cm
Urethane on F.R.P.
Orchard Central Singapore

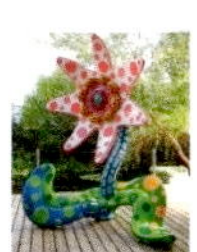

p.150
明日咲く花
Flower That Bloom Tomorrow
2011
H290×205×185cm
Urethane on F.R.P.
Installation view:
Victoria Miro, London

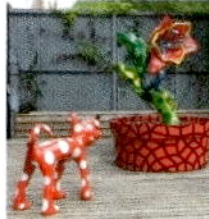

p.151
チューリップに愛を込めて
With All My Love for the Tulips
H236×231×110cm
2011, Urethane on F.R.P.
カワイイ(犬)
Kawaii (Dog)
H80×101×48cm
2011, FRP
Installation view:
Victoria Miro, London

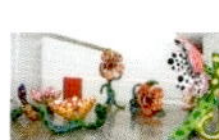

p.152-153
真夜中に咲く花
Flowers That Bloom at Midnight
2010
Urethane on F.R.P.
Installation view:
Gagosian Gallery, LA

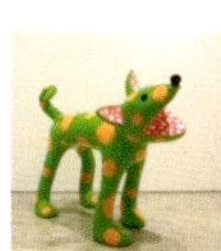

p.154
キャン キャン
Can Can
2010
H98×134×60cm
Urethane on F.R.P.
Installation view:
Victoria Miro, London

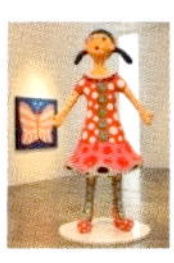

p.155
ケイちゃん
KEI-CHAN
2011
H260×135×100cm
Urethane on F.R.P.
Installation view:
Victoria Miro, London

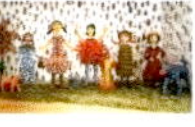

p.156-157
ハーイ、コンニチワ!
Hi, Konnichiwa (Hello!)
2004
Mixedmedia
Installation view:
Mori Art Museum, Tokyo

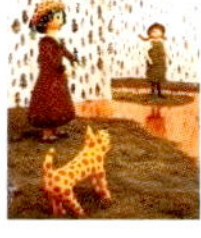

p.158
ハーイ、コンニチワ!
Hi, Konnichiwa (Hello!)
2004
Mixedmedia
Installation view:
Mori Art Museum, Tokyo

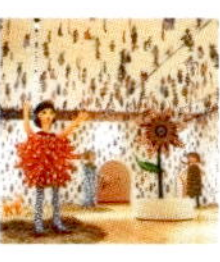

p.159
ハーイ、コンニチワ!
Hi, Konnichiwa (Hello!)
2004
Mixedmedia
Installation view:
Mori Art Museum, Tokyo

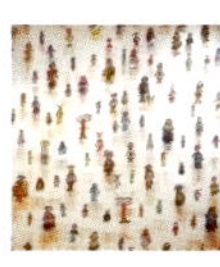

p.160
ハーイ、コンニチワ!
Hi, Konnichiwa (Hello!)
2004
Mixedmedia
Installation view:
Mori Art Museum, Tokyo

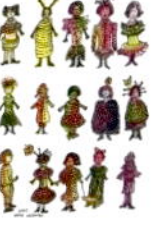

p.161
野にあそびにいこう。
Let's Go to the Field and Play.
2003
Acrylic, marker pen on paper board

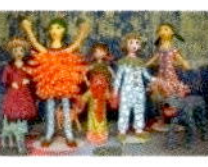

p.162-163
ハーイ、コンニチワ!
Hi, Konnichiwa (Hello!)
2004
Mixedmedia

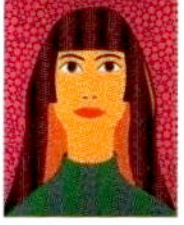

front cover
SELF-PORTRAIT
[TWAY](部分 detail)
2010
H227.3×181.8cm
Acrylic on canvas

Index of Kusama

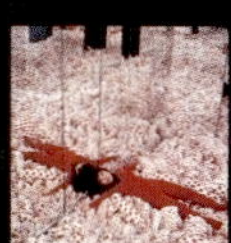
p.169
“無限の鏡の間-ファルスの原野”の中で
“Infinity Mirrored Room-Phalli's Field”
at Richard Castellane Gallery, New York
1965

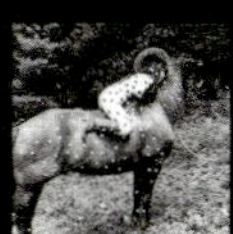
p.170
自己消滅　ホース・プレイ
"Kusama's Self-Obliteration Horse Play"
1966, Woodstock

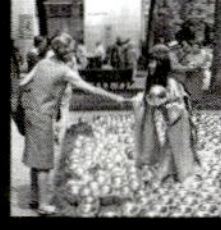
p.171
ナルシス・ガーデン、第33回ヴェネチア・ビエンナーレにて
"Narcissus Garden" at the 33rd Venice Biennale
1966

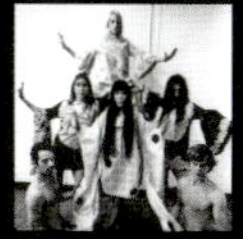
p.172
草間のファッション・ショー
"Kusama's Fashion Show", New York
1968

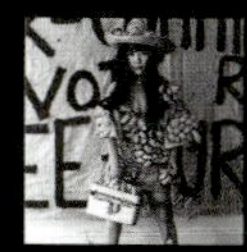
p.173
草間の前衛ファッション
Kusama's Avant-Garde Fashion, New York
1971
Photo by Tom Haar

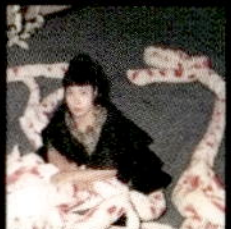
p.174
大阪フォルム画廊（東京）での個展会場にて
At her solo show at Osaka Form Gallery
1976

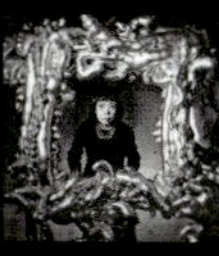
p.175
"21世紀への扉"と
Kusama and the "Door to 21st Century" at Yokohama
1993
Photo by Yuichi Hiruta

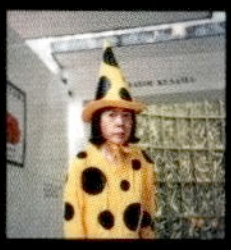
p.176
第45回ヴェネチア・ビエンナーレにて、日本館での個展
Solo Show for Japan Pavilion at the 45th Venice Biennale
1993

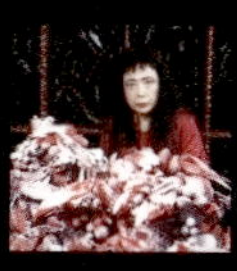
p.177
“クサマズ クサマ”個展会場にて
"Kusama's Kusama" Exhibition at Ota Fine Arts
1997

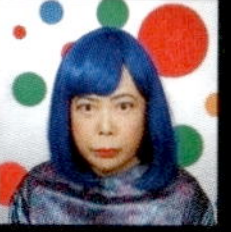
p.178
ドッツペインティングと
With Dots painting
2005

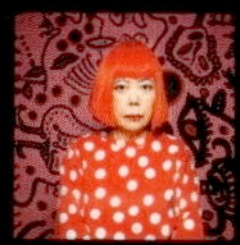
p.179
“わが永遠の魂”シリーズの絵と
With "My Eternal Soul" series painting
2011

Information about each work is listed in the following order:

Page where work appears in book
Title of work
[Portion of larger work shown]
Year work produced
Size
Material
Place where work is held
Photo credit

Published by Kodansha USA Publishing, LLC
451 Park Avenue South, New York, NY 10016

Distributed in the United Kingdom and continental Europe
by Kodansha Europe Ltd.

Originally published in Japanese in 2013 by Kodansha Ltd. under the title
Kusama Yayoi Art Book, Hi, Konnichiwa.

Creative Direction and Design: Yoshiro Nakamura (Yen Inc.)
Editorial supervision: YAYOI KUSAMA STUDIO Inc.
Cooperation: Ota Fine Arts
Translation: Gavin Frew
Editorial cooperation: Junko Kuboki

Photo Credits:
Pages 85, 173 © Tom Haar
Page 90-91 Photo by Peter Moore © Barbara Moore / Licensed by VAGA, NY
Page 138, 147 © Benjamin Thacker
Page 175 © Yuichi Hiruta

Text excerpted in this publication originally appeared in
Mugen no Ami — Kusama Yayoi Jiden, published by Sakuhinsha.

All photographs which are not specifically credited in the book
belong to Yayoi Kusama, YAYOI KUSAMA STUDIO Inc.

ISBN: 978-1-56836-538-1

First edition, 2014
22 21 7 6

kodansha.us